LITTLE PINK HOUSE

Also by Jeff Benedict

The Mormon Way of Doing Business: How Eight Western Boys Reached the Top of Corporate America
Out of Bounds: Inside the NBA's Culture of Rape, Violence, and Crime
No Bone Unturned: The Adventures of a Top Smithsonian Forensic Scientist and the Legal Battle for America's Oldest Skeletons
Without Reservation: How a Controversial Indian Tribe Rose to Power and Built the World's Largest Casino
Pros and Cons: The Criminals Who Play in the NFL
    (with co-author Don Yaeger)
Athletes and Acquaintance Rape
Public Heroes, Private Felons: Athletes and Crimes Against Women

LITTLE PINK HOUSE

A True Story of
Defiance and Courage

JEFF BENEDICT

GRAND CENTRAL
PUBLISHING

NEW YORK   BOSTON

Grand Central Publishing
Hachette Book Group
237 Park Avenue
New York, NY 10017

Visit our Web site at www.HachetteBookGroup.com.

Printed in the United States of America

First Edition: January 2009
10 9 8 7 6 5 4 3 2 1

Grand Central Publishing is a division of Hachette Book Group, Inc.
The Grand Central Publishing name and logo is a trademark of Hachette Book Group, Inc.

Library of Congress Cataloging-in-Publication Data
Benedict, Jeff.
    Little pink house : a true story of defiance and courage / Jeff Benedict. — 1st ed.
    p. cm.
    ISBN: 978-0-446-50862-9
    1. Kelo, Susette—Trials, litigation, etc. 2. Eminent domain—Connecticut—Cases.
3. Eminent domain—United States—Cases. I. Title.
    KF229.K45B46 2009
    343.746'0252—dc22   2008017650

To Josephine, my grandmother.

I wrote much of this book in the attic of her home. Many afternoons she trudged up the attic steps and quietly placed a grilled-cheese sandwich on my desk before saying, "You keep writing, kid." She knew I didn't have time to stop for lunch. My grandmother loved this story and couldn't wait to read the finished product. Sadly, she never will. On January 15, 2008, Josephine died suddenly, shortly before I finished writing. If only I could have written faster.

CONTENTS

AUTHOR'S NOTE

Eminent domain is the government's power to take private property for public use. Nobody particularly likes it. But occasionally it's essential to make way for roads, schools, hospitals, and the like. And Americans accept this practice as long as deprived property owners receive due process and just compensation. Under the Fifth Amendment, that's been the American way since the Framers drafted our Constitution.

But the Supreme Court changed the rules in 2005 when it decided *Kelo v. City of New London.* Now local and state governments can take private property from an individual and transfer it to a private developer in hopes of generating more tax revenue or creating jobs. The *Kelo* decision equated these public *benefits* with public *uses.*

Under this interpretation, there's no telling where the government's power to take private property ends. "The specter of condemnation hangs over all property," Justice Sandra Day O'Connor wrote in a blistering dissent in *Kelo.* "Nothing is to prevent the State from replacing any Motel 6 with a Ritz-Carlton, any home with a shopping mall, or any farm with a factory."

The *Kelo* case is infamous. But the stirring story behind what drove Susette Kelo—a divorced nurse—to take on a powerful governor, a billion-dollar corporation, and a hard-charging development agency to save her pink cottage is a hidden drama that begs to be exposed. On one level, it's a uniquely American saga about power and defiance that makes the Supreme Court decision even harder to swallow. But at its core, this story is about pride, a virtue that breeds self-respect and a condition that is first among the seven cardinal sins.

Little Pink House is an inside account of how a political street fight over a neighborhood escalated into a high-stakes federal case. It's the unsanitized version that the Supreme Court never heard. And it's told by the people who lived it—the residents whose homes were taken; the local officials who authorized the takings; the development agency that designed the plan; the state officials who supplied the money; a *Fortune* 500 company that stood to benefit; and lawyers who fought ferociously over whether this was right or wrong. All of these parties cooperated for this book.

Between November 2005 and March 2008, I conducted close to three hundred on-the-record interviews. I also received via e-mail well over one hundred written responses to factual queries I posed to participants. Most of these queries involved detailed follow-up questions to prior interviews.

I also had access to deposition transcripts, video and audio recordings of meetings and events, and many documents (internal corporate correspondence, internal government memos, and lawyers' private notes), as well as private papers and correspondence, such as journals, diaries, and e-mails. In all, I obtained enough documents—including voluminous records obtained under the freedom-of-information laws, court papers, press reports, and photographs and maps—to fill more than a dozen large, plastic storage containers.

My primary objective in this is to tell a compelling story that is true to the characters who shaped this historic case. I am deeply grateful to individuals on all sides who afforded me their time and helped me understand this complex story about people whose struggle ultimately shifted one of the most enduring principles of our democracy.

Perhaps no writer had more influence on English common law and American jurisprudence than seventeenth-century English jurist Sir Edward Coke. He penned one of the most famous lines of all time: "A man's house is his castle—*et domus sua cuique est tutissimum refugium.*" The Latin portion of the sentence is less well known. The loose translation is: "and where shall a man be safe if it be not in his own house?"

Amazingly, after *Kelo v. City of New London,* Coke's comment may be more relevant now than when the American colonists rebelled against the king.

Jeff Benedict
April 8, 2008
Buena Vista, Virginia

CAST OF CHARACTERS

THE PRINCIPALS

John G. Rowland, governor of Connecticut
Peter N. Ellef, chief of staff to Governor Rowland
Jay B. Levin, lobbyist and attorney
George Milne Jr., president of Pfizer, Inc.
Dr. Claire Gaudiani, president of New London Development
    Corporation and Connecticut College

Susette Kelo, lead plaintiff
Billy Von Winkle, plaintiff
Matt Dery, plaintiff
Rich Beyer, plaintiff
Byron Athenian, plaintiff
Michael Cristofaro, plaintiff

INSTITUTE FOR JUSTICE

Chip Mellor, president
Scott Bullock, attorney
Dana Berliner, attorney
John Kramer, communications director

CITY OF NEW LONDON

Lloyd Beachy, mayor
Tom Londregan, attorney
Tony Basilica, Democratic Party chairman

NEW LONDON DEVELOPMENT CORPORATION (NLDC)

David Goebel, chief operating officer
Stephen Percy, member of the board of directors
Mathew Greene, chief counsel
Edward O'Connell, outside counsel

COALITION TO SAVE FORT TRUMBULL

Kathleen Mitchell, speech writer and organizer for Susette Kelo
John and Sarah Steffian, financiers behind the litigation effort
Professor Fred Paxton, co-chairman of the coalition
Steve and Amy Hallquist, grassroots opposition leaders
Attorney Scott Sawyer, legal strategist for the local opposition

OTHER KEY PLAYERS

Reid MacCluggage, publisher of the *Day* newspaper
The Honorable Thomas J. Corradino, trial judge in
  Kelo v. City of New London
Jim Serbia, real-estate manager of Pfizer's research division

SUPPORTING CAST

STATE OF CONNECTICUT OFFICIALS

M. Jodi Rell, governor of Connecticut
Ron Angelo, special negotiator for the governor
Robert Albright, mediator for the governor's office

OTHER SUPPORT ROLES

Wesley W. Horton, argued before the U.S. Supreme Court on
  behalf of the City of New London
Aldo Valentini, head of the Italian Dramatic Club
Judge Angelo Santaniello, negotiator for the Italian
  Dramatic Club
John Markowicz, member of the U.S. Navy base reuse
  committee

LITTLE PINK HOUSE

ON CAPITOL HILL

September 20, 2005
U.S. Senate Chambers
Washington, D.C.

Clutching her notes and wearing heels, a gray skirt, and a white blouse, Susette Kelo approached the witness table, hoping the senators noticed her salmon-pink sweater. It matched the color of her house and had sneaker prints across the front, signifying "They walked all over me."

"Are you nervous?" her attorney, Scott Bullock, asked.

"Not too bad."

"You'll be fine," he said, patting her on the shoulder.

Facing a panel of senators, she sat down, grabbed a pitcher of water, and poured herself a drink. Bullock took a seat in the first row behind her.

Senator Arlen Specter pounded the gavel.

"Good morning, ladies and gentlemen. The Senate Judiciary Committee will now proceed with a hearing on the issue of the right to take private property under what is called the doctrine of eminent domain for public use. Our hearing is prompted by the recent decision just a few months ago, in June, by the Supreme Court of the United States in a case captioned *Kelo v. City of New London*, where private property was taken for the use of a private company, Pfizer."

Specter indicated that he and Senator Patrick Leahy had just been across the street in a conference with Supreme Court Justice

John Paul Stevens. They had been discussing the harsh criticism generated against the Court by the *Kelo* decision. As the author of the majority opinion, Justice Stevens didn't particularly appreciate all the fire the decision had been under. But Specter insisted the matter required congressional review.

"The Fifth Amendment," Specter continued, "prohibits the government from taking private property unless it does so for a public use and with just compensation . . . But the *Kelo* case goes a significant step further and takes it for economic development, where there are jobs, increased taxes, and other revenues. The issue, which the Congress has authority to act on—this is not a constitutional issue where the Supreme Court is the last word—is to determine as a matter of public policy whether this is a wise, appropriate taking of private property."

Specter yielded to Senator Leahy, who declared his respect for private-property rights. Leahy looked Susette in the eye and continued, "Ms. Kelo, I am probably one of millions of Americans who were distressed when we learned your story. We are concerned about what happened to you . . . It has been said that tough cases make bad laws. It can also be said that bad law can lead to bad remedies, and so we are going to have to figure out the best way to do this."

When the senators' preliminary remarks concluded, Specter introduced Susette as the first witness. "Despite her loss before the Supreme Court," Specter said, "she continues to inspire and advocate for a return to sensible eminent-domain policy. Thank you for what you are doing, Ms. Kelo, and we look forward to your testimony."

She took a deep breath.

"I want to thank Chairman Specter and the rest of the Senate Judiciary Committee for the opportunity to testify," she began. "My name is Susette Kelo, and I live in New London, Connecticut. I am the Kelo in *Kelo v. City of New London*, the now infamous U.S. Supreme Court case."

She cleared her throat and went on, "The battle against eminent-domain abuse may have started as a way for me to save my little pink cottage. But it has rightfully grown into something much larger—the fight to restore the American Dream and the sacredness and security of each one of our homes."

1

GIMME SHELTER

Spring 1997

M edic Eleven, come in."
Forty-year-old EMT Susette Kelo grabbed the paramedic truck's radio receiver. "This is Medic Eleven."

"Respond to a man down at First Avenue and Niantic River Road."

Susette's partner, Jeff Douchette, whipped the wheel around and headed toward Niantic Bay, an inlet off Long Island Sound in southeastern Connecticut.

"Medic Eleven en route," Susette said.

Married with five sons, Susette Kelo had become an EMT a few years earlier, after a drunk driver crashed head-on into her seventeen-year-old son's vehicle, nearly killing him. Paramedics had helped save her boy's life. Susette had begun volunteering on ambulance runs as a way of giving back.

The experience ultimately convinced her to become a medic. Emergency response offered Susette an escape from her unfulfilling home life in Preston, a small farming community twenty miles from the Connecticut coast. Susette and her husband, John Jorsz, had a ranch house, a barn, and farm animals on four acres. It had been a great place to raise boys. But now all of them except her youngest lived on their own. And with high school graduation approaching, he would soon be gone as well.

She was thinking about moving on, too. Her marriage had

soured, the relationship reduced to constant bickering. She felt like her husband showed more affection for the bottle than for her. He felt like she didn't appreciate how hard he worked to provide for them. But it didn't matter who was right; the romance was drained. And with the kids gone and the animals sold, the ranch felt empty and cold.

Susette knew she needed a change in scenery when the highlight of her week had become weekend EMT shifts. Most calls took her to waterfront communities on Long Island Sound. The water had a way of brightening her day.

"There he is," Douchette said, pulling up beside an elderly man sitting on a sidewalk curb, his feet resting on the street. Sweat saturated his shirt. An elderly woman and some pedestrians huddled around him.

"Grab the monitor," Douchette said.

With the summer temperature pushing eighty-five degrees, Susette had her long red hair pinned up in a French twist. Her form-fitting, navy blue uniform stuck to her tall, slender figure as she grabbed an oxygen bag, a heart monitor, and the drug box from the truck. But even while doing this she couldn't help noticing the attractive beach cottages lining the avenues along the water.

"Boy, it's beautiful down here," she said to her partner.

He headed straight for the patient, whose wife explained that they had been out for their routine morning walk and her husband had collapsed with chest pains. The man labored to breathe.

Susette gave him oxygen and applied cardiac-monitor cables to him while Douchette checked his vital signs. She saw fear in the elderly couple's eyes as an ambulance arrived.

"You were probably overcome by the heat," Douchette told the man, reassuring him that he would be okay. "But just to be safe, we're going to bring you to the hospital. And I'm going to go with you."

Susette helped the patient onto a stretcher before packing the equipment back in her truck and taking the keys from

Douchette, who climbed into the ambulance. "I'll meet you back at the hospital," he told her.

Pulling away, Susette spotted a house with a private dock, a small patch of beach, and a "For Sale" sign. That afternoon, when her shift ended, she returned to the scene to get the Realtor's name and phone number off the sign and take a closer look at the house. The setting sun put a sparkle on the ocean water that lapped up to the property's sandy shoreline.

I really have to move down here, she thought.

For more than a year, Susette had been trying to talk her husband into selling the ranch and moving closer to the water, convinced she could cope with an unfulfilling marriage if she had the water as a friend. But Jorsz consistently resisted. A machinist at a paper-recycling mill, he spent sixty to seventy hours per week at work. The ranch offered a place to unwind on the weekend doing what he enjoyed—tinkering on engines and fixing things. Besides, his job was only fifteen minutes from the house. He really had no interest in leaving a rural town for a more congested coastal community close to an hour away from his job.

Susette called the Realtor and got the price for the beach house: $170,000. If her husband would agree to sell the ranch, she figured, they could pay cash for the beach house and still have enough left over for a small retirement nest egg. She hoped a house with a private boat dock might be enough to finally persuade him. That evening, Susette approached her husband in the yard while he worked on a piece of farming equipment. She described the house.

"You wouldn't have to work anymore," she told him.

"I don't want to leave," Jorsz said, not bothering to make eye contact.

She could tell he had been drinking. "You know, you might like this place," she added. "There's a dock. We could get a boat."

He ignored her.

"I'm going to ask you again for the last time," she said in desperation.

"I'm not leaving Preston," he said.

Susette took a step back. "Well, if you don't want to go, I'm going anyway."

He showed no expression. Neither did she.

She had been let down her entire life. It had begun with her father, William Stevens, who had walked out right after Susette's birth on June 14, 1956. Stevens had left Susette with nothing, not even a last name. Destitute, Susette's mother, Josephine Chasse, had waited tables at a diner to support her six children in Millinocket, Maine, a remote rural town over sixty miles north of Bangor, not far from the Canadian border.

While her mother worked, Susette and her siblings fended for themselves during the long, hard winters. Her older brothers often fed her water with chocolate flavoring for breakfast. She wore socks on her little hands for mittens. At age four, Susette learned to keep warm inside their frigid house by climbing under the kitchen sink to be near the hot-water pipe. She had few friends and very little to look forward to.

In need of more steady work, Susette's mother moved to New London, Connecticut, before Susette's tenth birthday. She enrolled Susette in a Catholic school. After getting pregnant at age sixteen, Susette married Michael Kelo. By the time Susette turned twenty-five, she and Kelo had five sons.

Two years later, she divorced Kelo but kept his name. When her ex-husband failed to pay child support, Susette and her sons ended up on welfare for a short time before she found employment as a shipyard electrician at Electric Boat, a division of General Dynamics that manufactures submarines. With her five boys, she moved into a small house next to a chicken farm in Preston.

That's when she met thirty-two-year-old John Jorsz, who lived down the road, alone on his ranch. He had never married. At thirty-one, Susette had a body that defied the fact that she had delivered five children. Her fiery red hair ran all the way down to her waist. After a hurricane took down a tree in her yard, she asked Jorsz to cut it up, which he gladly did. Then when her boys' dog died, Jorsz helped them bury it. He even made a grave marker—a wooden cross bearing the dog's name.

In 1988, Susette married Jorsz and moved into the ranch

house, along with her sons. Although the marriage never sizzled, it suited their needs. Jorsz provided a roof and three square meals a day, and he cared for the boys as if they were his own. Susette brought livestock to the farm and used her green thumb to dress the place up with gardens and crops.

Things worked for eight years. But when Susette hit forty, she yearned for something more. Tired of the day-to-day grind of maintaining the ranch and a marriage headed nowhere, she wanted to pursue something for herself. Childhood poverty had cheated her out of an education. Early pregnancy and a determination to be a good mother had negated any chance of a career. She had worn out her life raising five sons and trying to make two unfulfilling marriages work. There had to be something better out there. To figure it out, she needed a fresh start.

But the beach house wasn't the answer. It was nothing but a pipe dream without her husband's help. She knew she could never afford it on her own. *That's all right*, she figured. One way or the other, she'd find a place of her own by the water. And when she did, she'd leave Jorsz.

Any hope of landing near the water rested in New London, one of the oldest cities in America. Established in 1658 and named after Great Britain's main city, New London, at the juncture of the Thames River and Long Island Sound, thrived as a colonial port. Whaling made it a commercial power in the 1800s. In the twentieth century, though, New London was transformed into a blue-collar, industrial city, with the defense industry exploiting the city's seacoast for U.S. Navy and Coast Guard installations. But as the cold war wound down and the defense industry cut back, New London's unemployment rose, and its property values fell.

Susette's EMT unit had its home base at New London's city hospital, where Susette spent most of her weekends. A few weeks after her husband insisted he'd never leave Preston, Susette and Jeff Douchette got called to an emergency at New London's Naval Undersea Warfare Center, a thirty-two-acre vacant campus of buildings and laboratories on the banks of the Thames. The call turned out to be a false alarm. As they left the base, Susette asked Douchette for the keys and suggested a scenic route back to the hospital. Douchette agreed.

Susette exited the base onto East Street, which ran between the base and a civilian neighborhood settled by Irish and Italian immigrants in the early 1900s. Some homes on East Street had views overlooking the base and the water. Susette coasted to a stop sign at the end of the street.

"Wow, look at that house," she said, pointing at a two-story Victorian that occupied the corner of East and Trumbull streets.

Douchette was not impressed. The house looked abandoned and had no yard or driveway.

Susette parked the truck to get a closer look. Vines and overgrown brush concealed a set of brick steps leading from the street to the front door. Dreary beige paint, cracked and peeling, covered the exterior. A weathered "For Sale" sign dangled from a fence.

"I think I'd like to buy that," she said.

"Are you crazy?" Douchette said.

"No, I'm serious."

"You gotta be out of your mind."

The front of the house's foundation abutted the cracked sidewalk on East Street. The left side of the house went right to the edge of Trumbull Street. Fewer than ten feet separated the right side of the house from an almost identical Victorian that also had a "For Sale" sign on it.

Susette didn't care. The place had a water view. The fact that it needed work convinced her she just might be able to afford it. She jotted down the phone number and the address "8 East Street" on a scrap of paper and stuffed it in her pocket.

BIG AMBITIONS

John G. Rowland had reason to smile. The Republican governor's polling numbers had top Democrats backing off from challenging him in his upcoming bid for reelection. Rowland had strung together an improbable series of convincing victories at a remarkably young age. After winning election to the state legislature at age twenty-three, Rowland had become a U.S. congressman at twenty-seven. Then in 1994, the state had elected him governor at age thirty-seven. Handsome, charismatic, and immensely popular, the governor had established dominance in a blue state in the heart of the northeast.

His meteoric rise had not gone unnoticed by the Republican National Party. Another four-year term as the state's chief executive would solidify his hopes of reaching the national stage. In this campaign, however, Rowland had more in mind than just winning: he also wanted to carry some of the state's most Democratic cities.

No Connecticut town voted more Democratic than New London, where Democrats outnumbered Republicans more than four to one among registered voters. Democrats absolutely dominated local, state, and federal elections there. But these overwhelming odds only fueled Rowland's ambition. He figured the city's economic woes gave him an opening. New London's unemployment rate was twice as high as the statewide average. Industry and business had fled the city. The crime rate was up, and a feeling of hopelessness had set in.

Rowland had in mind a massive urban-renewal project along the city's waterfront. But he didn't want to deal with New London's Democratic city hall. To wrest redevelopment authority from the city, Rowland looked to his loyal friend Peter Ellef, the head of the state's Department of Economic and Community Development.

Tall with silvery-black hair and deep-set eyes with bushy black eyebrows, fifty-three-year-old Ellef had a big say in the state's construction projects, as he controlled the purse strings for urban development. Ellef used his position to establish himself as the governor's toughest political ally. He liked control, loyalty, and results.

Ellef elected not to bulldoze the governor's agenda into the city. After all, the city's Democratic Party leaders despised Rowland and distrusted anyone closely associated with him. And if the city suspected the state was trying to invade its turf, there would be immediate opposition.

Ellef needed a foil—an envoy, a person of influence with an inside track to the city's political players. He needed a Democrat, but not just any Democrat. The task called for a powerful Democrat willing to help a brutally partisan Republican governor circumvent other Democrats—someone more loyal to personal ambition than to the party.

Jay B. Levin had wanted to be governor of Connecticut, and he had made all the right career moves to get there. After graduating from law school in 1976, he had served as staff legal counsel to Democratic Congressman Chris Dodd before becoming a prosecutor and then a partner in one of New London's most respected law firms. He had served two terms in the state legislature, but in 1990 he had run unsuccessfully for attorney general.

His defeat had marked the end of his statewide political aspirations. Yet his interest in politics remained, and in the mid-1990s Levin got elected mayor of New London. But then, at age forty-five, he abruptly walked away from politics to make some money. He joined the prestigious Hartford law firm of Pullman

& Comley and was appointed chair of its governmental-affairs department, the firm's lobbying arm.

Ellef didn't have to go far to find Levin. Pullman & Comley had its office within blocks of the state capitol. No one had better political connections in New London than Levin, especially in Democratic circles. A lobbyist who made a living off his Rolodex, Levin fit Ellef's needs to a T. The trick would be the job title—"lobbyist" was too blatant.

On March 15, 1997, Ellef posted an official request for proposals for a consulting job to assist the state in developing New London's waterfront. The posting described the job as analyzing the factors affecting this development and providing an assessment of the political support needed to complete it. "The contractor must fulfill the duties listed to the satisfaction of Peter N. Ellef," the posting said.

All the action was headed to Levin's hometown. Within three weeks, he submitted a two-volume proposal, promising to devote himself to directing the project until completion. Levin's proposal spoke of the political landscape in New London. He warned that numerous public and private boards, along with the city's influential local newspaper—the *Day*—had the ability to derail the governor's initiative even before it started. No one, Levin suggested, was better positioned than he to navigate the city's politics and local media.

Levin was offering just what Ellef wanted: connections. His price was $196,000.

Ellef didn't hesitate. He didn't need to study the voluminous appendices and paperwork stuffing Levin's binders—those were just bureaucratic nonsense. If Levin succeeded in steering the state around the city's politics, his price was cheap.

Eleven days after Levin submitted his proposal, Ellef awarded him the contract, along with a $65,000 up-front payment. Effective April 21, 1997, Jay Levin answered to Peter Ellef, who answered to Governor John Rowland.

3

THIS OLD HOUSE

Summer 1997

Real-estate agent Geoff Haussman had just obtained his broker's license. He had yet to sell his first house when the phone rang in his agency's main office on a slow Saturday morning. Haussman picked up and identified himself.

"Hi," said the person on the other end. "My name is Susette Kelo, and I want to look at the house at 8 East Street in New London."

Unfamiliar with the property, Haussman put her on hold and grabbed a listing sheet. It indicated the house was 107 years old and had a stone foundation and an unfinished basement. Total living space amounted to barely 1,100 square feet, with just two rooms on the first floor—a kitchen and living room—and two bedrooms upstairs. Each floor had a bathroom. The asking price had been reduced to $59,000 after the place had sat on the market for years.

Haussman got back on the line and asked Susette when she wanted to see the house.

"Today," she said.

"Okay, great," he said. "Let me give you directions."

"You don't need to give me directions. I'm already here."

"You're at the house now?"

"I'm standing in front of it."

Haussman said he'd be right over.

Before leaving the office, he told a colleague where he was headed. The colleague joked that he was going to show the house that no one could sell.

Waiting for Haussman to arrive, Susette put on some gardening gloves and took a pair of hedge clippers from her car. In sandals and shorts, she carved a path through the overgrown brush that blocked the front steps to the house. Eager to reach the door, Susette ignored the thorns that scraped the tops of her feet and the bottoms of her legs.

Haussman pulled up and removed the lockbox on the front door. "You're bleeding," he said.

"I'll be all right."

Just inside, a narrow staircase led to the second floor. Susette scooted past it and into the dark, empty front room. Haussman went through the house, looking for light switches.

Susette pulled back the old, drab curtains covering the front windows. Sunlight immediately flooded the room, revealing a breathtaking view of the water and of boats sailing on the Thames River.

Overcome by an instant, strange sense of belonging, Susette stared out the window. She felt like she had been there all her life. *This house is calling me*, she told herself.

Embarrassed, Haussman emerged from the unfinished basement, trying to figure out how to talk up a house he felt needed to be demolished.

"There's not much to see here," he said.

She kept looking out the window.

The rooms are small, he reported. Besides being unfinished, the basement had a boulder in it. The kitchen had only an old gas stove.

"I want to buy this house," she said, her back to him.

"This place?"

She spun around. "Yes, this place."

Haussman suggested she consider some other options and offered to show her other listings.

"No," she said, determined to defend the house, "I really like this place. This is my house."

Haussman hesitated. For more than a year his agency had been unable to talk anybody into looking at 8 East Street, much less buy it. Now he couldn't talk Susette out of leaving the place alone.

"Look," he said, "if you are going to buy it, you need to at least see what you're buying."

"That's fine. But I'm not changing my mind."

She followed him upstairs. Both bedrooms felt cramped, but one of them offered an even better view of the water than the living room did.

This is my room, she decided.

Without even bothering to inspect the basement, she offered $42,000 for the house, $17,000 below asking price. She had nothing to lose; the house had been on the market for years without an offer.

Haussman escorted Susette out, locked up, and hustled back to his office to write up a contract.

"I sold the house," he announced when he arrived at the office.

"Which house?" a colleague asked.

"Eight East Street in New London."

Nobody in the office believed him.

The prospect of owning her own home left Susette excited but anxious. She started researching the property. The only thing between it and the water was Fort Trumbull, an eighteenth-century octagon-shaped stone fort used by George Washington's troops in the Revolutionary War. In 1781, Benedict Arnold had led a British assault on New London and captured the fort before setting fire to the city. The navy then acquired the fort when it built its thirty-two-acre base between East Street and the Thames River. Neglect, though, had reduced the historic treasure to a decaying fortress.

The cottage had originally been constructed in 1890 in a more residential part of the city. It had been relocated to the Fort Trumbull neighborhood just after the turn of the century and jammed onto a vacant, postage-stamp-sized lot not much bigger than the footprint of the house. John Bishop, one of the city's most prominent carpenters, had built the house. After Bishop died in 1893, the house had passed through many hands until fifty-year-old Avner Gregory, a preservationist, had bought it in the late 1980s. Gregory had restored more than thirty-five historic homes in New London.

At 8 East Street, Gregory had removed the crumbling cement-block steps leading from the street to the front and brought in a mason from San Francisco to build redbrick steps. Gregory then accentuated the brick with a white picket fence that he ran across the front porch. He replaced the house's asphalt siding with cedar clapboard and installed all new doors and windows. Inside, he upgraded the plumbing, added a baseboard heating system, and added a bathroom with a nineteenth-century bathtub to the second floor.

Then he bought the house next door and did all the same things to it. When both houses were completed, Gregory sold them to an individual who bought them as investments. But the investments never panned out, and eventually the two houses ended up back on the market. The longer the homes sat unoccupied, the more overgrown they became. Ultimately, the outside appearance deterred potential buyers from examining the insides.

The neighborhood's tough appearance didn't bother Susette. A hodgepodge of industrial properties, warehouses, and old, small homes, the Fort Trumbull neighborhood was cut off from the rest of New London, sandwiched between Amtrak rail lines on the west and the abandoned naval base on the north. In the late 1800s and early 1900s, European immigrants—first Irish and then Italians—settled in the dirty, urban stretch, turning it into a close-knit community of shops, gardens, and pubs. Over the years, the immigrant families never left, passing their homes from one generation to the next. At the height of the cold war, two thousand people worked in the neighborhood at the Naval Undersea Warfare Center, then known as the Naval Underwater Sound Laboratory. Some of the Defense Department's top physicists, nuclear scientists, and sonar specialists studied and monitored underwater acoustics in relation to submarine warfare. But after the cold war died down, the Pentagon closed the base in 1995, and the neighborhood began to resemble a ghost town.

Undaunted, the more Susette learned about it, the more she felt she had in common with the house. It needed her, and she needed it.

Haussman called with bad news: the seller had rejected the offer. She wanted $56,000.

Susette did the math. Her joint bank account with her husband had plenty of money in it, more than enough to afford the house. But she never considered that money hers. Her husband had put away a lot of money before they married, and he had earned all the money since then. Besides, she didn't want him to know she was pursuing her own home.

Instead, she secured preapproval for a first-time homebuyer's loan for up to $53,500, on the condition that the home gets a paint job before the closing. But she had no money saved for closing costs, let alone a paint job. She told Haussman her final offer for the house was $53,500 if the seller absorbed the closing costs and paid for the paint job.

The seller agreed.

A friend loaned Susette $2,500 for the down payment. She turned to another friend—a painter who specialized in historic home restorations—to paint the place. Together, they read up on the house and examined paint colors that fit the time period and building style. Susette settled on Odessa Rose, a subtle shade of pink.

4

WE NEED A VEHICLE

Peter Ellef's instructions to Jay Levin were straightforward: identify and determine ownership of all the sites with strategic-development potential around the area of the state pier and then recommend a comprehensive plan of development for the area.

Levin had a lot to work with. The nearby infrastructure gave the waterfront a big upside for development. Interstate 95 ran right alongside the pier. Two major rail lines—the Central Vermont Railway, which ran all the way to Canada, and the Amtrak line running between Boston and New York—connected to the pier area. And a major ferry service occupied a portion of the waterfront.

First, Levin identified the owners of each parcel around the pier. Then he set up individual meetings with the railroad and port operators, with the ferry services and shipyard operators, and with the various city, state, and federal agencies that had interests along the waterfront. The meetings were fruitful. Vacant land existed for development, and all parties had ideas and enthusiasm for redevelopment. The pieces were falling into place fast. For Levin, the challenge was now to identify a device, a legal mechanism that would somehow enable the governor's administration to control a massive development project without interference from the city.

It didn't take long to come up with a solution. In 1978, the city had established the New London Development Corporation

(NLDC) to assist in planning economic development. Set up as a nonprofit corporation, the NLDC had its own by-laws and operated under the direction of a president and a board of directors. But after a strong start, the NLDC had faded into dormancy. It had been years since the agency had been registered with the state to do business. Yet nothing stood in the way of reviving it.

The NLDC was a familiar entity to city officials and therefore would not generate unnecessary suspicion or opposition. Ellef liked the concept. The governor did, too. But Levin's idea raised a concern: who would run the NLDC?

The selection of the agency's president had a lot riding on it. From the state's perspective, this individual would essentially become the governor's agent in New London and would be expected to advance the most massive, ambitious redevelopment project in the city's history. The situation called for someone with clout and popularity, yet who was not under the thumb of the current Democratic leadership. This was a tall order.

Always one step ahead, Levin already had a candidate in mind.

No New London institution had more prestige than Connecticut College, a private school that occupies some of the most valuable real estate in the city, on a hill overlooking the Thames. The school came off like an ivory tower in a blue-collar town, fostering resentment from many of the city's political leaders.

But in 1988, the school hired a new president, Dr. Claire Gaudiani. She arrived with impressive credentials: a Ph.D. in French literature, a slew of published articles, the Rolodex of a socialite, and a knack for fund-raising. Under her hard-charging leadership, the school's academic ranking and its endowment soared. Her star rose quickly in the city's social circles, too. She stole the show at the city's annual birthday gala when she showed up in an elegant, sleeveless red dress, showcasing just enough to tantalize. When the music started, she kicked off her shoes and danced, revealing her red toenail polish. Men couldn't help admiring her look.

A press photographer couldn't help himself, either. The next day, Claire's picture appeared on the front page of the *Day*. She was the closest thing New London had to a diva.

Some faculty didn't like the message Claire was sending. It simply wasn't dignified for a college president to be on the front page, dancing barefoot in an eye-catching red dress. Claire knew her ways weren't always politically correct. She characterized herself as "a feminine misfit in my own generation."

But she was unafraid and unashamed of her beliefs and her ways. While president of Connecticut College, she contributed a chapter to a book on Italian Americans, in which she wrote about one of her private rituals. Shortly after getting married, Claire began setting her alarm for 4 a.m. While her husband slept, she'd get out of bed to freshen up, do her hair, and apply mascara and blush. Then she'd get back in bed. When her husband awoke, he'd find Claire looking desirable, closer to what she wanted him to see. She followed this routine for years. Lack of self-confidence, vanity, and a desire to keep romantic love alive with her husband were all reasons she cited for this practice. But her upbringing had a lot to do with it, too. "My grandmother had always told me," Claire wrote, "to take precious care of my husband, to try to please him in what she mysteriously called 'personal ways,' and never do or say anything to break his heart."

Claire stood out in New London, and she knew it. But she seemed to relish that. And people in the community loved the idea that she wasn't afraid to get her hands dirty trying to help solve some of the city's financial and educational problems. On top of her college duties, she started spending time mingling with minority leaders, local churches, and other civic officials in an attempt to build bridges between the campus and the community.

Then, in early 1997, around the time that Jay Levin signed on to work for Peter Ellef, Claire had an epiphany that convinced her to take a more hands-on leadership approach in the city's affairs. That spring, she taught a course about service and social reflection. One day, an African American student publicly challenged her during a lecture. Pointing out that Claire had done so much to help the college financially and otherwise, the student asked why she hadn't used her standing to help the swelling number of minority students in the city that were on federal assistance and attending substandard schools.

At this same time, Claire read an opinion piece in the *Day* that lamented the city's poor political leadership and cried out for a new leader to emerge. A Roman Catholic who was unafraid to acknowledge her belief in Christ, Claire felt like the newspaper piece spoke to her. "It seemed like the hand of God in my life," she later said.

Jolted by her student and the Op-Ed piece, Claire embarked on a mission. She met one-on-one with more than two dozen of the city's most respected businessmen, civic leaders, and clergy. She asked each of them what was needed to help turn the city's economic fortunes around. The consensus answer that emerged was to take some of the city's most successful, civic-minded residents and create an organization that could produce an economic-stimulus plan for the city. To Claire, this was the best way to ultimately improve the educational opportunities and social services for the city's poor and underprivileged.

As an alumnus of Connecticut College, Jay Levin knew Claire well. And as word of her effort spread through the city, Levin talked with her privately. He told her an organization capable of mobilizing some of the city's civic leaders outside the elected political process already existed—the NLDC. Claire had heard the NLDC mentioned in her talks with city officials. But realizing it had been dormant for years, she had dismissed its significance. "Jay said that he could bring it out of mothballs," Gaudiani said.

Levin made it sound easy. Living members of the original organization would have to be contacted to get their blessing. Some paperwork had to be filed with the secretary of state, along with a registration fee to reactivate the agency's corporate nonprofit status. And then Claire could be elected the agency's new president. The way Levin explained it to her, Claire simply had to say yes. Levin and others would handle all the details.

When Levin floated Dr. Gaudiani's name past Ellef, it didn't mean much to him. It wasn't immediately clear why the governor should entrust a massive redevelopment project to a woman already tasked with running a liberal-arts college with 1,700 students. Did she have the juice to push the state's agenda through City Hall?

Levin believed she did. Claire was no typical academic—she possessed an uncanny power of persuasion and a captivating presence. Claire's combination of brains, charm, and relentless ambition made her an irresistible force in New London. Everywhere she went, Claire had the ability to win over people, especially men. Numerous men's organizations in New London made Claire an honorary member. "Blue-collar men understood what I was trying to do," Claire said of herself. "They were terrific with me."

Perhaps most important, Claire knew just one speed—full throttle.

Ellef had heard enough to take the next step. He agreed to meet with Claire.

Claire didn't know Ellef. She didn't know about the governor's big plans for New London. And she had no idea Levin worked for Ellef. She agreed to meet with Ellef only after Levin said Ellef wanted to meet her.

When Levin brought Ellef to Claire's office at Connecticut College, Claire kept them waiting. Ellef didn't appreciate it; he wasn't used to waiting for anybody.

"I didn't know who he was, and I didn't care about him," Claire later explained.

Irked after standing around for roughly half an hour, Ellef threatened to leave. Before he did, Claire emerged and invited Ellef in. A quick study, he didn't take long to size her up. Attractive, energetic, and articulate, Claire came across as advertised.

After the meeting, Ellef wanted Claire at the helm of the NLDC. The governor was persuaded, too.

Only one nagging question remained: *could she be controlled?*

Ultimately, they determined she could be. After all, the state had adequate incentives to keep her in check. Along with the prestige of overseeing a very high profile development, Claire would receive a lot of the credit if the project succeeded. An opportunity of this nature would enable her to punch her own ticket for her next career move. As long as Claire remembered the source of her power, the governor had nothing to worry about.

Levin now anticipated some opposition from one of the city's most influential political forces—attorney Tony Basilica, the chair of the city's Democratic Party. Husky and balding with dark eyes, Basilica had the looks and vocabulary of Tony Soprano. He spent his career defending criminals as a trial lawyer. When he wasn't in the courtroom, he was in a back room practicing politics in a way that would make Machiavelli proud.

Basilica had established himself as New London's kingmaker. In that role, he had fought and won a lot of political fights alongside Levin. Basilica had even managed a couple of Levin's campaigns. The two were tight.

Levin wanted Basilica's blessing before revamping the NLDC and turning it over to Claire, so he and an associate met with Basilica and one of his associates. Basilica listened while Levin explained his consulting role with the governor's office.

Hearing nothing that sounded problematic, Basilica said little while Levin talked up the idea of reviving the NLDC. Then Levin got to the hard part—he wanted to appoint Claire Gaudiani to lead it.

Basilica grinned and shook his head from side to side. "No way," he said.

Levin attempted to explain.

Basilica cut him off. "No way," he repeated. "You're not doin' that. No way." Basilica reminded him that Levin had previously convinced him to work with Claire on a city initiative to improve the public schools. Reluctantly, Basilica had gone along but felt that Claire had embarrassed him. Basilica had not forgotten. "Look, we've already had our experience with her," Basilica said. "We don't want her. It's a bad idea. Tell her to stick to French history or whatever the hell she teaches."

Levin left the meeting unsuccessful, even though, Basilica later recalled, "He told us, 'It's the only way Rowland is going to send money to the city.'"

GETTING TO YES

Buoyed by Levin's suggestion to jump-start the NLDC, Claire started rounding up people to fill board seats at the agency. She didn't have trouble finding takers. Many of the key civic leaders she'd been brainstorming with were eager to volunteer. None was more enthused than Steve Percy, a New London real-estate broker who specialized in businesses and marinas. Percy had written the essay calling for leadership in the city that had prompted Claire to take a hands-on role months earlier.

Claire had asked Percy what resources the city had to put against its economic problems. Among other things, Percy suggested a twenty-four-acre peninsula known as the New London Mills property, a prime piece of vacant real estate along the city's waterfront. Other people Claire polled said the same thing. Claire didn't know anything about the land in question or why it was vacant. Percy knew the background well.

The New London Mills property had been home to a linoleum manufacturer. Before that, cotton mills and other industries had occupied the land. But all the brick mill buildings had since been demolished, leaving behind nothing but piles of rubble atop land contaminated with all sorts of industrial pollutants.

A few years earlier, a company called Ocean Quest had approached the city and proposed building a $41 million aquatic facility on the site. Ocean Quest promised to build a water camp for kids, complete with a mock submarine and other tourist attractions.

Eager for jobs and tax revenue, the city embraced the project. The state took an active role, too, pledging millions of dollars to rid the site of environmental contaminants as preparation for development. But after all that, the Ocean Quest backers lacked the money to carry out the project. Suddenly, the twenty-four-acre brownfield was available. It wasn't the prettiest piece of real estate, but it had a grand location—right on the water, at the mouth of the Thames.

Claire, Percy, and the others in the small group emerging to take over the NLDC quickly settled on the idea that one of the agency's primary objectives should be to try to lure a *Fortune* 500 company to the site. Something like that could generate some instant momentum. But no one Claire was talking to in New London knew what it would take to attract such a company.

Claire didn't know the answers either, but she knew someone who did—George Milne Jr., an executive at Pfizer, the world's largest pharmaceutical company. Pfizer had a massive research facility in nearby Groton, just across the river from New London. As president of central research, Milne ran the Groton facility and ranked among the most respected corporate executives in southeastern Connecticut. He also served on the board of trustees at Connecticut College, which his son attended. And Claire's husband, Dr. David Burnett, worked under Milne at Pfizer and ran the company's corporate university. These kinds of connections were among the reasons Levin had recommended Claire to lead the NLDC.

Claire figured she had to get someone like Milne to join the board of directors and help them figure out how to market the New London Mills property to a major corporation. She decided to call him at home and request a face-to-face meeting.

George Milne hadn't become president of Pfizer's central research by accident. He had a chemistry degree from Yale and a Ph.D. in organic chemistry from MIT. After joining Pfizer in 1970, he spent eleven years doing chemistry and pharmacology research until being appointed director of the company's department of immunology and infectious diseases. Milne turned out to be a promising corporate leader, too. Intense, driven, and polished, he had all the right attributes for a successful executive in his industry. Pfizer made him a senior vice president in 1988 and then eventually president of the central research division and a senior vice president in charge of the company's global interests in human and veterinary medicine.

Under Milne, the research division's annual investment rose from $493 million to over $2 billion. During that same period, the scientific staff doubled to more than eight thousand people. With a unique blend of scientific smarts and corporate savvy, Milne knew the importance of translating breakthrough medicines into financial windfalls for shareholders.

He also knew something the rest of the pharmaceutical industry didn't: Pfizer was sitting on a drug that promised to take American culture by storm and propel Pfizer past all its rivals. A few years earlier, Pfizer conducted clinical trials for a drug called sildenafil, which was intended to expand blood vessels, enabling greater blood flow to the heart. But the response in alleviating suffering from heart problems was insufficient. At the close of the clinical trials, the female patients returned their surplus medication, as required, but many male patients did not. When clinicians investigated, they discovered that sildenafil had a powerful effect on men who struggled with impotence.

The accidental discovery had enormous potential. Millions of men in the United States struggle with impotence. If men could overcome the condition by simply taking a pill, this drug promised to be a rainmaker. Pfizer commissioned a new round of clinical trials for sildenafil and assigned the drug a new name: Viagra.

While Governor Rowland was busy trying to propel his political star higher by redeveloping Connecticut's urban centers, George Milne had aspirations of his own. The emergence of Viagra elevated him to a position of great prominence in the company as he led the effort to promote it to the nation's medical community.

"Impotence has a major, and sometimes devastating, psychological and social impact on patients and their partners," Milne told the American Urological Association at its annual meeting in 1997. "Effective drugs currently available involve injections and for that reason have not been widely accepted." Milne insisted Pfizer had the answer to this dilemma: "Viagra, because it is a pill and enhances the normal sexual response, offers advantages to these patients in terms of both convenience and safety."

Busy as he was, Milne graciously welcomed a call at home from Claire. After explaining the NLDC and its virtues, Claire informed Milne she had agreed to serve as its president. Impressed, Milne was not surprised. He knew Claire's penchant for taking on big initiatives and going full tilt.

Claire briefly indicated that one of the NLDC's top priorities would be to market the former New London Mills property, and she wanted to meet with him about it.

"It will have to be at seven in the morning in my office," Milne said.

"That's fine. I'll come in."

They agreed on a date.

August 28, 1997

Giddy, Susette arrived at a law firm in New London to sign the closing documents on her new home. There, for the first time, she met the seller, who indicated she had driven by the house and seen the new paint job.

"Doesn't the house look great?" Susette said.

The seller looked disgusted. "Pink?" she asked, then insisted it was not right for the period of the house.

"That's not true," Susette said. "I got the color right off the historic paint chart at Benjamin Moore."

The seller was not impressed.

"Besides," Susette said, "the color is Odessa Rose, not pink."

"Well, it will certainly brighten up the neighborhood," the seller said sarcastically.

Susette grinned. "And . . . so . . . won't . . . I," she said.

A half hour later, Susette had the keys to the front door and the title to the property. And at that point, she didn't care what the previous owner thought of her or the new paint color. The place was hers, and that was all that mattered.

That night, she drove to the house. It was empty and dark inside. From the porch, she could hear and see the water. She plopped down in a rocker.

For the first time in her life, she owned property in her name. Even her husband didn't know she had purchased the place. He still hadn't figured out she was leaving. She'd tell him eventually.

The house afforded her a sanctuary, a place where she could come and go as she pleased, a place to be alone. She pinched herself. She hadn't experienced that kind of freedom since before she had had her first child at age sixteen.

On a notepad, she scribbled some thoughts: "I don't think my life could be better and I know I have never been happier in my life than I am now, sitting on the porch rocker watching the water go by."

August 29, 1997

Claire considered George Milne a vital player to have on board if the NLDC was going to make a sudden impact. She had to get him to commit, so her pitch had to impress him. But heading into her meeting with Milne, Claire had more on her mind than simply getting him to join the NLDC's board of directors. She'd been doing some thinking. Milne's Groton office was directly across the river from the vacant mill site in New London. It was no secret that Pfizer had outgrown its Groton facility and had been hunting for a large tract of real estate to build more clinical office space. Never one to miss an opportunity, Claire planned to make the most of her one-on-one audience with the man ultimately in charge of site selection for Pfizer's new home. She figured that luring Pfizer to a contaminated brownfield was a pipe dream, but she had to ask.

Milne welcomed her warmly and listened politely as she explained in more detail the plan to revive the NLDC as an agency committed to helping reverse New London's economic misfortunes. She rattled off the names and credentials of those who had already pledged to join the agency's board. But, Claire explained, the one thing she didn't have in the NLDC's ranks was the CEO of a major corporation.

Milne needed more information to understand why a local development agency needed a major corporate executive on its board. Claire told him about the New London Mills property, describing it as a splendid piece of acreage sitting dormant right along the river.

"You may even want to think about it for Pfizer," she said.

It was a soft pitch, designed to see if Milne would swing. He didn't. Pfizer's site-selection team had been reviewing potential sites for a year.

"Well, it wouldn't work for us," he said, dismissing the idea at once. "We're down to two sites."

"Well, okay, even if it wouldn't work for you," she said, "you would still be an important person to the board because you would know the kinds of things that a *Fortune* 500 company would look for in a building space."

Joining another board wasn't something Milne really had time for. His plate at Pfizer was pretty full: decision day was looming for selecting a development site for the new research-and-development facility, and the company was ramping up to put a full-court press on the federal Food and Drug Administration (FDA) to fast-track Viagra through the approval process. With Pfizer projecting hundreds of millions in revenue from the impotence drug, a lot was riding on the FDA application.

But Claire pressed, stressing the virtues of the NLDC and the fact that she and Steve Percy were already committed to doing what it would take to market the mill property. "It's a great piece of land, and it needs to be developed," she explained. "But the people in the city don't actually know how to do that. We are people who can make this happen."

Milne found it hard to say no. "What's the commitment?" he asked.

"I'm going to tell everybody at the first meeting that we're going to stay together one year," Claire said. "If we can't get something dramatic going in twelve months, we'll abandon."

As a personal favor to Claire, Milne pledged six months. That's a long enough period, he suggested, to determine whether he had anything worthwhile to contribute.

Claire accepted that.

6

POWER STEERING

September 10, 1997

Become an RN without classes. The advertisement on the hospital bulletin board caught Susette's eye. She folded one up and put it in her bag.

After finishing her EMT shift, she went home to work on the house. In her mailbox she found a letter from the law firm Conway & Londregan, which had handled the closing on her house. She opened the envelope and found a bunch of papers and a cover letter. "Enclosed you will find your owner's title insurance policy," the firm's real-estate paralegal had written. "Please file this with your other important documents. If you should have any questions, please do not hesitate to contact our office."

Thinking nothing of it, Susette set the policy aside and retrieved the advertisement from her bag. The idea of going to school didn't thrill her, but Regents College in Albany, New York, offered a nursing degree through correspondence courses; she'd never have to set foot in a classroom. That sounded good to her. After all, she had to find a way to make more money. A nursing career seemed like a natural choice, especially with her education as a paramedic. In a little over a year she could complete the courses and become licensed as a registered nurse.

She decided to apply for admission.

The same day, across town

Jay Levin liked what he saw. Under Claire's leadership, a competent group had already started assembling around her. Levin knew Steve Percy well—the two were friends. Despite having no track record in large-scale urban renewal, Percy knew a great deal about commercial real estate. Much of the NLDC's time would be spent acquiring properties and redeveloping them, so Percy's connections and experience would be a major asset. Levin didn't know Milne well, but he certainly knew his reputation. As Levin had promised Claire, all necessary paperwork had been filed with the secretary of state to reestablish the NLDC as a legitimate nonprofit agency. Levin prepared a confidential memo to Peter Ellef in order to update him. Levin's contract with Ellef didn't include scoping out the old mill site for development possibilities. In fact, the mill site was a long way from the pier area that the governor had his eye on. But it didn't take an insider to realize that the governor would welcome a *Fortune* 500 company at the mill site.

"A focused development vision is already emerging," Levin told Ellef. "As you are also aware (and we are pleased to have happen) we have pursued additional projects for you." He continued: "Although not originally our primary concern, these efforts have involved extensive diplomacy with City officials and discovery of facts relating to the apparently collapsed Ocean Quest project at 36–90 Pequot Avenue.

"Of additional significance is the rapid revitalization of the New London Development Corporation under the direction of Dr. Claire Gaudiani, President of Connecticut College."

Levin assured Ellef that he would personally draft the new by-laws for the NLDC. "City leaders are divided on its relevance and Dr. Gaudiani's leadership," he wrote, "but we will work with you and the Governor's office to insure it . . . carry out the ultimate plan approved by you and the Governor."

Levin requested more money for all the extra work. "Difficult local personalities and circumstances rendered our time frame overly ambitious," he explained. "Yet we believe that we have the vehicle to carry the project into the future, but we need to strongly manage the final production of that New London Development Corporation vehicle."

The word "vehicle" was appropriate. Levin had put the governor in the driver's seat in New London. And by carefully managing Gaudiani, the state would be able to control the project from Hartford, steering around the Democratic-controlled city government.

Ellef approved another hundred-thousand-dollar payment to Levin.

It didn't take Claire long to figure out that her primary opponent in New London was Democratic Party chairman Tony Basilica. Although Levin's efforts to appease Basilica had failed, Claire decided to reach out to him. She called his office and left a message inviting him to the NLDC's first board meeting, explaining it would be organizational in nature in order to map out the agency's vision and objectives.

A few days later she got a voice-mail message from Basilica, telling her he didn't give his permission for such a meeting. Claire didn't let that stop her. She knew plenty of Italian American men who thought Italian women needed their permission. She called his office back and left an equally direct message: the meeting would go on, and he was still welcome to attend.

September 19, 1997

Claire convened the NLDC's first board meeting in a downtown building. After her rousing pep talk, the group elected officers and issued committee assignments. George Milne and Steve Percy agreed to co-chair the commercial-development committee. Tops on their to-do list was mapping out what it would take to attract a major corporation to the mill site. Milne decided he needed to see the site to get a better feel for its potential. Claire had never actually seen the site either. Percy agreed to take them to it.

Milne wasn't quite sure what to say when he first set foot on the property. It had been described to him as exquisite, but all he saw was acres of weeds and litter. The site looked a lot like a dump. It smelled like one, too. The neighborhood contained a big sewer-treatment facility, which essentially consisted of some oversized cesspools. Under the summer heat, the plant threw off a horrific odor.

"It smelled like you were in a toilet with someone who had a terrible illness," Claire said.

Milne observed another problem: a huge scrap-metal junkyard next door to the mill site. The place was an eyesore and no doubt had its own environmental issues with oil, grease, rubber, and other contaminants. Even the nearby historic Fort Trumbull was in shambles. Its overgrown brush and neglected buildings cast a depressing shadow on the entire landscape.

By the time Milne left, he had serious concerns about the prospects of marketing the site. "The whole setting was not particularly attractive," he said. "It was one with enormous liabilities."

Just the price tag for environmental remediation would scare off most corporations. Then there was the issue of indemnification. No company would settle into a site without some guarantees that it would not be liable for previous contamination. Milne saw other problems, too. "The whole environment was so unattractive that it was unlikely that any serious investor would ever come in," he said.

Claire heard all that. But she remained convinced that a junkyard could be erased. A sewer plant could be upgraded and capped if necessary. A fort could be refurbished and even turned into a tourist attraction. And soil could be removed and replaced. To her, the bottom line was that twenty-four acres of waterfront real estate weren't easy to come by. This land was ready to be had. It was simply too valuable to give up on.

While Milne stressed that all these costs were simply too much for a corporation to take on, Claire relied on her other strength—finding money. Jay Levin had given her reason to anticipate state assistance. "Jay said to me, 'Ellef promised that you are forty-eight hours away from a face-to-face with the governor if you can bring a *Fortune* 500 company to that land,'" Claire said.

This made the prospect of state funding real. It also got Milne focused on what kind of state commitment was necessary. "My entire focus," he explained, "was on trying to answer the question: 'If this was the one key empty piece of land and asset that might attract major commercial development, what would have to happen to make that even plausible?'" He agreed to compile a list.

Privately, Claire hadn't given up on the idea of Pfizer ultimately landing on the mill site. Although Milne had offered her no hope that that would happen, three things remained true: Pfizer needed land; the city had land; and the state had the power and the resources to make that land financially attractive. There was still a long way to go, but once Milne identified the needs, the governor simply had to be convinced to fill them.

Claire had more ambition than both men. She came from a family of high achievers who were all about overcoming long odds. Her grandfather Augusto had arrived in the United States from Italy in 1889. Determined to become a doctor, he had attended Columbia College of Physicians and Surgeons and become the school's first Italian American graduate. He opened his practice in East Harlem, where he had an endless number of patients who spoke his native language.

Augusto and his wife, Rosa, clung to their Italian heritage. They spoke, ate, and prayed in Italian. Yet all six of their children were taught to speak perfect English outside the home. Together Augusto and Rosa helped Italian immigrants get into college and medical school; they helped found Cabrini Hospital; and they helped start schools for immigrant children in New York City. In 1919, with Rosa stricken with pneumonia, Augusto turned to his best friend for help. Dr. Vincent Gaudiani, a brilliant Italian American surgeon who had received his medical training in Rome, saved Rosa by operating on her at home. Augusto and Rosa went on to have one more daughter, Vera, who grew up and married Gaudiani's son, Vincent Jr., himself a doctor.

Vincent Gaudiani Jr. and Vera had six children. Claire was the eldest. Her father had a profound influence on her. Highly educated and an extremely demanding perfectionist, Dr. Gaudiani wasn't satisfied when Claire came home from school with a 98 on a test. If any other student had a 98 or higher, Claire had not done well enough. He taught her an order of priorities: ambition, focus, and intensity.

Claire's life became a quest to satisfy personal drives and ambitions. Everywhere she went she broke barriers and stirred controversy. At Indiana University, she became the first married woman with a child to complete a Ph.D. in the French and Italian department. The department had to take an unprecedented vote to grant special permission when Claire insisted on breast-feeding her baby during her doctoral exams.

Getting Pfizer to New London was just another barrier to clear.

7

WELCOME TO THE NEIGHBORHOOD

September 27, 1997

Her red hair tucked under a wide-brim sunhat, Susette rested on her hands and knees on the sidewalk in front of her house, surrounded by piles of weeds she had dug up. Sweating within a long-sleeved shirt, she yanked on a root as she heard a car pull up behind her. Remaining on all fours, she looked over her shoulder. A shiny Jaguar stopped at the curb, a few feet from her.

A middle-aged man wearing jeans and a loose-fitting, short-sleeved T-shirt got out.

"I heard this place got bought up," he said, looking down on her.

She stood up. "Yeah, I bought it," she said, wiping the sweat from her face. "Who are you?"

"Billy," he said. "Billy Von Winkle. I own some buildings in the neighborhood."

"I'm Susette Kelo."

"It's pretty hot to be working in long sleeves," he said, grinning.

She removed her hat, letting her long red hair fall over her shoulders. "Redheads burn easy," she said. "I have to cover up when I work in the sun."

He nodded.

"So you live in the neighborhood?" she asked.

"I used to," he said. "What do you do?"

"I'm a paramedic. What do you do?"

"Nothing," he said, laughing.

Von Winkle had spent much of his adult life in the Fort Trumbull neighborhood. At one time, he had worked at the Naval Undersea Warfare Center. Twenty years earlier, he had quit his job there and started buying up rundown buildings around the fort. He moved into one of the places. One by one, he renovated the others, installing new heating and plumbing systems and converting them to apartments.

"I drive around all day because I have a bunch of rental properties in the area," he said. "And I own the deli on the corner."

"You married?" she asked.

"Yeah, I've got two teenage sons, and my wife, Jenny, is a registered nurse. I call her 'Do-what.'"

Susette gave him a puzzled look.

"Every time I tell her to do something, she says, 'Do what?' So I call her 'Do-what.'"

Susette burst out laughing.

"What about you? You married?"

She stopped laughing. "I'm divorced," she said. "I came down from Preston. I'm starting over."

"You got any kids?" he asked.

"Five sons. They're all grown."

Von Winkle ran his eyes up and down Susette. She looked too young, and her figure looked too good for a mother of five grown boys. She grinned.

"Well, welcome to the 'hood," he said.

"Thanks."

"Do you want to go for coffee?" he asked.

She explained she really needed to finish removing the brush from the sidewalk.

"Don't bother cleaning that up," he said. "Just call the city and tell them to clean it up."

She laughed. He smiled. "C'mon, Red. Hop in," he said.

No one had called her that in years. And she'd never been in a Jaguar. She brushed the dirt off her knees and got in. A couple of blocks from Susette's house, they passed the city's sewer plant, noting the smell. Neighborhood residents had complained about its odor for years. The city basically ignored them. Von Winkle couldn't resist boasting what he had done just one month earlier.

Fed up with City Hall's inaction, he had sent a fax to the city manager that read: "It stinks down here. Can you smell it in your office yet? In time you will!" A week later, during a public hearing at City Hall, Von Winkle entered the building with big buckets of chicken manure. He dumped some on the steps and put the rest in the elevator, along with a bag of Glade air freshener. The stench forced people to evacuate the building, and it shut down City Hall.

Susette laughed hysterically.

"Didn't you hear about this incident?" he asked.

"No," she said, trying to regain her composure. "I don't know anything about this."

Von Winkle couldn't believe it. The case had been all over the news. Even Jay Leno had joked about it in his monologue. After a monthlong investigation, the police had arrested him just a couple of days earlier for reckless endangerment and breach of peace.

Susette explained she hadn't paid much attention to the news lately. And she hadn't really met many people in the neighborhood yet. But she admired Von Winkle's willingness to stand up to City Hall.

His tales of mischief kept her laughing until they reached Stash's, a neighborhood bar that occasionally hosted live bands. The minute they pulled up, one of the worst memories of Susette's life flashed through her mind.

On a wet evening in 1991, she had been at a neighbor's farm, looking at dairy cows when her son Nicholas—seventeen at the time—left the house to attend a sports banquet. It was a cold, wet night. When Susette got home, her thirteen-year-old son Jonathan met her at the door, his face ghost white.

"Nick was in a car accident," he said.

Just miles from home, Nick ended up in a head-on collision when a drunk driver crossed the median at high speed. After surgery and hospitalization, Nick survived. Days later, a newspaper story reported that a concert at Stash's had been canceled due to an injury to a band member, the same guy who had crashed into Susette's son. Susette felt the story had a sympathetic tone.

Livid, Susette called the paper. "I screamed bloody murder at the reporter," she recalled. "'Do you have any idea what this man has done?'"

The injury to her son put Susette on a crusade. A drunk driver had taken something away from her. She vowed to make sure the driver was brought to justice. But in the end, she felt the system had wronged her; a failure to administer an alcohol test at the accident scene ended up hampering the prosecutor's case, and the driver served very little jail time. Unable to let go, Susette joined Mothers Against Drunk Driving (MADD), and she never allowed her older boys to bring alcohol into her home.

While Susette talked, Von Winkle ordered a beer. He had an edge to him, she thought. His off-the-wall antics and the fearless, distant look in his eyes made him irresistibly unpredictable. She couldn't help but like him, especially his sense of humor. He might be the perfect friend in a new neighborhood, she figured.

An hour later, Von Winkle dropped her back at her house and gave her his cell phone number.

"If you need anything, Red, call me."

8

VIAGRA TIME

September 29, 1997

For George Milne and Pfizer, the big day had arrived: the pharmaceutical company filed its new drug application with the FDA. "VIAGRA . . . is indicated for the treatment of erectile dysfunction," the application letter read. "The physiological mechanism responsible for erection of the penis involves the release of nitric oxide in the corpus cavernosum in response to sexual stimulation."

Pfizer made a medical case for the drug's importance and asked the FDA to fast-track Viagra through the approval process. If approved, Viagra sales would easily pay for the company's new research facility.

While Pfizer pressed the FDA, Claire continued working on Milne. Over a series of private meetings and conversations with him, she had hammered home the idea that Pfizer could become New London's economic savior. A decision to build a research facility in the city would be akin to getting Macy's to anchor a newly constructed mall, only on a much larger scale. Rather than just generate jobs and revenue, Pfizer could really improve lives.

The idea of leading an urban renaissance in New London had some appeal to Milne. So did the site's close proximity to Pfizer's existing labs. Claire suggested the two facilities could be linked by water vessels transporting employees back and forth. If the state was willing to sweeten the pot enough, certainly Pfizer could at least consider the possibility.

Milne agreed to visit the property again.

Kurt Cobain's nihilistic voice wasn't one Susette would have instinctively chosen to drone through her stereo while she diced vegetables on a wooden cutting board in her kitchen. But years of listening to her sons' music had turned her into a Nirvana fan. The habit of preparing large meals had stuck with her too, although she now lived alone. She dumped the vegetables into the giant soup pot on the stove.

Suddenly she heard a loud rap at the front door. It was Billy Von Winkle.

"C'mon in," she yelled over the music.

"Hi, Red."

"How's Jenny?" she asked, smiling.

"Oh, Do-what? She's fine," Von Winkle said, inspecting the house. "Well, this is a nice place. To think it was for sale for eight years and I never bought it." They both smiled. "Then I would have owned all the houses in the neighborhood," he said.

"It didn't look this way when I bought it," she said, explaining how she had replaced all the curtains and window shades, puttied all the nail holes, and stripped and refinished the hardwood floors.

He asked what she had used to sand the floors. Sandpaper, she told him. "I did it on my hands and knees."

"Why didn't you use a machine?"

"Had someone showed me, I probably would have used a machine," she said. "I just did it the hard way. Then I polyurethaned the floors."

Impressed, Von Winkle nodded.

She showed him the staircase leading to the upstairs. "The steps are one hundred years old," she said.

"They look good," he said.

She had had to pull up the carpet and remove layers of old paint to expose the original stair treads. "This time I got smarter and used a heat gun," she told him. "Then I stained them with a whitewash, and I painted the molding hunter green."

"You've done a lot here," he said.

Only two major projects remained, she said: furnishing the rooms with antiques and putting in raised flower beds made of granite on the outside. But she didn't have enough money for antiques and granite, at least not yet.

Von Winkle liked her ambition. He opened a kitchen closet. It was jammed with vegetable cans. "What is this, the grocery store?" he said.

"Just about," she said, explaining that she still had not gotten used to buying for just herself.

"You got any beer?" he asked.

"No," she said, inviting him to come back later for stew.

He declined. He had stopped in only to check on her and say hello.

October 1997

Barely a stone's throw from Susette's house, Claire and Steve Percy accompanied Milne back onto the mill site. It was a sunny, brisk morning. Without the summer heat, the sewer plant's foul odor was not as obvious. The surrounding scenery was still ugly, but this time Milne focused on something else—the stunning tip of the property that poked into the Thames River.

"You know, Claire," Milne said, "I can just see the Pfizer ferry going back and forth from that point of land to our site in Groton."

Percy got a rush. He sensed that Milne was on his way to trying to bring Pfizer to New London. Claire had broken through. Milne was finally looking at the site in a different light.

"Having seen the possibility," explained Milne, "I warmed to the notion that if enough pieces could come together, that in fact this would be something that Pfizer might be interested in." He wanted to look into the matter more thoroughly.

9

CAN YOU GUYS LOOK INTO THIS?

Jim Serbia specialized in assessing environmental health and safety risks associated with real-estate development done by large corporations. In 1997, he had left Anheuser-Busch in St. Louis to become the real-estate manager for Pfizer's research division. He reported to George Milne.

When he arrived in Connecticut, Serbia became acquainted with Pfizer's previous construction project and the company's immediate needs, which were directly related. In the early 1990s, Pfizer had expanded its hundred-acre research-and-development campus in Groton. At the time, one hundred acres had seemed more than adequate. But the drugmaker enjoyed phenomenal growth in a five-year span and by 1997 had maximized the capacity of its research facilities. It desperately needed more space, especially for animal labs.

This time, the company wanted a large, continuous tract of land with plenty of potential for future growth and development. The New England real-estate market had plenty of options. When word got out that Pfizer was on the hunt for property, proposals poured in. The company ranked potential development sites according to four criteria: expansion potential, schedule, cost, and risk.

Over a one-year period, Serbia and his colleagues reviewed many proposals. By the fall of 1997, Pfizer had narrowed its list of candidates to a few sites. Serbia and his team then met with

Milne, who listened thoughtfully to their presentation. All of the sites under consideration had upsides for Pfizer.

Then Milne posed an unexpected question: "What about the old New London Mills site?"

Serbia thought Milne had to be kidding. The site hadn't even been discussed, much less looked at. It had a fraction of the acreage offered by the other sites. And the land had been home to an industrial mill, a proposition that promised significant environmental-cleanup hurdles. None of the top sites under consideration required significant environmental remediation. The cleanup in New London would delay the start date of construction. The other sites were ready to go right away. To Serbia and others, it was hard to see an upside to the mill site.

"Can you guys look at this site?" Milne asked.

Serbia dutifully agreed. The company's architects and project designers were also not enthused. They had spent months analyzing and accessing the other sites. It would require a big effort in a very short time period to evaluate the New London site. Those already familiar with it thought even considering it was nuts. Nonetheless, Serbia and his associates went all-out to find the answers Milne had requested.

Susette checked her caller ID. It contained a number she didn't recognize. She dialed it. A man answered.

"I had your number on my caller ID," she said.

"What's your number? he asked.

She told him. He insisted he had called Susette's number only after someone at her number had called him and left a message.

"Well, I didn't call you," she snapped. "Perhaps one of my sons called your phone from my house. Do you have any kids?"

"No," the man said, "I don't have any kids."

"Well, I didn't call your damn house," she said before abruptly hanging up on him.

A few minutes later the man called back. Susette was about to tell him where to go, but before she could, he apologized for the misunderstanding and suggested the mix-up was probably on his end. "I hand out flyers because I buy junk and antiques," he said. "I thought maybe someone called about antiques."

"You like antiques?" Susette asked.

An hour later, they were still talking. Susette finally introduced herself to Tim LeBlanc, a forty-year-old bachelor who lived alone about twenty miles from New London. Besides collecting antiques for a hobby, LeBlanc worked as a professional landscaper. His specialty was stonework.

Susette told him she was in the hunt for some antiques and wanted to have some raised flower beds put in around her house. LeBlanc offered to help, and he invited her to visit his place and check out his antiques collection. She accepted.

It didn't take long for Jim Serbia and his team to complete the analysis Milne had requested on the mill site. The picture wasn't pretty. Environmentally, the ground beneath and around the site had the signs of being a toxic dump. At a minimum, tons of hazardous soil would have to be excavated and removed. New soil would have to be trucked in.

Legally, the polluted land posed a bigger challenge. Once taking over the site, Pfizer could become liable for any environmental problems that surfaced in the future. The only way to fully protect against future claims would be to get the state to indemnify Pfizer, a highly unlikely proposition. There was no precedent for the state's assuming environmental liability on behalf of a corporation.

Beyond these hurdles, the mill site presented problems that were completely outside Pfizer's ability to solve. First, the city-owned sewage-treatment plant bordered one side of the property. In addition to emitting a terrible odor that would regularly overwhelm the mill site, the plant needed upgrades and modifications to make it more environmentally safe and aesthetically appealing.

Second, a huge scrap-metal junkyard abutted another border of the mill property. A terrible eyesore, the junkyard also made access to the mill site nearly impossible.

Third, the city's infrastructure around the site—from roads

to utilities—was nowhere near sufficient to support a state-of-the-art, global research facility. On top of all this, the site failed to satisfy the primary immediate need for more lab space. The city's infrastructure wasn't capable of handling all the effluent that would be produced in the animal laboratories. New London barely had sufficient sewage capacity for its residents as it was.

The site had one final, overarching deficiency: size. The number one criterion on Pfizer's wish list was that the land had to be big enough for future expansion. Anything under a hundred acres was too small. The mill site consisted of just twenty-four acres.

By every vital criterion at the time, the New London site failed the test. New London was the absolute worst choice for Pfizer.

The detailed analysis that Serbia's team provided was in stark contrast to Claire's assessment of the site. She preferred to focus on the possibilities, not the drawbacks. And she had a much grander perspective than the singular needs of a corporation. That was immediately clear to Phil Michalowski, a leading land-use design expert working as a private consultant for Pfizer. At Pfizer's request, Michalowski helped prepare some land-use concept plans for the area around the mill site. He also started meeting with Claire.

"I remember discussions with Claire," Michalowski said. "It starts out as a global picture. Think of the Web site Google Earth—it's a mapping program that starts with the globe and works down to New London. That's the way Claire's mind works." He continued, "I was trying to focus on physical land-use issues in New London. She was looking at the status of the state economy for the next hundred years and trying to use the project as a mechanism to steer resources to educational and social service in the city. Early on she was trying to make those connections. I lauded those ideas."

The more Claire and Milne talked about Claire's vision, the more Milne began to laud her ideas too. And by helping the city, Pfizer could also benefit. The possibilities were endless. For instance, the thirty-two-acre Naval Undersea Warfare Center next door to the mill site could be acquired and redeveloped into something to complement Pfizer. With the base closed down, the navy wanted to unload the real estate. Better still, a lot of the land around the fort and the mill site could use a makeover. With Pfizer's commitment and state backing, the NLDC could assemble a massive chunk of waterfront real estate and transform this entire area into an upscale, corporate area.

"As cities go, New London is sized where a single investment of this type coupled with other downstream investments could make all the difference in the world," Milne said. "You could in fact at least contemplate a transforming set of investments that would do what the city badly needed, which is to build up its tax base."

For that to happen, Claire maintained, Pfizer had to develop the mill site.

For that to happen, Milne insisted, the state would have to be a partner and commit to a sizable investment.

Claire agreed. She called the governor's office.

Weeks earlier, Governor Rowland had elevated Peter Ellef to be his chief of staff. Ellef took the call. Claire told Ellef that Pfizer was ready to consider New London. Ready to deal, Ellef scheduled a meeting for Claire and Milne with the governor.

10

THE THINGS WE WANT

A stack of nursing manuals under her arm, Susette arrived home and found antiques on her porch. Instantly she knew where they had come from. It had been only a few weeks since she had journeyed to Tim LeBlanc's apartment. He had a lot of antiques and a great deal of knowledge about them. They started talking on an almost-daily basis and getting together a couple of times a week. He had even volunteered to help her put in raised flower beds alongside her house.

As soon as she got inside, she called him to thank him for the delivery. Toward the end of the call, LeBlanc's voice took a serious tone.

"I love you, Susette," he said.

The phrase jarred her. The words "I love you" had not been spoken to her as a child. Her first husband had never told her that. Neither had her second husband. She didn't know how to respond.

"What the hell is the matter with you?" she snapped.

"What?" he asked.

"You don't just walk around saying that to people you just met," she said. "Don't say that unless you mean it. Good-bye."

She slammed down the phone.

Governor Rowland was eager to hear what Claire and Milne had to say about the prospects of attracting a *Fortune* 500 company to New London. They did not disappoint.

After sharing some brief overview of the possibilities, Claire left most of the talking to Milne. As he would have in a corporate setting, Milne got right to the point with the governor.

"We spent thirty minutes with him," Milne recalled. "We outlined what would be possible broadly and what would be required to make all of this attractive to anybody, including Pfizer. That included such things as accelerating renovation of the fort, which at that point was just an overgrown jumble of trees and discarded junk; the Calamari junkyard; the whole sewer-treatment center; and all of the issues associated with permitting the site."

The governor listened intently. Milne made clear that no company—not Pfizer nor anyone else—would take on the mill site unless the state stepped in.

Sharp and shrewd, the governor got the picture. Like Claire and Milne, he preferred to move quickly when opportunity knocked. The governor planned to visit Fort Trumbull himself. In the meantime, written proposals and schematic drawings were needed to take the discussions from a conceptual level to something more concrete.

After meeting with the governor, Milne knew that the prospect of Pfizer's going to New London was real. He and Claire talked about his role with the NLDC.

"I have to leave the board," Milne told her. On one hand, he was trying to obtain real estate for his corporation to develop. On the other hand, he was chairing a real-estate development committee for a nonprofit board that was courting his company.

"No, you don't have to leave the board," Claire insisted. "You can recuse yourself from everything related to that site."

Milne did just that. And in his Pfizer role he mapped out in more specific terms what Pfizer needed from the state in order to say yes to New London. Pfizer wanted nearby Fort Trumbull renovated and turned into an attractive state park. It wanted the city's sewage treatment upgraded and capped to contain the odor. And it wanted the scrap-metal junkyard out of the picture entirely; the state should buy out the business or do whatever else was necessary to make it vanish.

The biggest demand came with a strong push from Claire: that money be set aside for the NLDC to assemble an additional ninety acres of real estate next door to the mill site for developing a five-star hotel, state-of-the-art conference center, office space, and upscale housing and shops to complement the Pfizer facility. Pfizer wanted the city to acquire the large naval base (thirty-two acres) and the properties in the residential neighborhood between it and the mill site (roughly sixty acres). The state would have to appropriate millions of dollars to the NLDC, which would in turn buy up all these properties, clearing the way for redevelopment in line with Pfizer's wishes.

If the state agreed to this approach, Pfizer could then serve as the gateway to a renaissance in New London. But without the state's willingness to help secure and redevelop the additional ninety acres, Pfizer would not come to the mill site.

"The notion that this could become a key unlocking piece already had been in discussion with the governor," Milne later explained.

The terms and conditions left little room for misunderstanding. Claire made sure that the state understood that timing was critical. Milne didn't want a new Pfizer facility surrounded by a perpetual construction site. To avoid this, Claire insisted everyone had to work fast, coining the phrase "Pfizer Time."

Claire and Milne's proposal was appealing to the Rowland administration. It certainly was not what Ellef had originally asked Jay Levin to help with, but by working in concert with Pfizer and the NLDC, the Rowland administration had the potential to get much faster results. And the idea of constructing new waterfront housing on the Thames apparently appealed to Ellef personally. In a memo, Claire wrote that Ellef had asked her to save him a condo: "Two bedrooms, two baths, ocean view."

"His name," Claire assured the state's commissioner of economic and community development, "is on the list with numerous others who decided they wanted priority housing in the new New London."

The governor pledged a strong state commitment and promised to come back with a written set of incentives that the state would be willing to provide Pfizer in exchange for its commitment to develop in New London.

Lloyd Beachy had never had aspirations of political power. The son of a Pennsylvania farmer, he joined the navy in the 1950s and became an intelligence officer specializing in naval aviation. After stints in the Pacific theater, Vietnam, and Hawaii, Beachy got assigned to the Pentagon. He finished his naval career at the Sound Lab at the Naval Undersea Warfare Center. In the midst of the cold war, the navy figured out that its top scientists weren't communicating with the intelligence community. Beachy served as a liaison between the two.

When he retired in 1979, Beachy and his wife, Sandy, decided to stay in New London. The small coastal city seemed like a great place to make a permanent home. They became involved in the local historical society and volunteered for all sorts of civic groups and initiatives. Their commitment to local causes didn't go unnoticed. One day Beachy's neighbor, a member of the city's Democratic Committee, asked Beachy to run for local office. The Democrats had candidates for all the city-council seats except one. Reluctantly, Beachy agreed to fill the final spot.

The Democrats never expected Beachy to win; they just appreciated his willingness to fill the ballot spot. Even Beachy didn't expect to win. But he did. His eventual reputation in the city for quiet, tireless service made him very popular.

Two years later, he was chosen to be the mayor. Days after taking the oath of office in December 1997, Beachy got a call from Claire. She congratulated him and invited him to her residence on the Connecticut College campus, saying she wanted to share hopes and dreams for New London. Beachy had never visited the president's private residence. He agreed to meet.

Sporting a gray beard and a yellow windbreaker, Beachy could easily have been mistaken for the captain of a fishing vessel. When he arrived, Claire greeted him at the door and ushered him inside. He noted the nice furnishings and perfect order.

"Would you like a cup of coffee?" she asked.

"Sure."

"C'mon in the kitchen."

As they entered the room, Beachy immediately spotted an easel with a bubble diagram depicting a new hotel, a conference center, and office buildings.

Claire opened cupboard doors in search of coffee cups and a coffeepot.

Beachy stared at the bubble diagram, trying to figure out the whereabouts of the buildings depicted. The geography looked very familiar, but the landmarks looked foreign. Then it dawned on him; the diagram depicted the Fort Trumbull neighborhood and surrounding peninsula, minus the existing homes and buildings. Stunned, Beachy glanced at Claire. She still had not found cups or a coffeemaker. The cupboards were empty.

She doesn't live here, Beachy thought to himself.

Determined, Claire rounded up one mug and a package of instant coffee. She boiled some water on the stove and made Beachy a cup of coffee before leading him to the dining-room table. While he sipped coffee, Claire explained each bubble on the chart.

Two and a half hours later, Claire escorted Beachy to the door. He had never gotten to share his vision for the city. That was the point, he realized, once he stepped outside.

December 11, 1997

George Milne received a letter marked "CONFIDENTIAL" from the commissioner of Connecticut's Department of Economic and Community Development.

"On behalf of the State of Connecticut and Governor John G. Rowland, I am pleased to provide this letter offering assistance to Pfizer, Inc. for development of a new facility in New London, Connecticut," it began. "This letter represents the State's commitment to ensure Pfizer's ability to select New London for a new Headquarters operation by defraying the cost of that development and improving its value through a comprehensive, State-funded waterfront improvement and development project."

These were the words Milne wanted to see.

The governor offered to:

- Release $4.5 million in liens currently held by the state against the twenty-four-acre New London mill site.
- Spend up to $2 million to relocate the Calamari junkyard to another site purchased by the state.
- Spend up to $20 million to develop historic Fort Trumbull into a state park.
- Provide a low-interest $7 million loan to the City of New London for improving the nearby sewage-treatment facility.
- Acquire the navy base with state money. "The State will develop a timetable to meet Pfizer's needs," the letter read.
- Provide $8 million to the NLDC for operating costs and acquiring properties in the neighborhood located between the mill site and the navy base.

"Please know that the State will continue to work with you to refine this proposal," the letter continued, "in order to meet the specifications of Pfizer, and to support their decision to locate their new facility in New London."

Claire followed up a few days later with her own commitment letter to Milne. "This commitment is presented in conjunction with the State of Connecticut and the City of New London," she said. The city had agreed to transfer the mill site, evaluated at $5.4 million, to Pfizer at no cost. It had also agreed to modify its zoning regulations to ensure that the mill site, the navy base, and the surrounding neighborhood could be redeveloped. Claire mapped out a comprehensive development scheme:

> In addition to your facility the project includes the development of the state's fourth biotechnology incubator, the refurbishment of historic Fort Trumbull, the reuse of the vacant Naval Underwater Warfare Center and the development of mixed retail and residential space that will be fully integrated into the surrounding neighborhoods of the City of New London.

In order to achieve these goals, it will be necessary to relocate the Calamari Bros. scrap dealer, upgrade utilities and infrastructure, and acquire a number of surrounding properties.

Claire promised that the NLDC would acquire the residential and commercial properties within the parameters of the redevelopment design plan. "We will work with you to refine this proposal to meet Pfizer's requirements," she said.

11

NATURAL-BORN LEADERS

January 18, 1998

Reid MacCluggage and his wife had just finished unpacking suitcases at their winter vacation spot in Florida when the phone rang. It was nearly eleven o'clock at night, but as the publisher of New London's newspaper, the *Day*, MacCluggage never really escaped the news. Even on vacation, his job always seemed to catch up with him. Expecting an editor, he picked up the phone and said hello.

"Reid, this is Claire."

MacCluggage couldn't believe she had tracked him down in Florida.

She insisted she had something very important to discuss, some inside information on a developing news story. Pfizer, she reported, had decided to build a large research lab and office building on the New London mill site.

MacCluggage wasn't too surprised. One of his reporters had a source saying the same thing. The paper had been seeking a second source for confirmation. But Claire wanted MacCluggage to delay reporting the news until Pfizer was ready to announce its plans at a large media event. MacCluggage didn't like the idea of holding back the news.

"I'm going to invite you to be on the inside," she told him, offering to grant access to a reporter. "But you can't report until the announcement."

Unwilling to pull his beat reporter off the story, MacClug-gage countered, "Here's the deal. I'll assign one reporter to come in and get the inside story on how this deal comes through. And we'll report that after the announcement—sort of an anatomy of how the deal was made."

Claire had no problem with that.

"But," MacCluggage continued, "I've already got a reporter working on this, and if she nails it through other sources, we're going to break the story before you announce it."

"Well, I don't want you to do that," Claire said.

MacCluggage didn't know what to say. He wasn't used to being told how to run his newspaper. Claire wasn't used to being told no. For nearly two hours they went round and round, each trying to get across his or her point of view.

Exhausted, MacCluggage finally said, "I'm not going to make any agreements that tie the hands of the newspaper."

Dissatisfied, Claire said she had to talk to her assistant and would get back to MacCluggage. She never did.

The *Day* broke the story a few days later.

January 21, 1998

Decision day had arrived. Pfizer's board assembled at cor-porate headquarters in Manhattan to vote on a number of mat-ters, including whether to authorize funding for George Milne's recommendation to construct a new research-and-development laboratory in New London.

Milne had briefed the board earlier and made the case for investing $300 million to develop the site. This bold, unorthodox move would enable the pharmaceutical giant to lead the revital-ization of an economically depressed city. Governor Rowland had made up his mind, too. He wanted Pfizer in New London badly enough that he had promised $75 million in incentives.

Claire had persuaded both men to raise the stakes in order to close the deal. By embracing her vision, Milne and Rowland were taking big risks. Pfizer specialized in making drugs, not trans-forming small cities. How would shareholders and the board of directors react if more than $300 million in corporate treasure ended up squandered on a social experiment? The state was taking an even bigger risk. Rowland had committed taxpayer money to a grand plan that ultimately hinged on the NLDC's ability to carry it out. And the head of the agency had no track record for a project of this nature.

But everyone was bullish.

With Milne in New York to meet with senior officers at Pfizer headquarters, Rowland's economic-development commissioner, James Abromaitis, dispatched a last-minute, confidential letter to Milne, saying it superseded his previous letter in December.

"This letter represents our continued interest in working with you to craft an assistance package that will allow Pfizer to choose New London," Abromaitis began. "It is our goal to reduce your development costs and to assure that the selected site provides an appropriate environment for Pfizer and its employees."

In addition to giving Pfizer the twenty-four-acre mill site at no cost, Abromaitis promised additional land to Pfizer, including the nearby scrap-metal facility and junkyard owned by Calamari Brothers: "We are in the process of funding the New London Development Corporation's effort to purchase the adjacent Calamari site at a purchase and testing cost of $4.7 million. This site would be provided at little or no cost to Pfizer." Abromaitis also promised the state would get control of the massive navy base property: "The Department of Environmental Protection will work to assure control of the Naval Undersea Warfare Center to accommodate your expectations for the waterfront area." And he offered up more money—now $26 million—for the NLDC to buy out and demolish homes and businesses in and around the Fort Trumbull neighborhood.

The state's willingness to help acquire the junkyard, the navy base, and the nearby neighborhood homes and businesses sealed the deal. The total package from the state, including tax abatements and the improved value of the land after cleanup, crested at about $100 million. That translated to the state's spending one dollar for every three pledged by Pfizer.

Early in the evening, Mayor Beachy received a call at home

from a friend at City Hall. He had important news: Pfizer had called an urgent meeting with city officials and senior Pfizer employees in the area. George Milne was on his way back from New York and planned to address them in an hour.

Beachy figured the news had to be good. He threw on a jacket and tie. Minutes later, his friend picked him up and drove him to the meeting. More than thirty of the city's top business leaders, lawyers, and political officials were on hand, along with several senior Pfizer executives. Waiters and waitresses served cocktails and hors d'oeuvres. Everyone eagerly awaited Milne's arrival.

Just after dark, guests were invited to take seats around an oversized conference table. Milne entered, shook some hands, and formally announced that the company had approved plans to construct a four-hundred-thousand-square-foot clinical-research laboratory on the mill site. Beachy and his colleagues applauded.

Construction was to begin in a few months and had an expected completion date of the year 2000. Up to two thousand new jobs would be generated by the project.

Milne displayed some bubble diagrams for the audience. Beachy recognized them instantly: he had seen the same ones in Claire's home a month earlier. Milne pointed to improvements planned for the area around the mill site. One by one, Milne asked each city official to support the Pfizer plan. Everyone agreed.

Pfizer planned an elaborate public announcement in early February involving Governor Rowland. Until then, the company planned to make no statements on its plans. It hoped city officials would remain quiet, too.

At the conclusion of Milne's presentation, Beachy approached and shook his hand. "Your people really know how to run a development," he told Milne.

Milne smiled and thanked him for his support.

The following morning, the newspaper ran a headline announcing that Pfizer had interest in the mill site, though the story quoted a Pfizer's spokeswoman who insisted she had no information about her company's possible plans to build in New London.

A couple of days later, the newspaper planned a follow-up story, reporting that the state's Bond Commission, chaired by Governor Rowland, planned to review a request for $185 million to fund a New London waterfront project. The bonding request indicated the NLDC planned to spearhead the project, which involved an unconfirmed *Fortune* 500 company. The paper planned to report that Pfizer was the company. It called Claire for a comment.

Claire declined to talk. Instead, she dispatched a Connecticut College spokesman, who told the paper there was no firm commitment from Pfizer. "The funds would get the site ready for marketing," the spokesman told the *Day*. "It could be any business or corporation."

The last time Tim LeBlanc had tried telling Susette he loved her, he had gotten an earful. This time, he decided to write his feelings down. He left a letter on her kitchen table.

Tears ran down Susette's face when she read it. She couldn't deny how strongly she felt for him. As a little girl, daughter of a single mother, Susette had learned to take care of herself. Then she had taken care of five sons. She had even cleaned up after her two husbands. As a medic and an aspiring nurse, she felt like she would always be taking care of somebody.

LeBlanc offered something she had never found in anyone, much less in a man: someone to take care of her. She looked forward to that for a change. She just couldn't bring herself to verbalize affection.

That night she penned him a letter.

Dear Tim,
   As I read your letter I wept.
   You asked me to reveal what you saw in my eyes.
   They are telling you that I am in love with you.
         Suz Q.

She wiped away a tear and tucked the letter in her notebook. She never gave it to him.

February 3, 1998

A chilling breeze swept off the water at the New London port. Claire boarded a ferry dressed in a short skirt, displaying her legs on a cold February day. The weather didn't faze her. The glances she got buoyed her, as did her company, Governor Rowland and George Milne. Hundreds of VIP guests were on hand for the formal announcement that Pfizer had selected New London for its new research and development headquarters.

As the most powerful political and business leaders on board, Rowland and Milne dressed the part: fashionable business suits, pressed shirts, power ties, and neatly tailored haircuts. But Claire stole the show. Her knack for the spectacular turned a press conference into a coronation. She had arranged for a ferry to transport the crowd down the Thames River during the announcement. Food, beverages, and entertainment abounded. Reporters and photographers were on hand. And every person of influence in the city had gotten an invitation. Even members of Connecticut's congressional delegation showed up. No one staged an event like Claire did.

On board, the governor announced the sweeping package of financial incentives and commitments to the city and Pfizer. "This is going to make this a formidable location, with a quality of life second to none," Rowland said. "I've never seen a community come together with such force, creativity, and vision."

Anticipating press questions about the amount of money he had committed to helping Pfizer, Rowland insisted the spending was justified. "What I saw in this community was a spirit, a hunger, an interest in doing something good for this area," Rowland said. "I saw a community really willing and able to develop, with some natural-born leaders." He singled out Milne and Claire.

"This will be a center for clinicians and scientists who lead worldwide research," Milne told the crowd. "The relationship between Pfizer and southeastern Connecticut is solid. There's an enormous opportunity for continued growth. This allows us to remain very competitive on a global level."

Satisfied, Claire smiled before speaking. Without her, Pfizer would never have selected New London, and the state would not have committed nearly $100 million. She had transformed a pipe dream into a massive development backed by big business and state government. Yet she deflected the credit. "It was teamwork and a commitment to 'on time, on budget, and on goal' delivery that created the momentum," Claire told the crowd.

The politicians smiled. It was party time. New London's ship had finally come in. And Claire was the captain.

"We thought of the idea of putting everybody on the ferry and taking them to the site," Claire recalled. "People cried. It was like a dream come true was right around the corner."

12

BAD BLOOD FORMING

"Pfizer to Expand into New London."

Susette saw the headline the minute she walked into a convenience store to pay for gas.

Why would Pfizer want to come to New London? she wondered, but she didn't give it much more thought.

Later that day, she saw Von Winkle. "So, you're all dressed up today," she said, making fun of the fact that his shirt was tucked in.

He brought up the Pfizer story.

She asked what he thought about it.

He laughed. "Maybe I can finally get out of here and get paid for my buildings," he said. Susette sensed he was serious.

Von Winkle was way ahead of her. He explained that he had already talked to Steve Percy at the NLDC and told him his price for all of his buildings in the neighborhood: $700,000.

Susette didn't get it, so he spelled it out for her: if Percy came up with $700,000 and dealt fairly with him, Von Winkle would sell.

"Well, I'm not planning on going anywhere," she said. "I just got here."

The NLDC set an ambitious timetable to acquire the properties in and around the Fort Trumbull neighborhood. In all, it wanted close to one hundred properties. The responsibility for coordinating the acquisitions fell to Steve Percy, whose real-estate office employed agents who were capable of knocking on doors and offering money to property owners in exchange for options on their property.

Besides all the commercial and industrial properties around Fort Trumbull, between seventy-five and one hundred people resided in the area. The occupants had a median annual family income of $21,250, ranking them among some of the poorest people in the city. While waiting for the purchasing funds to arrive from the state, the NLDC had a plan to persuade the residents to sell out fast. It authorized Percy's real-estate agents to offer $1,000 to each property owner who optioned his or her land to the NLDC. To motivate the agents to go after the options aggressively, the NLDC established a compensation scale for the agents. For the first twenty-five options secured, agents received $3,000 per property. For the next sixteen options secured, agents received $4,000 per property. Any additional options would net agents $6,000 each.

The financial incentives touched off a frenzy among real-estate agents. Within a week, brokers knocked on nearly every door in the neighborhood. Confused and scared, the residents didn't know what to do. Approximately twenty homeowners immediately granted options on their land. Most indicated they would sell if they had no choice.

Percy gave Claire and Milne a progress update: "An incomplete review of the 55 properties not under option indicates the following," he wrote. "Twenty-four of the properties should be under option within two to three weeks. Seven more may be under option within five weeks. Nine properties would require a higher than fair market price for the option. The remaining properties would be difficult."

With so many properties changing hands so quickly, Percy's firm stood to make a bundle on the transactions. The closings also promised a windfall to the NLDC's law firm, Waller, Smith & Palmer. Percy provided the firm a list of the addresses of the properties. The law firm agreed to perform title searches, to prepare all closing documents, and to represent the NLDC at approximately seventy closings at a minimum fee of $550 per closing.

*   *   *

His winter vacation finished, *Day* publisher Reid MacCluggage headed back to Connecticut. While away, he had kept a close eye on the events unfolding between the NLDC and Pfizer. He liked the fact that Pfizer had selected New London—the city needed a boost.

Only one item gave MacCluggage pause: his paper reported that real-estate agents were attempting to buy out every property owner in the adjacent neighborhoods, which would enable the NLDC to carry out a redevelopment vision that went far beyond simply bringing Pfizer to New London.

God, I hope we don't use eminent domain to do this, MacCluggage thought.

Then, on his first day back at the newspaper, MacCluggage heard that Claire had been telling people he had broken his agreement with her. He figured he'd deal with the situation head-on. After all, Claire had never been shy about calling him up when she had a complaint about press coverage. "Reid, this is Claire," she had begun one phone call to his office shortly after becoming president of Connecticut College. "You know that story you had today was bull-a-sheet-a," she had said, mimicking the way her Italian father used to say "bullshit."

As far as MacCluggage was concerned, Claire had the story wrong this time. He called her at the college to arrange a meeting. Claire insisted she was too tied up to meet with him. MacCluggage said he would come at the soonest opening in her schedule. She said she'd have her chief of staff get back to him to arrange a time to meet.

That evening, MacCluggage and Claire were scheduled to be dinner guests at the home of Rear Admiral Malcolm I. Fages, commander of Submarine Group 2 at the naval base in nearby Groton. Both their spouses also attended, along with a number of other guests. MacCluggage and Claire exchanged chilly greetings. Otherwise, they confined their dialogue to superficial cocktail talk. At the end of the evening, they said good-bye. It was the last time the two would speak to each other.

*   *   *

Susette usually didn't bother reading the newspaper. But after spotting the Pfizer headline and talking to Von Winkle, she started buying it every day. A couple of weeks after the Pfizer news broke, she read a story quoting Steve Percy. He said he hoped the NLDC wouldn't have to resort to eminent domain to take property from owners who refused to sell. But he wouldn't rule it out.

Eminent domain? Susette had never dealt with eminent domain, the government's power to take private property for public use. States and municipalities can legally seize an individual's land, but the Fifth Amendment of the U.S. Constitution limits the power to instances of public use, and it requires just compensation.

Susette put down the paper and called Von Winkle. He had seen the story, too. "You know what this means, don't you?" he asked.

"I know what eminent domain is," she said. "It's when they come in and take your farm and put in a road."

He laughed. The city had its eye on much more than a farm. Von Winkle remembered the last time New London had used eminent domain, in the 1970s. The city had cleared entire blocks, wiping out neighborhoods under the banner of urban renewal, but the city had never carried out its development plan; it had left acres of vacant lots. Like so many urban-renewal plans, it had run out of money, and the results never materialized. "It's not like New London is a stranger to eminent domain," Von Winkle said. "The city takes everything it wants."

He repeated his intention to sell as long as the city offered him a fair price.

"But I don't want to leave," Susette said.

"You're probably going to have to sell," he said.

"Or what?"

"Or you'll get nothing."

News of the paper's reference to eminent domain swept through the neighborhood. Most residents were scared. Aldo Valentini got mad. He ran the Italian Dramatic Club (IDC), a private men's club located two blocks from Susette's house. Built by Italian immigrants after World War I, the club had been a cultural center for Italian musicals and plays in the thirties, forties, and fifties. More recently it had become a hot spot for politicians seeking votes and financial support. No elected official made it through New London without attending ziti-and-garlic-bread dinners and making speeches at the IDC.

Valentini ran the IDC with an iron hand, controlling everything from exclusive membership rules to visitation rights. Only certain families could obtain membership, and women were forbidden on the premises except to prepare and serve food. The idea that the NLDC or Pfizer might take his club didn't sit well with Valentini. He called Jay Levin, a frequent visitor to the club. Valentini wanted Levin to absolutely guarantee that his club would be protected. Levin gave Valentini his word. Valentini wanted it in writing.

February 23, 1998

It was a busy day for Jay Levin. First, his firm and the state amended the original consulting contract between Levin and Ellef. Levin had done a lot more work since that contract had been signed. The amendment reflected the additional work and resulted in an additional payment of $120,000 to Levin's firm.

Also that day, Levin sent Valentini a letter on his law firm's letterhead. "It is widely and completely known that the Italian Dramatic Club is not to be touched by anyone," Levin wrote. "It is the understanding of every agency of State government from the Governor through DECD through DEP through DOT. It is an absolute complete understanding. Anyone who says otherwise is lying to a member of the Club and I will confront that person personally who is spreading the rumor."

When Valentini received Levin's letter, he framed it and hung it on a wall inside the club, displaying it like a trophy.

Steve Percy made sure Claire and Milne knew the deal. "We are not pursuing the Italian Dramatic Club," Percy told them in a personal letter he faxed to them.

Every other property in the neighborhood, however, remained on the get list.

With pressure on them to secure options from homeowners who hadn't said yes on the initial approach, Realtors descended on the Fort Trumbull neighborhood again.

Seated at the kitchen table, her head buried in nursing manuals, Susette heard a knock at the front door. A woman identified herself as a real-estate agent representing the NLDC. Eager to find out the NLDC's plans, Susette invited her in.

"Oh, it's very nice in here," the agent said, looking around.

Susette told her a little about the house. The agent offered her $68,000 to sell.

"I'm not interested in selling my property," Susette said.

If she didn't sell, the agent warned, the property would be taken by eminent domain. Susette said nothing.

The agent insisted she knew how Susette felt. Years earlier, she said, her grandfather's farm had been taken by eminent domain to make room for a road.

"Well, if you know how I feel and you already know about eminent domain," Susette said, "then you have a lot of nerve doing this kind of work."

The agent headed for the door, telling Susette to keep in mind the city's intention to move forward with its plan. "It's better to take the money now," she said, "knowing you'll get this amount now rather than having to fight for it later."

A couple of weeks later, the same agent showed up on Susette's doorstep again.

"Oh, you're back," Susette said.

This time, the agent offered $78,000 for the house, a $10,000 increase from her last offer.

"I'm not interested in selling my property, and I'm not interested in talking to you about selling my property," Susette said. "And if you come here again, I'm going to throw you off the porch. So get out."

"But—"

"Get out before I throw you off."

Retreating, the agent said she'd follow up by mail.

"Whatever," Susette said, before slamming the door in her face.

Days later, Susette got a letter from the agent. "I'm getting in touch with you again to bring to your attention some additional information," she said. The letter included a document titled "NLDC GUIDELINES." It listed the reasons the NLDC wanted Susette's neighborhood and what it would do to facilitate her departure:

1. *The NLDC is interested in developing the property around the area of Fort Trumbull in support of the recently announced Pfizer development.*
2. *The plans around that area have not been developed yet, but will attempt to create an appropriate complement to the Pfizer development.*
3. *Agents will exhaust all reasonable possibilities to relocate displaced persons and businesses to locations within New London prior to locating them elsewhere.*

Susette stopped reading. *These people aren't going to give up,* she thought.

She looked back at the cover letter from the agent. "I urge you to look over this material carefully, and stand ready to be of any assistance I can," it said.

Angry, Susette tossed the letter in a stack of correspondence she had received since the Pfizer project had been announced. Days later, Susette got a letter from Claire that hyped the news of Pfizer's building a four-hundred-thousand-square-foot clinical-research facility less than a block from Susette's house. "I hope that you are as pleased and proud as I am about the news of these major commitments from all involved," Claire had written. "The state is providing funding to the New London Development Corporation to buy property in the area. The properties that NLDC is interested in are . . . all of the properties in the Fort Trumbull area from the Amtrak rail line to the NUWC property line."

Claire made a point of emphasizing that Pfizer was not the

buyer of the properties. Susette laughed. "The NLDC doesn't intend to cause any unnecessary hardships," Claire said. "Every effort will be made to make your move as convenient as possible for you."

At the close of the letter, Claire left a phone number for her and Steve Percy and invited Susette to call if she had questions that couldn't be answered by the real-estate agents.

Worked up, Susette called Von Winkle. "She isn't even asking me," Susette said. "She is telling me: 'Pack up and get the f—— out.'"

Von Winkle had gotten a letter, too. But he wasn't angry. As long as the NLDC met his price, he'd go.

"Claire Gaudiani thinks we're all indigents," Susette said. "Who in the hell is this woman? She thinks I would give up my house and move into welfare housing?"

Von Winkle didn't know Claire, either. "They can *buy* my property from me," he said. "But they're not going to take it from me." He insisted he would not budge from his demand for $700,000.

"She doesn't want to 'cause any unnecessary hardships' and 'every effort will be made to make my move as convenient as possible'?" Susette said. "Give me a break."

Von Winkle laughed.

"Who in the hell does she think she is telling me I have to leave?" Susette said.

13

DO I HAVE A REASON TO
BE CONCERNED?

The price tag for altering the neighborhood around Pfizer's new headquarters kept going up. But the NLDC had no worries—it was playing with other people's money. Pfizer didn't have to worry over money, either. On March 27, the FDA and the Department of Health and Human Services approved the sale of Viagra to treat erectile dysfunction. Pfizer's projections indicated it would do about two hundred million in sales the first year. The profits from Viagra alone could pay for Pfizer's new research facility.

Pfizer had another reason not to worry: it had the state on the hook. At Milne's insistence, the governor had pledged to go after the vacant thirty-two-acre naval base next door to the land given to Pfizer. As events developed, this was no easy promise to honor. The state didn't control the federal property, and the navy had other plans for its base. Still, under federal regulations, the City of New London established the Naval Undersea Warfare Center Local Reuse Authority (LRA), a federally funded committee charged with producing a plan for discharging the property. The city appointed Tony Basilica to head it.

After extensive studies, analysis, and negotiations, Basilica's committee agreed that a public auction held the best benefit for the navy and the city. Milne and Claire hoped to stop the public auction in order to ensure the land got redeveloped in a manner that complemented the Pfizer development. As a result, they asked the state to intervene. The state promised to do its part.

Under rare circumstances, navy guidelines allow a state environmental-protection agency to acquire navy land at no cost, provided the land is used for a public purpose. Claire secured a confidential letter from James Abromaitis, at the DEP. "The DEP is willing to take this property utilizing the public purpose provisions allowed by the Navy," Abromaitis told her. "This would provide for a no cost transaction, but limits the use of the site."

The good news came with some bad news. "It appears that the local Reuse Committee is still considering public auction as an option," Abromaitis told Claire. "As you know, we made a commitment to develop the site on a concurrent timetable to that of Pfizer."

The message was clear enough: the state would go after the navy base, but someone had to go after Basilica and get him to back off his public-auction plan. Navy officials were scheduled to arrive in town within days to meet with Basilica's committee and to finalize the auction plan. Any hopes of stopping them required immediate action.

With a mock test sheet in front of her, Susette rested one elbow on a green paperback edition of *Taber's Cyclopedic Medical Dictionary*. Yellow Post-its with handwritten notes stuck out of the badly worn pages. She started filling in the blanks next to the abbreviations.

QD: Daily.
QOD: Every other day.
BID: Twice a day.
TID: Three times a day.
QID: Four times a day.
ACHS: . . .

Her mind went blank. "Oh, my God," she said. "I have to focus."

ACHS: Before meals and before bed.

She checked her answers. All were correct. She pushed aside her study manuals. Unable to stop thinking about the letter Claire and the broker had sent her weeks earlier, she called City Hall and asked to speak with the mayor. Beachy took the call. Susette introduced herself and provided her street address.

"Do I have a reason to be concerned?" she asked.

"Yes, you do have reasons to be concerned," Mayor Beachy told her.

Beachy had spent the previous day in Hartford, meeting with the governor's economic-development team overseeing the New London project. He didn't like what he had heard. Pfizer, the NLDC, and the state were on a fast track to clear the Fort Trumbull peninsula. The city had no intention of saving any of the houses in the neighborhood. Beachy came away convinced the project had taken on a new course, one that spelled trouble for anyone standing in the pathway of progress. Susette's house was in the way.

"What can I do?" Susette asked.

Beachy paused. Pfizer and the state had already committed hundreds of millions of dollars to the plan. Powerful business and political forces were combining to remake the neighborhood. The only way to stop the momentum would be to stir up a real controversy, a political storm.

"There's only one person I know that can help you fight this," Beachy said.

"Who?"

"That would be Kathleen Mitchell."

"Who's she?"

Beachy hesitated.

Fifty-three-year-old Kathleen Mitchell had grown up in nearby Groton. When she was a child, her mother wouldn't allow her to visit New London, calling the place a ghetto. But as an adult, Mitchell had moved to New London and become a social worker and a political activist working on behalf of the poor and underprivileged. When the government had threatened to cut off funding for day-care centers in the city, she had organized protests and walkathons. The press had come, and the day-care centers had been saved.

Beachy viewed Mitchell as a bit crazy, crass, edgy, and unpredictable. But she cared deeply about people, especially the poor and the powerless. Poor herself, Mitchell volunteered much of her adult life, helping the disadvantaged. And she had a gift for drawing a lot of attention to a problem.

"Kathleen is a stirring stick," Beachy said. He gave Susette her number.

Susette called Mitchell immediately and introduced herself. "I live in Fort Trumbull," she said. "There's a development coming, and Pfizer is behind it."

Mitchell had been following the news coverage. Always itching to fight for the underdog, Mitchell assured her the NLDC could be stopped. "There's ways to go about fighting this," she said.

"How?" Susette asked.

Mitchell suggested an initial strategy meeting at Susette's place. She recommended inviting Mayor Beachy to join them. Susette agreed, and they set a date.

14

PUSH BACK

Rich Voyles lived two doors up from Susette. He had moved into the neighborhood eleven years earlier and remodeled his home, and he had just eight years remaining on his mortgage. For him, East Street offered a dream location: a quiet, dead-end road with great neighbors and an unobstructed view of the Thames River. He kept a telescope on his porch and spent lazy afternoons looking at boats coming into and going out of Long Island Sound.

Middle-aged and balding, Voyles had recently been laid off from nearby General Dynamics, where he had helped build submarines. The loss of income had forced him to invite his brother to move in to help him keep up with the mortgage payments.

Voyles spotted Susette working in her flower bed one afternoon.

"Did you get a letter in the mail?" he asked her.

She laughed. "I have a bunch of letters." She took him inside and showed him. None of them resembled the one he had just gotten.

"I'll be right back," he said. Moments later, he returned and handed her a letter addressed to him.

"The time is rapidly approaching when those fort area properties not already optioned will be moved into the governmental process," the letter began. "The implications of this are considerable and I believe not in your best interest.

"We are empowered by the New London Development Corporation to offer you the City's Appraised value of $67,300." The letter outlined two conditions for getting the appraisal price raised. It continued:

> *We anticipate demolition and construction to begin in April with the removal of the powerhouse in Fort Trumbull, removal of unneeded buildings at the NUWC site, repairs to the City Waste Water plant, removal and remediation of the salvage yard, and ground breaking for the Pfizer building at the New London Mills property.*
>
> *Rich, I am very concerned that your best opportunity will slip by for lack of action. If there is any question you might have, or any assistance I might provide, please do not hesitate to call. I want to make the inevitable dislocation as easy and stress free as possible.*

The letter had come from Hamilton (Tony) Lee, a broker working for Steve Percy at the New England Real Estate Group.

"This guy can't say this to us," Susette said.

"Are they going to evict me?" Voyles asked, fearing he'd end up homeless if he got forced out. "I don't know what I'm going to do."

"Well, I know what I'm going to do," she said.

"What?"

"I'm going to bring this letter to the newspaper, and everyone will see what's going on down here. And then we'll get help."

Voyles let her keep the letter.

"They think they're going to push us around," she said. "Well, we're going to push right back."

Later that evening, Susette showed Voyles's letter to Von Winkle and told him her plan. "Once this becomes public, they'll have to stop because this is illegal," Susette said. "They can't do this to us."

Von Winkle liked Voyles; he didn't like the letter. He agreed that the public needed to know about the NLDC's tactics. But he really didn't think public exposure would stop it.

The next morning, Voyles's letter ended up on the desk of a reporter covering Pfizer and the NLDC.

April 2, 1998

With a shiny silver pen in his shirt pocket and wire-rimmed glasses to go with his perfectly groomed, graying black hair, fifty-five-year-old John Markowicz could easily have passed for a chief financial officer at a Wall Street bank. With corporate experience and military training, Markowicz had been tapped to serve with Tony Basilica on the LRA. Basilica had the political and business connections in the city, while Markowicz was an expert on the defense-industry and navy regulations.

Selling off a navy installation is not easy. Over a two-year period, Markowicz had worked with Basilica to form a plan. The northern and southern tips of the base property had environmental problems that made the entire parcel unmarketable. As a result, the committee had decided to partition the thirty-two-acre base into three parcels.

The southern tip containing the old Fort Trumbull would go to the state for a public park. The Interior Department had already signed off and the state's Department of Environmental Protection had approved the plan too. The northern tip of the base would go to the city for a marina. All the federal and state approvals were in place for this transfer too. The middle parcel of the base property, which included all the buildings and labs, was the most marketable piece. The committee planned to sell the middle parcel to the highest bidder at public auction. The city stood to harvest millions in tax revenue once the buildings were sold and reoccupied.

Basilica and Markowicz were nearing the end of their work. The navy had already audited the plan. Early in the evening on April 2, Markowicz left his downtown office and walked the two blocks to City Hall. Numerous officials from the navy's real-estate and budget offices were in town to iron out details. Markowicz anticipated an uneventful meeting focused on procedure and timelines.

But inside City Hall he found Basilica standing outside the council chambers, seething.

"What is it?" Markowicz asked.

Basilica showed Markowicz a copy of Hamilton Lee's letter to Rich Voyles. While Markowicz read, Basilica vented. It infuriated Basilica that the NLDC felt it had the power to take homes. Eminent domain was one of the most sweeping powers held by government. Things were about to get ugly fast.

To Basilica, the letter signaled a major political power shift in the city. Governor Rowland, he felt, had found himself a Trojan horse: Claire and the NLDC. Basilica knew no real-estate agent would write that kind of letter without direction. He also knew that the agent worked for Steve Percy and that Percy held a seat on the NLDC's board. Basilica understood that Percy planned to attend the meeting with the navy officials.

"What are you going to do?" Markowicz asked.

"I'm gonna confront his ass."

A strategic thinker, Markowicz preferred a more diplomatic approach to his adversaries. He also didn't think a shouting match with Percy would provide the ideal way to kick off an important meeting. But he didn't bother trying to talk Basilica out of it.

Percy arrived in his customary sport jacket and tie. He had white hair, bushy, dark eyebrows, and a pug nose. Basilica pounced.

"Where do you get the balls to send something like this out?" he said, shoving the letter in Percy's face. "Who gave you permission?" Basilica shouted.

The NLDC had given it, Percy insisted.

"You can't threaten these people with eminent domain," Basilica shouted. "You don't have that power."

Basilica stormed into the meeting room. Markowicz was waiting for him inside the doorway. He had overheard most of the shouting. Without saying a word, Markowicz raised his eyebrows and nodded in the direction of the conference table in the center of the chamber. The seats around it were full. Basilica did a quick head count. More than fifteen people were on hand, all in suits and equipped with notepads and pens. Other than the two navy officials, most of the faces were unfamiliar.

"Who in the hell are these people?" Basilica mumbled.

Markowicz had no idea. He pulled out a pad and prepared to take minutes.

Basilica cleared his throat and took his position at the head of the table. He opened the meeting by asking the visitors to introduce themselves.

John Downes and Gary Timura said they worked for the Downes Group.

Basilica recognized the name. The Downes Group was a consulting firm and a subsidiary of the Frank E. Downes Construction Company. Members of the Downes family had donated heavily to Governor Rowland's election campaign.

"Why are you here?" Basilica asked.

Downes explained that the NLDC had hired his firm as consultants one month earlier.

Markowicz didn't get it. A construction firm with strong ties to the governor had been retained by Claire to work on the Fort Trumbull redevelopment project. *Why are they showing up at a meeting involving the disposition of a navy base?* Markowicz wondered.

Confused, Markowicz noted the other visitors. Most of them worked for Claire or the governor, including the head of the DEP and Claire's executive administrator at the college.

Basilica now got the picture. The governor and the NLDC had a sudden interest in the navy property. *But why? And why now, after two years of disinterest?* Basilica wondered.

"The purpose of this meeting is to get everything on the table and answer questions regarding the process for the disposal of the NUWC property," Basilica said. He turned some time over to one of the navy officials, who explained that the Department of the Interior planned to convey a portion of the base to the state for a park, but that the core of the navy base was set for public auction. The bids would be sealed, and the land and buildings awarded to the highest bidder.

Percy asked if the sale would be absolute. He was told it would be, as long as the bids weren't below the land's appraised value.

Representatives from the state and the NLDC began peppering the navy official with questions and scenarios designed to delay the public auction. Markowicz glanced at Basilica. The federal officials made it clear that the government had already appropriated $300,000 for Basilica's committee to analyze the situation and come up with a plan. The process was too far along to change course now.

The NLDC and the state suggested that Pfizer's recent entry into the mix was sufficient cause to reconsider the plan. The navy disagreed. Changing the plan now would require a new round of public hearings and another audit by the navy. The time to modify property-transfer plans had passed.

The state indicated it now had an interest in the navy property. Basilica bristled. His committee had already planned to transfer the southern tip of the property to the state for a park. If the state acquired the rest of the property as well, the city might not get any tax revenue at all from the land or the buildings.

Markowicz couldn't understand what the state would possibly do with the land or how it would pay for it.

Federal rules and regulations permitted only four methods of transferring navy property: a public sale, a negotiated sale, an economic-development conveyance, and a public-benefit conveyance.

The state officials expressed interest in the last one.

But federal law permitted public-benefit conveyances only for uses such as airports, educational and public-health purposes, port facilities, and public park or recreation areas.

The state suggested it would use the land for a marine school.

Markowicz had his suspicions. He sensed that the state planned to flip the property to a private developer when nobody was looking.

This is a smoke screen, Markowicz thought.

Basilica didn't plan to play along. "We dropped three hundred grand of fed money on the plan we've put in place," Basilica said. "If somebody wants to come forward, we've got to have money to redo the plan. Otherwise, it doesn't make any sense to stop what we are doing."

The meeting closed with the navy officials reiterating their intention to conduct the public auction in June, enabling the city to start collecting taxes on the property six months later.

Afterward, Basilica and Markowicz huddled. Markowicz sensed a connection between the threatening letter sent to Fort Trumbull property owners and the presence of state and NLDC officials at the meeting. "These people want our property," said Markowicz. "And they want it for free." Basilica agreed.

Markowicz wondered if there was any chance the public auction would be delayed.

"Screw them," Basilica said. "We're going forward unless they produce the coin."

"Broker Pressures Fort Trumbull Residents to Sell"—Susette loved the headline in the Sunday paper. The story exposed Hamilton Lee's threatening letter. "It was an unfortunate use of words," Steve Percy told the paper, after being confronted with the letter, which at least four homeowners had received. The threat of eminent domain had left residents fearful and anxious.

Angry at the prospect of being connected to a public-relations mess, the governor dispatched his press secretary, who took a shot at Claire and the NLDC. "They have received specific directions from our office not to use that kind of tactic," Chris Cooper told the newspaper. "The use of eminent domain is not even on our radar screen."

Elated, Susette showed off the article to Voyles and her other neighbors.

Publicly, Claire called the incident unfortunate and said the homeowners deserved an apology. Privately, she fumed. Few things angered her more than bad press. The newspaper, she concluded, had established itself as an adversary. But she had two other adversaries to contend with first: Basilica and Markowicz. The NLDC needed a way around their control of the navy-base property. The city council offered the best bet: it had the power to alter the composition of Basilica's committee by adding new members. Basilica's longtime nemesis on the council, Peg Curtin, was an old political warhorse who wasn't afraid to battle her Democratic counterpart.

The night after the news report on the Hamilton Lee letter broke, the city council met at City Hall. Around 10 p.m. the council dismissed the public and the press and went into executive session. Flanked by two top officials from the governor's administration, Claire made a hard pitch for the NLDC to be given the authority to oversee the development of the waterfront area, including the navy property. Peg Curtin suggested the city form a new committee to develop a concept plan for the property, a committee that would present an alternative option to the reuse committee chaired by Basilica. Claire supported a committee of six members: two members from the existing committee, two from the NLDC, and two from the governor's administration.

Two and a half hours later, the council emerged from executive session. With hardly anyone from the public on hand, the council voted overwhelmingly to support Claire's plan, nicknamed the "Committee of Six." Only Mayor Beachy opposed the motion. "I'm voting against this because I feel we're giving up our obligations and responsibilities," he said. Peg Curtin criticized Beachy, pointing out that Governor Rowland had invested millions in New London.

Claire flattered Curtin and the other council members who supported her plan, calling them "intelligent councilors."

Susette had never met with a public official, much less had one in her home, but Mayor Beachy showed up at her cottage.

"It's a pleasure to meet you, Susette," Beachy said, smiling and extending his hand. She shook his hand and invited him in.

Kathleen Mitchell arrived right after him. With disheveled hair and bags under her eyes, she looked like she had just rolled out of bed. Her baggy sweatpants and sweatshirt did little to hide her excessive weight. She smelled like cigarettes. "I'm Kathleen," she said in a hoarse voice.

Susette didn't care what Mitchell looked like. She ushered Mitchell and Beachy to the kitchen table, an antique surrounded by four black Hitchcock chairs she had picked up at a yard sale for twenty-five dollars. Beachy began with an update on where things stood with the city and the NLDC. He got right to the point. "The city, the state, and the NLDC want your house, and they'll stop at nothing to get it."

Susette nodded.

"So you have a decision to make," Beachy said. "It's very simple. Either you take their money and go, or you stay here and fight."

"Well, I wanna keep my house," she said.

"You will have to do everything you can and more," Beachy said. "And you're going to have to stay the course."

"Okay."

While Beachy talked, Mitchell sized Susette up as naïve, completely unschooled in how politics work. But Mitchell also saw something she liked—a fearless streak, almost a reckless, risk-everything approach. She figured Susette was either borderline crazy or had suffered some pretty serious personal pain. Mitchell could relate to both.

"So how do we get started?" Susette asked.

Beachy turned to Mitchell. The first step, Mitchell suggested, was organizing a neighborhood association to oppose the NLDC. They would have to mobilize the neighbors into action and draw attention to the plight of the residents by using the media. Mitchell suggested they call the group the Fort Trumbull Neighborhood Association and that they make Susette its president.

Beachy liked the idea. But Susette had no idea how to form a neighborhood association. She didn't know how to mobilize. And she had no experience working with the press.

"It's not that hard," Mitchell assured her. Susette should start, she suggested, by finding out how many people in the neighborhood were willing to join such an organization.

Other than Von Winkle and a couple of people on her street, Susette barely knew anyone in the neighborhood. She had moved there to start over, to go unnoticed, and to maintain her privacy, not to become a political activist.

"You wanna save your home?" Mitchell asked.

"Yeah," Susette said.

"Then go door-to-door and see how many neighbors you can enlist to the cause."

Beachy nodded in agreement.

"All right," Susette said.

Beachy had another suggestion: when going door-to-door, she should ask every property owner to write a letter to the city council and to the mayor's office indicating that they didn't want to give up their homes.

Mitchell liked that. "We could present all the letters at a city council meeting," she added.

"That's a good idea," Beachy said.

Mitchell offered to organize a series of events that would generate media coverage. She suggested activities like a neighborhood walk with a tour guide to point out historic landmarks. Each event would include press releases and build public opposition to the NLDC's plans to demolish the neighborhood.

After an hour, the meeting broke up with each pledging to take on certain assignments and tasks. Susette felt comfortable with Beachy and especially liked Mitchell.

"This is going to be a battle from hell," Beachy said, grinning at Susette.

Susette flashed an uneasy grin.

"And you are going to become the poster child for eminent domain," he told her.

15

OFFING TONY

Tony Basilica was convinced that the NLDC would gain control of the Fort Trumbull neighborhood one way or another. He planned to make damn sure they didn't get hold of the navy-base property, too. He and Markowicz had worked hard and long to formulate a sale that would both protect the historic buildings and generate much-needed tax revenue.

And more was at stake: power and control. Two weeks after the state and NLDC officials had shown up at his committee meeting, Basilica had gotten a letter from Governor Rowland's commissioners of economic development and environmental protection. They wanted Basilica's committee to reevaluate its plan, pointing out that Pfizer's presence required a new approach. "We have therefore urged the City to request the postponement of any announcement of public sale by the Navy," the letter read. "We are, however, aware that it is the Local Reuse Authority which controls the conveyance and reuse process." The letter closed by reminding Basilica that the governor wanted the state to have a chance to develop the navy property, and the state would bring appropriate resources to the city for that purpose if the public-sale option went away.

But Basilica had never liked Rowland, and he ignored the governor's overture. The navy had made it clear that it would not suspend public sale of its facility without a formal written notice from the reuse committee to suspend, and without an alternative strategy for the property, Basilica refused to issue a formal notice. Instead, he told the navy it should proceed with its public auction, since no alternative plan for the site had emerged. Defiantly, Basilica sent a copy of his letter to Claire.

Before going door-to-door to recruit neighbors, Susette called Von Winkle. "Do you want to join the Fort Trumbull Neighborhood Association?" she asked him.

"Are you out of your mind, Red?"

"No. I'm trying to fight this."

"Well, you go ahead and fight it. We'll see what happens to you."

She didn't bother asking him to sign a letter saying he opposed the NLDC's plans.

Susette approached her other neighbors. Yvonne Cappelano owned the house next door. She and her husband had bought it as a weekend getaway. Rich Voyles lived next door to the Cappelanos. At Susette's request, both wrote letters opposing eminent domain.

A few doors up, she met eighty-five-year-old Helen Ballestrini and introduced herself: "I'm Susette Kelo. I'm a newcomer in the neighborhood, and I'm trying to save our homes." Ballestrini welcomed her. By the time they finished talking, Ballestrini had penned a letter and handed it to Susette.

> To The Honorable Mayor Beachy and City Council:
>   I am 85 years of age, have lived here all my life, and at this stage in my life I cannot even think of moving. I do not want to move.
>   Respectfully,
>   Helen Ballestrini
>   16 East Street, N.L.

Susette tucked the letter in her bag and approached a two-family, white Victorian with red trim. It had a meticulously maintained lawn with flowers. Walter Pasqualini, an elderly man, answered the door and invited her into his kitchen. It had a 1950s-era gas stove, a white porcelain sink, and a shiny metal kitchen table.

Susette explained the purpose of her visit. Walter introduced her to his wife, Cesarina, who had lost most of her sight and wore a hearing aid.

"Do you think they're going to make us leave?" Walter asked.

"I don't know," Susette said.

"Can you stop them?"

"I'm going to try."

He reached across the table and tore a piece of paper from a small notepad. He handed it to Susette and told her what to write.

> *To The Honorable Mayor Lloyd Beachy and City Council:*
> *I am a 93-year-old homeowner of Ft. Trumbull who has lived here all my life. This is our home. My wife and I do not want to leave here.*
>
> > *Respectfully,*
> > *Walter Pasqualini*
> > *Ces Pasqualini*

He asked Susette to hand him the letter. There was one thing he wanted to add. He penciled in the words "I was born on Smith Street" just above his name. He handed the letter back to Susette.

"Do you think this is going to work?" he asked. "Do you think you're going to be able to stop them?"

"I hope so."

Before Susette left, Walter told her to go visit his sister, Nora, who lived in a separate apartment on the first floor. She agreed to write a letter, too.

> *To The Honorable Mayor L. Beachy and City Council:*
> *I am a senior citizen who has lived here 27 years and I am not about to move.*
>
> > *Respectfully,*
> > *Nora Pasqualini*
> > *54 Smith Street. NL*

Each house Susette visited seemed to be occupied by elderly people. She had had no idea she lived among so many senior citizens. They all agreed to sign letters.

To The Honorable Mayor Lloyd Beachy, City Council:

I am 91 years of age. Live with my daughter in separate quarters who takes care of me. Have lived here for 27 years and cannot bear the thought of moving. We put so much time, effort & work into this house & the thought that the house could be razed is too much for me to take.

Very kindly yours, Mrs. Erica Blescus

Susette wondered if she'd find anyone her age, anyone truly capable of mobilizing serious opposition to the NLDC. At the top of her street, she approached a two-story house next to Von Winkle's deli. She rang the doorbell.

"Hello," a man shouted from a second-story deck. "Up here."

She looked up at the man. "I want to talk to you about what's going on in the neighborhood," she said.

Holding a beer, the man squinted. "Susette Chasse?"

She cocked her head back. No one had addressed her by her maiden name in more than twenty-five years.

"Yeah," she said. "Who are you?"

"Matt Dery," he said.

"Oh, my God, it's Matt."

They burst into laughter. They had attended high school together in New London and had not seen each other since.

"What are you doing here?" he said.

"I bought the house down on the corner, the pink one," she said.

"Well, c'mon upstairs," he said.

Dery introduced Susette to his wife, Sue.

"Susette, have a beer," he said.

A restaurant-size Coca-Cola cooler stood against the wall, stocked with Heineken, Michelob, Budweiser, and an assortment of other alcoholic beverages. Susette had avoided alcohol since her son's accident, but suddenly, a cold beer sounded good. She reached into the cooler and grabbed a can of Miller.

"Matt, do you know anything about what's going on in the neighborhood with the NLDC?"

"No more than what's been in the paper."

"What do you think about it?"

"I'm not really sure what to think about it."

Born and raised in the neighborhood, Dery didn't want to move. His mother, Wilhelmina, lived in the tiny house behind his. She had been born there on February 20, 1918, in the same room she still called her bedroom. She planned to die there.

Dery had renovated his house, and his family also owned two other properties. In all they had four properties and various tenants in the neighborhood.

"I'm forming a little neighborhood association to try and fight this," she said. "Do you want to join?"

"No," Dery said.

"How come?"

"Because I don't join groups."

Undaunted, Susette pressed on. But the more she talked, the more she got the impression that Dery and his family felt powerless to stop the city. They absolutely didn't want to go. If forced to vacate, they at least wanted fair compensation for their properties.

Susette exchanged phone numbers with Dery, and they agreed to start sharing information about developments in the neighborhood.

That night, Susette told Tim LeBlanc how much trouble she was having enlisting people. She used the Dery family as an example.

"These people busted their asses to have what they have," she said. "To other people it might not appear to be much. But they worked hard to get what they have."

"Who else have you talked to?" LeBlanc asked.

"Mr. Von Winkle."

"Which Mr. Von Winkle, the old one or the young one?"

"Well, he's older than I am. But he's not ancient."

"What's his first name?"

"Billy."

"That's the young Von Winkle."

"How do you know Billy?"

"My father worked for Billy's father," LeBlanc said. "My father was a nuclear physicist at NUWC."

Susette had never heard Von Winkle talk about his father. LeBlanc explained that Von Winkle's father had not only worked at the navy's underwater sound lab, he ran the place. In his day, Dr. William Von Winkle had established himself as the navy's top sonar expert. Billy had a bunch of brothers and sisters, and he had grown up in a very large home.

Von Winkle had never divulged any of this to Susette. He came off as a regular Joe who did all his own electrical wiring, plumbing, and carpentry on the buildings he bought and renovated. She hadn't realized he came from such a successful family. It gave her pause. Without people like him and Matt Dery standing by her, Susette wondered how far she'd get taking on the NLDC and Pfizer.

"What do you think I should do, Tim?"

"Get out while you can," he told her. "Besides, New London is a shit hole."

But she couldn't let go of the house. She understood Von Winkle's position—he was a businessman. His properties were investments. He'd sell as long as he received a good return.

But it wasn't that way for Susette. Her house represented her only possession. More than that, it was a refuge, the place she went to in hope of becoming the woman she had always put off being while raising five sons. She had remodeled the house to reflect her personality and tastes.

She called Mitchell to give her an update. Just about everybody except the senior citizens wanted no part of the association. The seniors were scared to death, but everyone else seemed uninterested in a public fight.

"It's every man for himself," Susette said. "Nobody wants to stick their neck out. Nobody wants to get retaliated against by the

NLDC. Only the elderly want to join and that's because they want protection."

Mitchell assured her the neighbors would come around.

May 16, 1998

Tony Basilica and his wife, Gwen, were in bed asleep when the phone started ringing at 5:45 on a Saturday morning.

Tony didn't budge. Gwen answered it. Then she tapped Tony's shoulder.

He opened his eyes, glanced at the clock, and gave Gwen an irritated look.

She put her hand over the receiver. "It's George Milne," she whispered.

"Get the hell outta here," he said, in no mood for humor.

She repeated herself, motioning for Tony to lower his voice.

"George Milne," he mouthed. "Are you serious?"

She nodded and handed him the phone.

Tony cleared his throat. "Hello," he said, trying to sound awake.

"Tony?"

"Yeah."

"George Milne."

"Good morning."

"I'm not getting you at a bad time, am I?"

Basilica looked at the clock again. "Oh, no, of course not."

"Can you make a meeting?"

"When?"

"Whenever you can get over to Pfizer."

Basilica paused. "You mean this morning?"

"Yes," he said, explaining that Claire was already in his office. "We're here. How about six-thirty or seven?"

Basilica sat up. He couldn't help thinking they were both nuts. "Would you mind if I bring John Markowicz if he's available?"

"No, not at all."

"We'll see you at seven-thirty or as soon as we can get there."

Basilica hung up and handed the phone back to Gwen, shak-

ing his head. He could not believe the president of Pfizer and
the president of Connecticut College were so intent on acquiring
land in Fort Trumbull that they were having a meeting before six
on a Saturday morning. He dressed and called Markowicz.

"Hey, how'd you like to go to a meeting?"

"When?"

"Now."

Markowicz waited for the punch line. Basilica explained. Markowicz didn't want to go in unprotected. Neither did Basilica.

Markowicz agreed to bring a one-page memorandum of understanding to the meeting. In it, Basilica would agree to ask the
Defense Department to suspend the public auction of the navy
base in exchange for Claire's promise to prepare, at the NLDC's
expense, an application to acquire the property under an economic-
development conveyance by August 31, 1998. If Claire refused
to sign the agreement, Basilica and Markowicz would know that
the NLDC and the state had no intention of paying for the navy
property. If Claire signed it, then Basilica and Markowicz would
be protected legally from any recourse that might come from
delaying the auction. And the NLDC would have to pay for the
navy property. Either way, both men figured the document would
tease out Milne and Claire's true intentions.

Just after eight o'clock, Markowicz and Basilica arrived at the
Pfizer complex in Groton. A security guard escorted them to
Milne, who led them to a private office. Inside, they found Claire
at the head of the conference table.

Markowicz and Basilica immediately spotted a series of oversized drawings positioned on easels around the room. They
depicted a conference center, a five-star hotel, high-end town
houses, a health club, and business offices.

What am I looking at? thought Markowicz.

Basilica recognized the area—a ninety-acre swath of land
stretching from the railroad tracks to the waterfront, which en-
compassed the Fort Trumbull neighborhood and the navy base.
He noted that the design plans carried the signature of a firm
under contract to Pfizer. Yet none of the land in the drawings
actually belonged to Pfizer. Basilica wondered why Pfizer had

designed plans to redevelop real estate it didn't own. Markowicz had the same question.

They took seats at the conference table, facing Claire and Milne. A couple of Pfizer employees and an NLDC official filled in the other seats.

While Milne and Claire took turns speaking, Markowicz began connecting the dots. At the committee meeting a few weeks earlier, state officials had asked a lot of questions about how the state could acquire the base property from the federal government without any cost under the public-use provision, suggesting the state might want the land for a marine-education facility. But Markowicz didn't see a marine-education facility on the schematic drawings; instead, he saw private commercial and residential uses, ones that would directly or indirectly benefit Pfizer.

"The issue that came up at the meeting," Milne explained, "was whether a public auction would be the best use of what was a key waterfront piece of property. If there was no infrastructure or other things that were going to support that site, would it attract a strong presence in the area? In other words, would it lock you into a more incremental move?"

But Milne didn't get anywhere with Basilica or Markowicz. "They were strongly recommending that the process proceed down the path they had already ordained," Milne said later.

Ultimately, Basilica looked to Markowicz, who pushed copies of his memo across the table to Milne and Claire. The heading read: "Memorandum of Agreement between Naval [Undersea] Warfare Center Local Reuse Authority and New London Development Corporation."

"This document is a compromise," Markowicz said.

All the elements of the agreement, including the dates, Basilica explained, were negotiable.

Without saying a word, Claire read the memo and then tucked it in her bag. The memo made it clear that Basilica and Markowicz weren't getting on board with her plan.

Markowicz attempted to explain the document, but Claire cut him off. She announced she had to catch a ferry into the harbor, where she was scheduled to meet George H. W. Bush, the former president, and escort him into New London. She said good-bye and walked out.

The meeting quickly lost steam and adjourned.

Claire never signed Basilica's proposal. Instead, she distributed it to members of the city council, along with a cover letter. "The attached is a Memorandum of Agreement that LRA Chair Tony Basilica gave to me recently," she told the council. "I am forwarding it to you for advice." Claire also took a shot at Basilica. "The Chair of LRA has known since November that a new plan for this land was preferable to Pfizer," she wrote. "I understand that neither the Executive Committee nor the full LRA has met since before the Pfizer decision was made. Consequently, the city has lost six valuable months for rethinking the land use and proper conveyance from the Navy."

She also gave the city council reason to get concerned about Basilica's demands on the NLDC: "If NLDC accepts Mr. Basilica's requests to undertake this work, citizens may see this as an NLDC 'land grab' and not as a request from Basilica."

Claire was tired of jousting with Basilica. The seeds for removing him from the committee had now been planted.

Days after the meeting at Milne's office, Markowicz received a letter from two of the governor's commissioners. "The Municipal Development Planning Process now underway for the Thames Peninsula area is a major community development effort that is needed in order to induce the Pfizer development project," they wrote. The plan to auction off the property came together before Pfizer announced its intention to develop in New London. "It is now prudent to re-evaluate this plan," they continued. "If we fail . . . we may jeopardize the maximum development potential of this site and possibly Pfizer's commitment to the region." Markowicz got the message: Pfizer didn't want the base sold at an auction; if the auction went forward, Pfizer might not come to New London.

The end of the letter went further, pointing out that the governor had just committed hundreds of millions of dollars to three other cities for massive redevelopment projects. "Clearly, this indicates that New London will no longer have the sole attention it enjoyed to date in these types of ventures," they wrote. "We will appreciate your cooperation." Markowicz noted the letter had been copied to Peter Ellef, Claire Gaudiani, and the city council.

Then Markowicz got a call from Jay Levin. He wanted to know why Markowicz wasn't supporting the governor's agenda in New London. Markowicz wasn't sure he knew the agenda. That was the problem. Levin advised him to be more open-minded.

Markowicz didn't care for Levin's strong-arm tactics.

The call ended abruptly.

The next day, Markowicz's secretary at the Corporation for Regional Economic Development knocked on his office door. Markowicz had been executive director for the nonprofit for a couple of years. His secretary told him a tall man in a business suit was at the front desk, asking to see him.

"What does he want?" Markowicz asked.

The names of every director on the corporation's board, she said.

Markowicz told her to find out who the man worked for. She came back a minute later with the answer: Jay Levin.

Markowicz knew what was coming. Levin planned to call board members and push them to pressure Markowicz to get behind the Rowland administration's wishes.

The receptionist turned over the list of names, and the man left.

June 1, 1998

The phone in Tony Basilica's law office was hot. His allies from City Hall informed him that a movement was afoot to force him off the committee overseeing the navy-base property.

Later that night, Basilica got a call at home from a reporter.

"Mr. Basilica?"

"Yes."

"Did you know you were removed from the committee?"

"No."

"Well, you were."

Without commenting, Basilica hung up.

Earlier that evening, the city council had voted 4–3 to dump Basilica and Markowicz from the committee. Peg Curtin, Basilica's political adversary on the council, was named as his replacement as the new chair of the navy base reuse committee. Mayor Beachy was one of the three who voted against Basilica's removal. "It's politically driven and politically motivated," Beachy told the newspaper. "It's a bad mistake."

The bottom line was that the fate of the navy property had been taken out of the hands of Basilica and Markowicz and placed in those of a committee of six people that included Claire, Milne, Curtin, and members of the NLDC and city council. Within days, Milne declared it was time to level the navy buildings that Basilica had planned to sell or lease. "You'd be better off tearing it all down and starting off fresh," Milne said. "They look sort of like basic factory buildings."

16

I'M SOMEBODY

Susette desperately needed followers. Door-to-door outreach in her neighborhood had yielded little result. Kathleen Mitchell suggested organizing a neighborhood cleanup day. Susette had spent her whole life getting her hands dirty and scraping her way through tough times. She posted signs on telephone poles and street corners, advertising free hot dogs and soda, and about two dozen people showed up at her house on the appointed day. She handed them garbage bags, rakes, and brooms. After the cleanup, everyone went back to Susette's place for a barbecue.

It wasn't a big turnout, but Susette and Mitchell were pleased. A number of people in attendance pledged to help fight the NLDC. Every little bit helped, they figured.

Days after Kelo held her neighborhood cleanup, the NLDC held its own event to build support. It reserved the Radisson Hotel and invited influential people capable of donating money. By the end of the evening, the NLDC had raised tens of thousands of dollars and added sixty new members.

Susette soon realized she was up against more than the NLDC. Ten days after she held the neighborhood cleanup, Governor Rowland appeared across the street from her pink house and held a press conference. He pledged $15 million in state money for relocating residents of the neighborhood.

That son of a bitch, Susette said to herself.

The letter from Claire still sat on her kitchen table. For weeks she had ignored its invitation to telephone Steve Percy.

I'm going to have a meeting with these people, she thought. *I'm going to tell them that I'm somebody and they aren't going to do this to me.*

She called Percy's office and scheduled a time to see him.

I have to look important, she told herself.

She pulled her best outfit from the closet, a greenish-brown, full-length sweater dress with long sleeves. She had picked it up for a few dollars at a secondhand store. The dress's earthy tones flattered her red hair. She slipped the dress on and looked in the mirror. Ribbed, it hugged her long, slender figure, accentuating the curves. She liked what she saw. She put on a pair of brown zip-up boots and headed to Percy's office.

It was an attractive red brick building with big windows and stylish green window trim. He greeted her in the lobby and led her into an office with easels holding maps and design plans. Percy introduced a couple of NLDC employees.

Feeling out of her element, Susette promptly forgot their names.

Percy asked how they could help her.

"I'm here to find out what's going on," she said. "What's the plan?"

Percy grabbed a pointer and started discussing a municipal-development plan while pointing at different areas on a map. Susette got lost. She knew nursing, not commercial-development lingo. Even the maps were confusing. Rather than using an aerial map or photograph depicting buildings, homes, and landscapes, Percy worked off a plot plan. All Susette recognized was the little square where her house stood at the corner of East and Trumbull streets. But her home was invisible. Maybe that was the point, she thought.

Yet nothing Percy said clarified why the NLDC needed her house.

"Is this for Pfizer?" she asked.

Percy acknowledged that Pfizer would receive some indirect benefits, but he insisted the takings were not directly for Pfizer.

Susette felt his explanation just didn't add up. Claire had told the newspaper about building space for clinics, along with biotech buildings, around the fort. That would directly benefit Pfizer. "What about eminent domain?" Susette asked.

"The plan is going to benefit the city," Percy insisted.

"But what about eminent domain?" she repeated.

He conceded that eminent domain remained an option in instances where people refused to sell.

Susette swallowed hard and clasped her hands to prevent them from shaking. She felt powerless. It was as if she hadn't owned the only home she had ever owned. She finally possessed something she could call her own—and these people were going to snatch it away from her.

They want us out, she thought. *They want to frighten us.*

Percy emphasized that the plans for the neighborhood were still in the conception stage. Nothing had been finalized or approved.

"If you try to take my property away from me," she said, "the whole world is going to hear about it."

Eager to hear how things had gone in her meeting with Percy, Von Winkle stopped by Susette's house that evening.

"So what happened?"

"They laughed at me."

"Did they offer you more money?" he asked.

"I told you. They laughed at me."

Von Winkle asked what she had done about it.

"I told them if they try to take my property from me, the whole world is going to hear about it."

"Red, you have to be careful. If you keep running your mouth they won't give you any money."

He waited for a reply. None came.

"If you try to take Susette's house," he joked, "the whole world is going to hear about it."

The harder Claire worked to accommodate Pfizer, the more Pfizer did to help the NLDC. On June 12, the pharmaceutical company made a no-interest loan to the NLDC for $150,000. It was a pittance compared to what the NLDC had agreed to do for Pfizer.

Two weeks later, the NLDC paid $4.75 million for the Calamari junkyard next door to the Pfizer property. The money had come from the Rowland administration. After the NLDC acquired the property, it transferred it all to Pfizer for one dollar.

The scrap yard wasn't the only property Pfizer had its eye on. Days after the deal closed on the Calamari property, one of Milne's representatives met with Claire's top representative to discuss other properties Pfizer hoped the NLDC would help the company acquire. The more Pfizer expanded its land interests, the more Claire resisted the *Day*'s attempts to access NLDC financial documents and other records. When the newspaper tried sending a reporter to cover an NLDC meeting, the reporter got locked out. The paper responded by filing a Freedom of Information (FOI) Act complaint with the state. Claire had no intention of complying with the request for information. In her view, freedom-of-information laws didn't apply to the NLDC, because she saw it as a private organization, not a public agency. Never mind that the agency got its funding from a public source. In 1998 alone, the NLDC received or requested nearly $21 million in state funding. And the NLDC's marching orders came from Rowland's administration.

The newspaper pressed its case, requesting a formal hearing by the state's Freedom of Information Commission, insisting the agency should be subject to public-disclosure laws on the basis that the NLDC functioned as an agent of state and city government. Claire did not back down. The NLDC submitted a brief, outlining why it should not be required to comply. The brief identified the NLDC as a nonprofit corporation with bylaws that didn't require participation by a government agency. It went on to claim that its director oversaw the day-to-day operations "with no input from any government agency. . . . The evidence clearly shows that the NLDC board members incorporated the NLDC, and it is not the creature of any government agency."

The Freedom of Information Commission set a hearing date.

17

WEDGES

August 1998

Steve and Amy Hallquist had fallen in love on a tour bus in New London in 1997. A paint contractor in her midforties, Amy had wanted a different line of work. She took a job as a tour-bus driver, and her first day on the job, she met Steve, the tour guide. A former teacher and the son of a preacher, forty-two-year-old Steve had a gift for oratory. They did their first tour together a couple of blocks from Fort Trumbull. She liked his over-the-collar-length hair and his neatly trimmed beard. He liked her wavy black hair and frequent smile.

A year to the day after meeting, they got married and bought a home just outside the ninety-acre peninsula targeted for redevelopment by the NLDC. The Hallquists closed on their home the same day Pfizer announced its plans to build its research headquarters in New London. They immediately got involved in the community. A few months later, they attended a public meeting hosted by the NLDC at a downtown church. The place was packed, but Amy managed to find two seats right in front.

Claire arrived in a white blouse with a colorful scarf, her hair pinned back, showcasing pearl earrings and a seasonal tan. Using maps and diagrams, she walked the audience through her vision for the future of New London. Amy and Steve thought she looked like the Vanna White of development. And they liked what she was pitching.

"What we want is a world-class, hip little city," Claire told the audience.

The Hallquists were captivated, along with most of the audience. The atmosphere felt like a pep rally.

As soon as the meeting broke up, Steve and Amy approached Claire and introduced themselves. She greeted them warmly. When she learned that Steve and Amy were community activists, Claire asked them to get involved. She asked Amy to write a letter to the newspaper in support of the NLDC's revitalization efforts, and Amy agreed.

September 1, 1998

Susette thought men in business suits looked silly wearing hard hats and wielding gold-tipped shovels. But she didn't laugh when VIPs were on hand to watch Governor Rowland and George Milne break ground on Pfizer's $220 million facility next door. Only eight months had passed since the two men and Claire had announced the development. The ceremonial start of construction illustrated the project's speed.

"Years from now," Governor Rowland told the audience, "this will be a case study in how to revive a community."

The implication insulted Billy Von Winkle. For years, the city had ignored the broken sidewalks, failed to make garbage pickups, and neglected a smelly sewage-treatment plant in the middle of the neighborhood. During that time, Von Winkle had quietly bought up old buildings with his own money and then rehabbed them on his own time. One by one, he had turned some of the neighborhood's most blighted structures into quality, affordable housing. He even moved into the neighborhood himself and opened up his own business. At no cost to taxpayers or the city, Von Winkle had probably invested and done more than anyone else to improve the neighborhood around the Pfizer property.

"We stayed through all the shit," Von Winkle told Susette. "Now they want to kick us all out and make the neighborhood nice for someone else."

The idea that she wasn't worthy of living next door to Pfizer left Susette feeling scorned and slighted too. "Rich white people don't like us," she said. "Claire and George drove down over the hill into Fort Trumbull one day and said, 'Look at this view. What are these scumbags doing living here?'"

From the moment the Pfizer project had been announced, Von Winkle had prepared to sell his properties. But resentment had begun to set in. He knew the NLDC had paid almost $5 million for the junkyard next door to Pfizer, which was way beyond fair market value. Other property owners closer to Pfizer had been paid far above the properties' appraised value, too. Yet the NLDC consistently refused to offer Von Winkle what his properties were worth. Enough time had passed to convince him that the NLDC would simply take his properties through eminent domain unless he agreed to sell for less.

Susette hoped Von Winkle had finally been persuaded to help her rally the neighborhood in opposing the NLDC, but Von Winkle had other ideas. Claire and Steve Percy were messing with his livelihood. He had his own ways of dealing with them.

After living apart from her husband for nearly a year, Susette told him she wanted a divorce. Although he'd been living without her, Jorsz took it hard. To him it felt like a death in the family. He vowed he'd never marry again. Susette figured she wouldn't either. With separation and the passage of time, she harbored no ill will toward Jorsz. Despite the problems between them, she recognized he had done a lot for her and her boys and had asked nothing in return.

Together, they hired an attorney to draft the necessary legal documents. One afternoon, the attorney telephoned Susette following a review of the couple's financial affidavits, disclosing personal income, assets, and liabilities.

As a full-time nursing student, Susette didn't have much to disclose:

Workers' compensation: $90
Unemployment: $297

Child support: $75
Total: $462 per month

Her assets included her house, valued at $53,000; a used car worth $8,000; $3,000 in a mutual fund; and a checking-account balance of $1,200.

Her husband, on the other hand, had a well-paying job, a fair amount of cash tucked away in savings, and a home and property worth a lot more than the pink cottage. The divorce lawyer asked Susette if she was sure she wanted to walk away from the marriage without taking some money.

"Yes," she said. "It's not my money." Her husband had inherited his money from his deceased father, long before Susette had come along. She didn't feel right about taking money that didn't belong to her.

The lawyer explained that she was also entitled to a percentage of Jorsz's house, but again she declined. Her husband had purchased the house with a portion of the money he had inherited from his father. This had happened before Susette entered the picture. Making him sell the house in order for her to obtain half its value would be like the NLDC's taking her house.

The lawyer drafted and had Susette sign a straightforward divorce settlement. It all felt anticlimactic. She had been living a separate life from her husband long before moving out on her own.

Her new friendship with Tim LeBlanc had more of what she had always looked for in a marriage. They spent weekends going to yard sales, hunting for antiques and used items to furnish her house. They spent nights eating at cheap, out-of-the-way restaurants. Both were frugal; both preferred privacy and simple pleasures. LeBlanc had quickly become more than a friend.

LeBlanc's easygoing personality had a lot to do with the relationship's success. Even Susette's escalating battle against the NLDC didn't seem to faze him. The more time Susette dedicated to saving the neighborhood, the more supportive he became. Beneath her tough exterior, Susette longed for a man to look out for her, but she didn't want to remarry.

"I have the patience of Job," he told her. "It doesn't matter how long it takes."

In lieu of marriage, she invited LeBlanc to move in with her. But he preferred his small home in the woods. Recognizing how much she loved being by the water, he didn't try to persuade her to move back to the country, so they agreed to maintain separate homes but to spend all their spare time together.

Believers in social justice, Steve and Amy Hallquist had quickly become big supporters of Claire's efforts. They started attending all kinds of meetings and began bumping into her at fund-raisers. Claire invited them to attend a dinner in her honor hosted by an Italian men's club in New London. They gladly accepted.

Amy ended up being one of the few women in the audience. Most of the men seemed to be over forty-five. None of that bothered Amy. Claire's speech did, however. While pushing the redevelopment plan, Claire was dressed seductively and made use of sexual innuendo, Amy thought. Claire had all the men in the palm of her hand. But it made Amy feel dirty, and she wanted out.

The scene had turned Steve off too. But he had zeroed in on something else. Someone had referred to Claire as an apostle on a mission to save New London. With his religious background, Steve figured that could be either really good or really bad. Watching Claire, he quickly determined it was the latter.

"She's really manipulating people," Amy told Steve. He agreed. They went home that night with serious doubts about Claire and her vision for the city.

The decision to build in New London had not been popular with some of the Pfizer officials who had worked on the site-selection process. Some felt the company's needs would have been better served at another location. Some also questioned the wisdom of a Pfizer official being on the board of the NLDC.

Meanwhile, state officials were getting impatient with the NLDC and its demands on behalf of Pfizer. The state wanted

Claire to back off. But at the same time, no one wanted to offend Milne.

There was another problem too. Press reports about the prospect of the NLDC's resorting to eminent domain were on the rise. The governor didn't need to be dragged into a politically unpopular issue. One of his senior officials privately reached out to Jim Serbia at Pfizer. As the point person for Milne on many aspects of the development, Serbia shared some of the same concerns. Pfizer could not afford to have the public or the media thinking that the push behind taking people's homes came from the pharmaceutical company. But Milne's presence on the NLDC board made it almost impossible to avoid this impression.

For months Serbia had been emphasizing that the Pfizer development needed to be kept separate from the NLDC's development plans in the nearby neighborhood. But the state made it clear that something more had to be said. Serbia agreed to intercede.

October 21, 1998

Serbia composed an e-mail to Milne: "Dr. Milne, There seems to be some confusion regarding the expectation that Pfizer (you in particular) has regarding development of the peninsula. This confusion has caused some friction between NLDC and DECD/DEP [Department of Economic and Community Development/Department of Environmental Protection]."

Serbia repeatedly referred to the NLDC as being at odds with the state. He also expressed concern about eminent domain: "The State, from a public policy perspective, has difficulty in supporting residential areas located in a flood plain, and in condemning/taking an existing residential area and replacing it with a more upscale residential district."

Serbia closed with a question: "Would approximately 70–80 high end residential units fit with your expectation?"

Satisfied, he marked the e-mail "High Importance" and hit SEND.

His e-mail did little to change things. Eight days later, Milne

and Claire presented Rowland and Ellef with a multipage plan
for "Team New London," including a diagram showing all existing houses in the Fort Trumbull area totally wiped out and new
condos put up in their place, along with a hotel.

Susette frowned when she saw a moving truck parked in front
of her next-door neighbor's house. Yvonne Cappelano and her
husband had bought their place shortly after Susette had moved
in. Residents of Virginia, the couple used the home as a weekend getaway. At first, the couple had supported Susette's effort
to save the neighborhood, but Susette could see something had
changed. She approached the truck and asked Cappelano what
was going on.

"We talked with our lawyer," Cappelano said soberly, holding
back her emotions, as she explained that she and her husband
had no choice but to sell. "There's nothing you can do."

Susette insisted she would never leave.

"Susette, you have to sell," she said. "They're going to put you
out on the street."

"Let 'em try."

18

FREEDOM OF INFORMATION

Under cover of night, Billy Von Winkle approached the NLDC's Dumpster. No one appeared to be around. Unsure what he'd find, he rifled through fast-food wrappers, coffee cups, and half-eaten sandwiches until he hit pay dirt: documents. Steve Percy's name was on many of them, including handwritten correspondence. Von Winkle dug further. He came across the original retainer agreement signed between the NLDC and its law firm, Waller, Smith & Palmer.

The Dumpster contained piles of NLDC internal documents. It turned out that Percy had a habit of handwriting letters, memos, and internal notes. He also saved files with minutes from internal meetings and confidential correspondence to and from George Milne, Claire Gaudiani, and top officials from the Rowland administration and Pfizer. Some documents were torn in half. Others were torn in four pieces. But most of them were easily reassembled.

Surprised that the agency had discarded so many original records, Von Winkle took them. The NLDC had been playing hardball with him. It was now his turn.

The documents showed Pfizer was working hand in glove with the NLDC, while the state gave its stamp of approval for the NLDC to essentially satisfy Pfizer's wishes.

Von Winkle even recovered a confidential letter written to Percy by Pfizer's director of facilities planning and management,

Paul Begin, who worked very closely with Milne. "Dear Steve, To maximize the benefit of the Pfizer investment in New London, we will need the land flexibility to add buildings beyond the initial 1200 person office building," Begin had written. "This land flexibility will enable us to ultimately reach an employee population of roughly 2000.

"Upon review of several initial design plans, it has become clear that the properties across from the former New London Mills site along Pequot Avenue are now of extreme strategic importance. Therefore, we ask that the NLDC obtain options on these properties as a top priority, adjusting market values as necessary to reflect this strategic importance."

Dated March 2, 1998, the letter confirmed that only a month after Milne and Claire had stood with the governor to announce the selection of New London for Pfizer's new facility, the company had already started eyeing more land. The letter also confirmed that the NLDC would pay above-market price for homes and properties when told to do so by Pfizer, something it had been unwilling to do with Von Winkle on his properties.

Other documents from the Dumpster revealed that the state had told Percy to honor Pfizer's wishes. Von Winkle found an NLDC confidential internal memo to Claire dated March 27, 1998. It reported on a meeting between top officials from Pfizer, the state, and the NLDC. At the meeting, one of the governor's top administrators, Rita Zangari, recommended that Percy's real-estate firm actively pursue the new properties on the top of Pfizer's get list. She also proposed a new passive strategy toward the holdout properties in Susette's neighborhood. "Rita explained that by continuing to negotiate options we were bidding against ourselves," the memo said. "With the MDP [Municipal Development Plan] process there will be plenty of time to acquire properties."

This strategy change seemed to make it more likely that the NLDC would resort to eminent domain to obtain properties from holdouts. If the NLDC paid above-market value for properties that had been added to Pfizer's wish list, funds for the Fort Trumbull neighborhood homes would dwindle.

At the state's request, Percy also put in writing an estimate of how much the New England Real Estate Group would make in commissions from the transactions. "A good planning number is probably $225,000 to $250,000," Percy wrote.

Another memo to Claire had one of Rowland's officials asking the NLDC to prepare another bond commission request for funding. The governor chaired the state's bond commission. Rowland's deputy told the NLDC to emphasize Pfizer's additional property needs as the driving force in the additional funding request.

Von Winkle also found a hand-drawn "Cash Flow Diagram" showing tens of millions of dollars going from the state through the NLDC to various properties and initiatives. It appeared to have been drawn by Percy and used at a private meeting he attended with officials representing Milne and the governor in March 1998.

Many of Percy's letters had to do with money. In a handwritten letter to Jay Levin in March 1998, Percy asked him for help with fund-raising for the NLDC. "We will need whatever funding assistance you can help us get from DECD," Percy said. "Nice to be working with you, as always, my friend."

Overall, the documents established a series of direct links between the governor's office, Pfizer, and the NLDC. Claire seemed to serve two functions. For Pfizer, she was a go-to person willing to charge hard for the corporation's interests; for the governor, she appeared to function both as a funnel and a shield. By piping money through Claire's organization for property acquisition on behalf of Pfizer, the state was using the NLDC as a layer of insulation between it and Pfizer.

Von Winkle brought plastic garbage bags full of documents to the basement of one of his buildings, where he hid them away for safekeeping. Recognizing the Dumpster as a gold mine of intelligence, he started making regular visits after hours.

Attorney Tom Londregan had finished law school in 1969 and joined a Connecticut unit of the National Guard, where he had served with another young law graduate, Christopher Dodd. Before the Vietnam War ended, Londregan and Dodd started practicing law in New London. While Dodd quickly transitioned to politics, Tom Londregan joined his brother Frank's law firm,

Conway and Londregan, in New London. After Frank became mayor of New London, Tom became the city's attorney.

Few people had better legal and political connections than Tom Londregan. Near sixty with gray hair and old suits, Londregan hadn't always appeared to be a powerful lawyer. But over a thirty-year career he had handled hundreds of cases and established himself as one of the most polished, accomplished lawyers in the city. Few things happened in New London political circles without Londregan's knowledge. And the mayor and city council took no significant steps without first securing Londregan's legal opinion.

Londregan strongly supported the Pfizer plan and the clearing of the peninsula. From the beginning he had been carefully examining each step in the process for the city council and the mayor. He knew it was only a matter of time before eminent domain would be used by the city, and he'd be busy defending it.

December 1998

Working at his desk, Tom Londregan got buzzed by his secretary. Claire Gaudiani was on the line. Londregan knew Claire well. Her husband, David Burnett, was Londregan's tennis partner. Londregan picked up the phone.

"I'm very disappointed in you," she snapped.

"For what?" Londregan snapped back.

"You refused to cooperate and be helpful to my attorney."

"When was this?"

Claire had retained Hartford lawyer Peter Hirschl to advise the NLDC. At Claire's request, Hirschl had called on Londregan for assistance in drafting a resolution on behalf of the city that would expand the NLDC's power. Londregan had explained that as the city's attorney he didn't draft resolutions for the NLDC. The NLDC had its own lawyers.

Claire told Londregan she didn't appreciate his refusal to help.

Londregan countered by saying he didn't appreciate that a Hartford lawyer making double what he made basically expected Londregan to do his work for him.

The conversation became ugly.

December 21, 1998

Publisher Reid MacCluggage paced the hallway outside the hearing room at the Freedom of Information Commission in Hartford. Normally he did not attend such hearings. This one, however, had taken on a personal element for him. Ever since MacCluggage had rebuffed Claire's attempt to influence how his paper treated the Pfizer announcement to build in New London, the NLDC had made life difficult for his reporters. Requests for documents had been denied. Meetings had been closed.

MacCluggage had not been called to testify before the commission. He had come to show moral support for his reporter Judy Benson.

Suddenly, a woman in a business suit approached and identified herself as a Connecticut College administrator working for Claire. She had driven nearly an hour to give MacCluggage a very urgent message.

"I talked to Claire this morning, and she wants you to drop the suit," the woman said.

MacCluggage didn't find that very urgent. "We're about ready to have the hearing," he told her.

"No, she wants to talk with you. She wants to talk with you. She thinks somehow we can . . . You have to drop the suit."

MacCluggage had little patience for these last-minute tactics. For nearly a year the paper had been trying to obtain documentation from the NLDC. A formal complaint had been filed. At one point the NLDC had offered to settle by promising to comply with FOI Act requirements. But it never did. The *Day* felt the NLDC had reneged on its promise, and the time for negotiating had passed.

"No," MacCluggage said, "we're going through with this."

"Let's talk some more," the woman insisted.

MacCluggage smiled. "There's no use talking any more because we don't get the straight story. So we're just going to the commission. We're going to get a ruling." He walked away.

Inside the hearing room, reporter Judy Benson testified first. Brief and to the point, she recounted how the NLDC had denied her access to meetings and documents.

The NLDC had a tougher task. The commission had a simple question to resolve: was the NLDC a public agency subject to freedom-of-information law? The burden fell to the NLDC to prove it wasn't. As its primary witness, the agency sent its brand-new chief operating officer, Navy Rear Admiral David Goebel, who had joined the NLDC board of directors back when Jay Levin and Claire had revived the agency, over a year earlier. Not long before the hearing was scheduled, the NLDC had hired Goebel as a full-time executive working directly under Claire.

A former deputy director for international negotiations for the Joint Chiefs of Staff, Admiral Goebel was all business when he stood to be sworn in. Tall and imposing, he raised his right arm, forming a perfect right angle, and promised to tell the truth. Then, in an authoritative, no-nonsense way, he succinctly answered questions from his lawyer.

"Does the State of Connecticut determine what your tasks will be?"

"No," Goebel testified.

"Does the DECD or any other part of the state provide you with any direction on your day to day activities?"

"No, they make a specific point not to."

"Who decides what consultants you will retain?"

"We do, NLDC."

"Do you need permission from the city or the state to get a consultant?"

"No."

"Or to retain a particular consultant?"

"No."

"Who decided what properties the NLDC would buy and how much they would pay for them?"

"The NLDC."

After Goebel's lawyer finished, the newspaper's lawyer cross-examined Goebel.

"Am I correct that the state agency, the Department of Economic and Community Development (DECD), attends your meetings? The NLDC meetings?"

"No, not correct."

"They never attend?"

"They do not attend NLDC meetings," Goebel said. "They do not attend board of director meetings. They do not attend group meetings, to my knowledge."

"Sir, am I correct that Fort Trumbull is part of a municipal redevelopment plan?"

"Yes, a portion of that area. Not all of it."

"Am I correct that there are state statutes and regulations which control how that can be done?"

Goebel's lawyer objected. After a brief discussion between the attorneys and the commission, Goebel confirmed that his agency was subject to the laws of the land.

Goebel didn't give an inch, insisting the agency did not take its marching orders from the state. But he couldn't get around the fact that the NLDC got its funding from the state.

In his closing remarks, the newspaper's lawyer took a shot at the NLDC's secretive approach to doing business. "Is there latitude by this agency that the city government doesn't have?" he asked. "That's exactly why we're here because a lot of the business they're conducting they're conducting in secret without following the rules. It's the business of the city and we want it brought out into the sunlight."

Pleased with the performance of his reporter and his lawyer, MacCluggage left the hearing confident the commission would declare the NLDC a public agency and his newspaper would get the documents it had asked for.

The chances of the NLDC's getting a favorable ruling out of the state's Freedom of Information Commission were slim to none, but Claire already had another feud brewing with city attorney Tom Londregan. She ended up firing off a letter accusing Londregan of being unprofessional and uncooperative for refusing to draft a resolution to her liking. Not one to be bullied, Londregan ignored Claire and stuck to the letter of the law. He went out of his way to make sure the resolution Claire wanted got drafted in public at a city-council meeting, a move that resulted in a final product that wasn't exactly what she had in mind.

Once again she wrote Londregan and voiced her displeasure with his actions.

Londregan had heard enough.

"After reading your letter . . . I feel that I must respond," Londregan began, before defending his actions and hammering her for wanting to avoid the public process. "You found the City Council meeting confusing with unprofessional moments as the resolution was edited in public," Londregan wrote. "I am sorry that you feel that way about the democratic process." Londregan reminded Claire that he didn't work for her; his client was the City of New London.

After getting Londregan's letter, Claire called him and demanded he come to her office at Connecticut College. Incredulous, Londregan couldn't wait to get there. City officials had been starting to feel that Claire had taken over the city and oversaw their roles in development and planning. In less than a year, she had announced sweeping redevelopment plans for downtown, the waterfront, the state pier, the largest beach in the city, and the Fort Trumbull neighborhood. The state had given her agency close to $100 million while telling the city it couldn't play with the state's money. Londregan's political clients were feeling put upon by Claire, and he wasn't about to let her browbeat him.

He took out some index cards and jotted down what he planned to say. He brought a member of the city council along. By the time Londregan got to Claire's office, he was in no mood to listen.

"What I did at the city council meeting was to answer questions proposed to me by my client," he said, with a bite in his tone. "I gave advice and counsel. If you feel such was unprofessional, then you and I have a difference in what is professional."

Claire had a different point of view. But for each point Claire raised, Londregan had an answer on his index cards. He didn't budge. "Anything else?" he said sarcastically. Then he left.

19

THE NEW NEW LONDON

March 8, 1999

D ear Claire."
George Milne didn't usually write letters to Claire on
Pfizer letterhead. But circumstances called for an exception. The
NLDC had applied for an economic-development conveyance
for the Naval Undersea Warfare Center property. If granted, the
NLDC would obtain the multimillion-dollar property at no cost,
and Pfizer would secure the assurance that the property would
be developed in accordance with its wishes.

"Our New London expansion requires the world class redevelopment planned for the adjacent 90 acres in the Fort Trumbull Municipal Development plan including the 16 acres of the
NUWC property," Milne wrote. "The Fort Trumbull area is integral to our corporate facility."

Milne spelled out his plans for the base property and the
neighborhood around it: a waterfront hotel with about two
hundred rooms; a conference center and physical-fitness area;
extended-stay residential units; and eighty units of housing. "We
will use the proposed hotel and conference facility as an extension of our facility committing to 100 of those rooms on a daily
basis for visiting international staff and other professionals,"
Milne said. "In addition we require conference space and are exploring a 'virtual' Pfizer University to keep our researchers up
to date on the most recent breakthroughs in biotechnology. The

extended stay housing will provide for researchers who often stay for periods of up to 3–6 months. Year round quality housing is also crucial to recruiting top scientists. The waterfront residential neighborhood envisioned provides a one-of-a-kind housing option desired by many of our employees. As a result, the NUWC property is and has been key to our investment in the area."

To date, Milne had not been so specific, so blunt, and so clear in expressing Pfizer's desires and motives for the ninety acres of private land around its new facility. He had enough confidence in what he and Claire were contemplating that he was willing to do what corporate executives typically shun: spell it all out in black and white. He even pledged a partnership with the NLDC.

"We are prepared," he told Claire, "to enter into agreements with the NLDC and developers to build the type of facilities we require . . . We have also requested the NLDC to expedite the development as quickly as possible to meet our schedule . . . for the unveiling of the new, New London."

Milne wasn't telling Claire anything she didn't already know. The real target of his letter was Governor Rowland. Milne sent him a copy. Claire and Milne needed the governor to redouble his support for the NLDC-Pfizer partnership. That meant stepping up the pace of development and squeezing more money out of the state for mounting costs.

The letter worked. Governor Rowland and Peter Ellef agreed to meet with Claire and Milne one month later. In the meeting Milne and Claire made a pitch for more money—a lot more money. It wasn't the first time the NLDC and Pfizer had come back to the Rowland administration for additional cash, but this time the governor had some reluctance. The project had taken on some messy overtones. Between fights with the newspaper and the homeowners, Claire and the NLDC had a black eye, and the governor wanted to avoid bad public relations. Rowland liked Claire's results; he just didn't like the dirty details that produced those results.

Before agreeing to more state funding, Rowland wanted proof that the expenditures represented "real numbers." And he wanted some assurance that there would be no more requests for money. The meeting ended with the governor's demanding answers in writing.

Claire and Milne had reason to be concerned when they left the governor's office: his enthusiasm had clearly slipped; his demeanor had changed. If the governor failed to go any further in his commitment, the plan to overhaul the peninsula might need to be scaled back. They had to convince him to stay on board.

A couple of weeks later they sent Ellef a jointly signed letter. "You challenged us eighteen months ago to deliver New London in the way that the private sector works—on time, on budget, and on goal," Claire and Milne said. "So far, we have not missed a trick. There is a significant risk that delay now will derail the project that you initiated and that we are implementing. We need you to stay with us as we continue to march forward."

Before committing to more funding, the governor now wanted to see proof that other investors were committing money to the plan. But the NLDC had no one to point to. Desperate for credible backers, Claire made a bold decision: she pledged a commitment from the Connecticut College board of trustees. With a little more time and another infusion of state money, she and Milne insisted, other private-sector investors would surface in New London. Reluctantly, the governor went along.

Part of the decline in the governor's enthusiasm stemmed from the fact that many homeowners still occupied homes in Fort Trumbull, and they had shown no signs of leaving. The prospect of resorting to eminent domain to evict them was starting to make the Rowland administration skittish. To keep the governor happy and the development on track, the NLDC had to deal with the holdouts. Claire asked the NLDC's real-estate acquisition team to come up with a recommendation. She received a memo with a plan. "To date," the memo said, "it appears that the process has been to purchase properties throughout the area. We have reached the point in the program where we need to move in a more coordinated fashion. The goal should be to get control of blocks of property."

With entire blocks, the NLDC felt, it could start demolition, wiping out entire rows of houses and buildings. Besides being cost-effective, this approach might dampen residents' desire to stick around in a neighborhood overrun by excavators and dump trucks. "If we can create a sense of inevitability," the memo said, "it may motivate additional property owners to sell."

July 8, 1999

The radio in Susette's emergency-response vehicle reported a fire on Trumbull Street.

"What did they say?" Susette asked her partner.

"There's a fire on Trumbull Street," her partner responded.

"Oh, my God! There's only one house on Trumbull Street. And it's right behind mine."

They sped to Susette's neighborhood. Smoke billowed from the area of her home. "Oh, my God, my house is on fire!" she yelled, jumping from the truck.

Firemen on the scene assured her that the flames had not spread to her house. Smoke had, however. And the heat from the fire had melted the paint on the exterior of her house. The Odessa Rose finish had been ruined. Firefighters were hosing down the outside of the house to cool it off.

"You better go upstairs and shut your windows," the fire marshal told her.

With firemen guiding her, Susette entered her home. It had filled with smoke and the inescapable smell of burning. Water from the fire hoses had seeped inside. The place was a mess.

Exiting the house, Susette looked around and tried not to cry. In one direction she saw cranes and construction vehicles erecting steel girders for the new Pfizer complex. In another direction she saw a burning house surrounded by fire trucks. The house on the other side of hers had been empty since it had been acquired by the NLDC. It all looked pretty bleak.

"This is one way to get rid of her," one fireman joked to another.

The comment left Susette unsettled. The African American family that owned the house behind hers had barely escaped the flames. Now homeless and too poor to find housing elsewhere, they ended up on the street, ultimately moving in to a relative's crowded apartment. The NLDC acquired the burnt home and left the charred structure standing. Susette couldn't look out her kitchen or bedroom windows without seeing it.

Fire officials concluded foul play had not been the cause of the fire. All Susette knew was that one more family that had refused to sell out was now gone.

20

THE TWEED CROWD

July 9, 1999

A bunker mentality quickly overtook the NLDC. The state's Freedom of Information Commission had just issued a final order saying the NLDC was a public agency and had to comply with the Freedom of Information Act. The ruling meant a big victory for the newspaper and more headaches for Claire.

For starters, the newspaper was pressing to find out what the agency had done with all the money it had received. One of the NLDC's biggest expenditures was for consultants. The biggest consultant contract involved the Downes Group, the construction firm with ties to the governor. One of the reasons the NLDC had hired Downes was the company's reputation for having the right connections to move a massive development project along. Pfizer's deadlines called for a firm that knew how to quickly navigate the state's permit and approval process. But by the time the Freedom of Information Act decision came down, Claire's view of the Downes Group had changed.

With the newspaper questioning the NLDC's finances, Claire decided to question Downes's billing. On July 14, she met with the firm's president, Joe Desautel, and asked for a detailed explanation of the work and services Downes had provided. The next day, Desautel faxed her a two-page memo, listing twenty-four action items. He included the negotiation of a $20 million bridge loan for the agency; acquiring buildings and business for

120

the NLDC; demolishing properties; drafting the municipal development plan for the peninsula; orchestrating a $16 million bond issue; and securing approvals and permits for all sorts of construction items, from the sewage-treatment facility upgrade to other developments along the waterfront.

Claire wasn't satisfied. "It didn't say hourly rates," she said later. "It didn't say who performed the work, when it was done, who supervised."

She insisted she wouldn't release payment until the firm sent her a more detailed, annotated bill. Her refusal to pay didn't sit well with the Downes Group. The state didn't like it either. Claire received a call from a member of the Department of Economic Development. She later recalled a very direct, testy conversation.

"You have state money, and we order you to pay the bill," Claire said the state official told her.

"I'm happy to pay the bill," Claire responded. "But I have to sign that I know state money is being appropriately spent. And I don't believe the bills are appropriate."

The governor had been monitoring the freedom-of-information dispute between the NLDC and the *Day*. It didn't take long for word about the tiff between Claire and Downes to reach his administration's attention. Claire appeared ready to fire one of the most powerful construction-consulting firms in the state.

"The governor was furious with me on a number of occasions," Claire later recalled. "It's the old thing: 'Are you going to do exactly as I tell you? Then I'm going to keep liking you.' It got very ugly. I think they thought I'd be dumber than I was because I was an academic."

After lawyers got involved and the standoff was on the brink of spilling into a public dispute that threatened to embarrass the NLDC, the Downes Group, and the Rowland administration, the three sides came to a truce. "They sent a different bill that was more explanatory," Claire recalled. "I paid the bill and I fired them."

But now Claire was clearly on the governor's blacklist.

* * *

Connecticut College history professor Fred Paxton had barely returned from a sabbatical in Cairo when he received word that Claire intended to appoint him director of the school's Center for International Studies and Liberal Arts. Paxton had long had his eye on the leadership post at the center, which Claire had founded shortly after becoming president of the college. Under her leadership, the center had quickly emerged as the college's signature program. The directorship promised prestige and a chance to work with top students and scholars.

The appointment surprised Paxton. As the former chair of the faculty steering and conference committee, he had the credentials, but he didn't have a particularly close relationship with Claire, who treated the program like her baby and tightly controlled its leadership reins. Nonetheless, when she asked to meet with him to discuss the position, he willingly agreed.

In his customary tweed blazer over a form-fitting, collarless shirt that matched his stylish corduroy pants and L. L. Bean shoes, Paxton dressed the part of a professor at a liberal-arts school in New England. Yet at forty-eight, he had the looks of a distinguished Hollywood actor. His receding hairline gave way to a modestly tanned forehead and face, along with a neatly trimmed gray beard. He expected Claire to be dressed provocatively for their meeting. Beyond that, he didn't know what to expect.

She did not disappoint on the dress. Claire invited him to discuss his leadership approach for the center. She also asked him to review the other interdisciplinary centers on campus to determine what could be done to improve their performance.

Shortly after taking on the assignment, he reported back to her in a phone conversation and said he had interviewed his colleagues and gathered their input on finances, curricula, and other matters. Paxton wanted to have the benefit of their knowledge and experience. He also wanted the support of his colleagues.

Paxton later remembered Claire saying, "Oh, no, Fred, that's not leadership. That's consultation. Consultation is like foreplay. But leadership is like sex. Then you have the baby down the road."

Paxton didn't know how to respond. But he thought he got the point: there was a long way to go, so he should get to work.

While starting in his new role, he read in the newspaper that the NLDC's municipal-development plan for the area around Pfizer's new facility would soon be ready for public review. Since he'd been out of the country on sabbatical, Paxton did not realize how involved Claire had become with the NLDC and in redeveloping parts of the city. Curious by nature and a bit self-interested because he owned a home not far from the Fort Trumbull neighborhood, Paxton decided to find out more about the development plans.

He drove to the NLDC office and asked to see the plan. The receptionist informed him that copies for the public weren't yet available. But she offered him an office copy to review. She handed him a massive binder. Paxton took it to a nearby table and began reading. The material was dense and technical. Most people would not have the patience to work through it, much less the knowledge to scrutinize it. But Paxton, a historian, made a living by breaking down long, complex documents.

He spotted a wide range of development schemes in the plan. But none of the alternatives included keeping the existing Fort Trumbull neighborhood in the larger redevelopment scheme. *How can that be the only alternative that doesn't belong in the plan?* he asked himself.

He read through the budget and noted the projected costs to acquire the homes, demolish them, and remediate the land they sat on. It occurred to him that tens of millions of dollars could be saved by simply preserving the neighborhood.

"No need to take this neighborhood," he jotted down on his notepad.

After a few hours, Paxton returned the document. The idea that the president of his institution was leading an effort to demolish an entire urban neighborhood didn't sit well with him. With the start of the fall semester still a few weeks off, Paxton figured he had time to find some support for opposing the idea. He drove directly to Landmarks, a nonprofit outfit dedicated to preserving the city's historic buildings and neighborhoods. He asked Landmarks director Sally Ryan if her organization shared his concerns. Ryan said her organization had grave concerns about the NLDC's plans.

Paxton asked what Landmarks had been doing to oppose the plan.

There was little Landmarks could do, Ryan indicated, explaining that Claire had all the momentum behind her.

Having expected to find a ready-made opposition plan, Paxton was disappointed. He thanked Ryan for her time and turned to leave. But before he got to the door, Ryan called Paxton back. "There's this architect who is talking about this and who is also very concerned," she said. Ryan handed him a piece of scrap paper with the name John Steffian and his home phone number. Not recognizing the name, Paxton stuffed the scrap in his pocket and left.

Instead of calling up a stranger, Paxton telephoned a fellow professor at the college, Jefferson Singer. When reviewing the plan, Paxton had noticed Claire had established numerous committees, some of which were led by faculty from the college. Singer headed up the NLDC's Social Justice Committee.

Paxton told Singer his concerns. "I don't understand why it foresees the total destruction of this neighborhood," he said. "I think there's a real possibility that a social injustice is going to be committed."

Singer agreed to accompany Paxton on a visit to the Fort Trumbull neighborhood a few days later. They parked a block from Susette's house and started walking. They found Matt Dery making repairs on his house. Paxton introduced himself and told Dery that Singer was affiliated with the NLDC.

"What's your perspective on this redevelopment idea?" Paxton asked.

Dery didn't mince words. "We're getting bulldozed," he said, explaining that his mother had been born in the family house and had hoped to die there. But the anxiety created by Claire and the NLDC was sending Dery's mother to an early grave, he said.

Paxton's blood began to boil. He asked what the residents were doing to oppose the NLDC. Dery pointed out that many of the residents were elderly and lacked the energy and resources to fight.

As soon as they left Dery's place, Paxton unloaded on Singer. The fact that Connecticut College had direct involvement in an effort to displace lifetime residents of a historic neighborhood was an outrage, he argued. Singer didn't disagree. His committee had a meeting coming up. He invited Paxton to make a presentation.

To prepare, Paxton read through press accounts of what had transpired during his sabbatical. He decided to pay one more visit to the neighborhood. This time he brought his wife, Sylvia Malizia, along. An Italian artist, she immediately recognized some of the architecture in the area. Italians from the Adriatic coast had settled some of the neighborhood, and Sylvia's ancestors had come from there as well.

"They are going to take all these properties by eminent domain," Paxton told her as he drove her up and down the streets.

"Oh, Fred, they can't do that," she said, dismissing his anger as an exaggeration. "This is not for public good. They can only do that for schools or roads or a hospital or something."

"I'm telling you the NLDC plans to demolish all of this."

"This is an intact piece of urban neighborhood," she said.

"I know it."

While at the stop sign in front of Susette's cottage, they spotted her on the front porch. Paxton recognized her from newspaper accounts. He parked the car and got out.

"Are you Susette Kelo?"

"Yes."

"Hi, I'm Fred Paxton. This is my wife, Sylvia. I teach at Connecticut College."

Unimpressed, Susette nodded.

"We've been away on sabbatical. We've been reading about what has happened while we've been away."

Unsure what "sabbatical" meant, Susette started talking about the NLDC's pressure tactics to drive out homeowners.

Paxton immediately sensed her combative demeanor. "We

are going to help you, Susette," Paxton said. "We are going to do everything in our power to not let this happen."

Susette didn't know what to think. Paxton and his wife sounded smart. They looked fashionable. *Why would people like that care about people like us?* she wondered. Appreciative, she told them about Kathleen Mitchell and provided her contact information.

As soon as the Paxtons drove off, Susette called Mitchell and told her that a professor from Connecticut College had agreed to help.

Paxton figured that Claire had told the NLDC's Social Justice Committee all about the good side of the redevelopment plan. He went to the committee meeting ready to tell them the dark side. He appealed to their liberal way of thinking and got them to reconsider displacing modest-income residents for the sake of a big corporation.

"So we are going to throw people out of their homes and demolish their homes to create a brownfield?" he asked. "For what? People don't develop like that anymore."

The committee broke up with an uneasy feeling. Word of Paxton's presentation quickly reached Claire. Then she found out he had contacted one of the project managers at the NLDC and got him to concede that it wasn't too late to modify the plan to preserve the neighborhood. Claire immediately went to work to defuse Paxton.

Kathleen Mitchell wasted no time in bringing Paxton on board. She arranged a strategy meeting for the two of them with Mayor Beachy. Together they determined the importance of getting Landmarks and the New London Historical Society involved. The mayor agreed. He belonged to both organizations. He explained the problem: the board of directors at Landmarks was split on the question of whether to get in the fight. Many of its members figured it was too late to stop the process.

A preservationist, Paxton knew some of the board members. He asked Beachy which ones were inclined to oppose the NLDC.

Beachy said the most outspoken board member in favor of opposing the plan was a fellow named John Steffian, an architect from
the neighboring town of Waterford.

Paxton still had the scrap of paper with Steffian's home phone
number. He decided to call him.

John and Sarah Steffian were among the wealthiest residents
in southeastern Connecticut. Sarah's great-grandfather had
founded Aetna, the insurance company. Sarah's grandfather had
served as chairman of the Hartford National Bank and Trust
Company. But her father had achieved the most success and had
the most far-reaching impact on the world: Dr. John Enders was
a professor of bacteriology and immunology at Harvard Medical School and the chief of the division of research of infectious
diseases at the Children's Hospital medical center. His landmark
research had led directly to the development of vaccines against
polio, measles, rubella, and mumps. In 1954 he had received the
Nobel Prize in Medicine, with two colleagues, after demonstrat-
ing how to grow the polio virus in tissue cultures instead of nerve
tissues. *Time* magazine had named him and fourteen other scientists Men of the Year for 1960.

Dr. Enders had maintained a summer estate on Long Island
Sound in Waterford, Connecticut, next door to New London. He
had died there in 1985 while reading T. S. Eliot aloud to his wife.
Sarah and her husband, John, had moved into one of the homes
on the estate and had also owned various properties in New London. They were heavily involved in historic preservation in the
city.

Paxton left a message on their answering machine. When
John Steffian called him back, they hit it off immediately. Like
Paxton, Steffian had spent his career in academia. He had served
as Chairman of the Architecture and Planning Department at
the University of Maryland's College of Engineering. He'd also
been dean of the School of Architecture. Steffian gave Paxton a
scathing critique of the NLDC's design plans for the Fort Trumbull peninsula. To him it was almost blasphemous to tear down
every home and building to accomplish urban renewal. He and

his wife, Sarah, he told Paxton, were determined to stop the NLDC from tearing down historic homes. Demolition, Steffian insisted, was completely unnecessary.

Steffian liked the fact that Paxton spoke his language and shared his philosophy about urban redevelopment. He also liked the fact that Paxton taught at Connecticut College, Claire's home base. The Steffians also had a close link to the top of the NLDC's power structure: Steve Percy, Claire's right-hand man in charge of real-estate acquisition, was Sarah Steffian's cousin, and he resided in the other home on the Enders estate. But despite being blood relatives and next-door neighbors, Sarah had no use for Steve. The Steffians despised what Percy had done with the NLDC.

Both Paxton and Steffian wanted to do their part to derail the plan. They agreed to work together and to do all they could to help Susette.

Susette opened her mailbox and pulled out a letter from her nursing school. In desperate need of some good news, she tore it open. It contained a letter informing her that she had successfully completed the nursing program.

She called Mitchell to share the news. Mitchell also had good news. Her meeting with the mayor and Professor Paxton had been very fruitful. "We're starting to build some real momentum," Mitchell said.

21

A HIP LITTLE CITY

Fred Paxton needed to be marginalized. Claire called a meeting for faculty and students on campus to promote the great things she had been doing in the city.

Paxton attended and listened to Claire explain that redeveloping a depressed part of New London would provide economic opportunity for the poor. "Social justice and economic development are two sides of the same coin," she said. Many in the audience nodded in agreement.

Paxton had heard enough. He raised his hand. "This is all well and good," he said. "But I'm really concerned about what's happening to that neighborhood down there."

The faculty and students turned to face Paxton.

"It doesn't seem to me," he continued, "that this fits into the goals of the NLDC, the idea that social justice and economic development are two sides of the same coin."

Some faculty looked down at their feet. No one said a word. Claire's presentation ended awkwardly. When the meeting broke up, a few of Paxton's colleagues gave him the cold shoulder. Claire followed him outside.

Paxton remembers her saying, "Look, Fred, this train has left the station. It's too late to do anything about this."

"But this is a *draft* plan," he said. "There are still public hearings to be held. It can't be approved until you have all these public hearings."

"No, no," she said.

"It's a draft," he interrupted. "Why not amend the plan?"

Paxton quickly realized Claire had heard enough. "Fred, the state is a blunt instrument," he recalled her saying. "The plan has to be approved the way it is."

It was clear the discussion was over.

For days, Paxton stewed over his exchange with Claire. Feeling Claire expected him to quash his true feelings on the project, he couldn't resist sending her an e-mail.

"Claire, let me be completely honest," he began. "As to the heart of our conversation, I have given the matter a good deal of thought. You are asking me to dissemble. But that is not my style. Nor is it yours, it seems to me. Did you dissemble with George Milne? With the City Council?"

It angered Paxton that Claire had gone to great lengths to help and stick up for Pfizer. But no one seemed to be standing up for the little guy—the homeowners. "Why didn't you go to them from the start and insist that no more homes and neighborhoods be sacrificed to development in New London?" Paxton wrote. "The state may be a blunt instrument, but one could have said the same about the City Council and Pfizer Corporation. Why should the governor or state agencies be spared the call to do things differently this time around?"

Paxton objected to Claire's apparently dismissing the neighborhood as a blighted community. "It's not a slum," he said. "But a viable piece of old New London with people who have lived there all their lives, who have invested in that part of the city when no one else wanted to, who fear they are being forced out just when their investment could pay off. It is not right.

"Right now, a lot of good people are questioning your integrity and the integrity of the NLDC. What I'd like you to do is amend the plan."

Claire didn't have to study Paxton's e-mail to realize he wasn't going away quietly. Without some quick intervention, Paxton's outspoken opposition could cause some real problems down the road. The NLDC set up a series of public presentations at different locations throughout the city. The presentations had a simple objective: lock up public support for the NLDC's plans and snuff out any opposition before any negative momentum picked up.

What's it like to have a newspaper reporter come to the house? Susette wondered. She was about to find out. Kathleen Mitchell had called Lee Howard, the editor of the *Day*'s real-estate section, and suggested he interview Susette. Howard had been following the eminent-domain dispute and agreed.

When Howard arrived he immediately put Susette at ease with his quiet, unassuming manner. Early on, he asked her about the NLDC's plan to revive the city through eminent domain.

"They can have my house when they can take the keys out of my cold, dead hands," Susette said.

Howard knew instantly that the NLDC was going to have its hands full with this woman.

When asked about the NLDC's argument that she could make a $16,000 profit by selling to it, Susette balked. "Look at this view," she said, pointing toward the Thames River. "How many people with a $70,000 house have a view like this? If I leave here, where can I go and get the same thing?"

Her point was simple, yet compelling.

Susette insisted she wasn't the only one in the neighborhood determined to stay. "The people that wanted to sell have sold," she said. "The people still here don't want to go."

The more she talked, the more sense she made. Susette had nothing to hide. And the resentment in her voice and on her face was raw, especially when Howard asked her about the negative perceptions about her neighborhood, such as its reputation for crime.

"The biggest crime here is what Claire has planned," she said, insisting that Claire was using code words to hide her true intentions. "You know that 'HIP little city?' To me, that means Higher Income People."

Howard left impressed by Susette's intensity and her candor. He called the NLDC for a response to her statements.

*   *   *

Pat O'Neil had been in charge of public relations at the NLDC for a year. Previously a reporter at the state capitol, he had heard about the opening at the NLDC from Jay Levin, and had agreed to come on board to help defuse the Freedom of Information dispute with the *Day*. Right away, O'Neil ended up handling one crisis after another and working closely with Claire. But he never bought into Claire's agenda. And he had a personal distaste for her approach. The steady sexual innuendo and the urgent Friday-night meetings got old fast, in his view. But like a good soldier, he kept his gripes to himself. It was hard to believe he had been on the job only a year; it felt more like a decade.

It fell to O'Neil to handle Howard's questions about Susette and her insistence that the NLDC was being unfair. O'Neil told Howard that he understood where Susette was coming from. "For people who have lived in houses for a long time, it is difficult," O'Neil said.

His honesty made an impression on Howard.

O'Neil also admitted that there were financial motives for the NLDC to act quickly in its attempt to obtain the homes in the fort area. "If you wait two years and Pfizer opens and people are desperate to move in, things like that do have an effect on the market," he said.

After interviewing Susette and O'Neil, Howard produced a cover story titled "In The Way of a Revival" for the newspaper's weekly real-estate section. It included color pictures of Susette's house—freshly repainted after the fire—and of its impressive views.

The article's slant and Susette's tough quotes were just the kind of press the NLDC was trying to avoid. A couple of weeks after the article appeared, Dave Goebel told O'Neil he wanted to see him in his office. O'Neil figured the agency had another crisis.

"This isn't working out," Goebel told him. "I'm going to have to give you notice."

Stunned, O'Neil said nothing.

"It's unfortunate," Goebel continued. "I feel bad about this.

But we've got budget issues. We need project managers and engineers. It's a problem that I have to deal with."

O'Neil liked Goebel and had always found him to be professional. But he wasn't buying Goebel's explanation. He was convinced it was something else.

"I'm not sure how or why I ran afoul of Claire," O'Neil said.

"I don't know either," said Goebel.

Steve and Amy Hallquist saw the feature story on Susette. It confirmed their growing reservations about Claire and the NLDC.

They decided to attend one of the public presentations Claire had scheduled.

Claire was partway through her speech when Susette suddenly stood up in the back of the room.

"This is bullshit!" she said.

All eyes shifted to Susette. Steve and Amy spotted a redhead in blue jeans and a flannel shirt. They recognized her as the woman in the newspaper.

"It's total bullshit," Susette repeated. "They're down here stealing our properties. They're trying to take our homes."

Civility instantly left the room. People mumbled under their breath. A woman toward the back of the hall insisted people in the neighborhood hadn't been included in the process. A man complained that Claire was messing with real lives.

Claire insisted that there were various alternatives and that no final decisions had been made.

Susette remained standing. "We're not against all development," Susette said. "But that doesn't mean you can push us around. We have a right to stay here. These are our homes."

Amy turned to Steve. "Wow," she whispered in his ear, "she just went off."

The audience didn't appreciate Susette's outburst. Most people wanted what Claire had promised.

The contrast struck Steve. Claire described teamwork, democracy in action, and everyone working together for a better city, but Susette's actions displayed anger over powerlessness.

When the meeting broke up, the Hallquists heard a community opposition group was planning a meeting.

"We have to do this," Amy said.

Steve didn't have to be persuaded.

November 18, 1999

When Susette walked into the Landmarks building she hardly believed her eyes. In the center of a large room with a wood floor, some tables had been pushed together to form a makeshift conference table. Mayor Beachy and Kathleen Mitchell sat around it, along with Fred Paxton and his wife, Sylvia; John and Sarah Steffian; Steve and Amy Hallquist; and many others. Most of the attendees had never met Susette. But her plight had a lot to do with everyone's presence. She quietly took a seat near the window, away from the table.

Mitchell hoped the meeting would be the beginning of a true neighborhood opposition group. Board members of the New London Historical Society and of the Landmarks group had shown up. A few people from Connecticut College were also on hand. The mayor looked ready to roll. This, Mitchell thought, is a group capable of having an impact.

After the mayor said a few words, Paxton made a presentation outlining the NLDC's plans to wipe out the Fort Trumbull neighborhood.

John Steffian pounded his fist on the table. "This is not going to happen," he thundered. He had looked at the NLDC's designs for the Fort Trumbull area and concluded they had failed to take into account a variety of ways to preserve and incorporate the historic residential neighborhood into the new development.

Steffian pushed for a joint resolution by the historical society and Landmarks that would oppose the forceful eviction of residents from their homes in Fort Trumbull. Both boards had previously resisted taking that stance, but the opposition had largely been based on the sense that it was too late in the game to stop the NLDC. The people in the room felt otherwise. Both boards now voted in favor of the resolution.

Next the group voted to establish a nonprofit organization to lead the drive. They settled on the name: the Coalition to Save Fort Trumbull Neighborhood. Committees were established and filled. Assignments were made. And the group settled on meeting weekly.

The Hallquists agreed to do legal research on the NLDC's actions. Paxton accepted responsibility for writing opinion pieces and letters to the editor. Another group of individuals agreed to pen letters to all elected officials at the local, state, and federal levels. Others agreed to mobilize more residents into action.

While protesting the NLDC's plans to wipe out a neighborhood, the group also agreed they had to offer a counterplan. John Steffian accepted that assignment. He promised to produce an alternative design that would preserve the neighborhood while still accomplishing the NLDC's goals.

Susette got emotional. This collection of talented, dedicated people overwhelmed her. Few of them knew Susette, yet they all were dedicated to helping her save her home. For the first time, she felt convinced the neighborhood could be saved.

The group asked Susette for a list of people who had moved out of the neighborhood under duress. They also asked her to write a letter to the editor of the newspaper voicing her anger with the NLDC's actions.

Susette had never written an opinion letter. Mitchell offered to help her, and that night they got together and wrote:

> *While other associations are battling for speed bumps on their streets and better lighting, sidewalks in front of their homes and drug-free streets, we in the Fort Trumbull neighborhood are fighting for only one thing—our homes.*
>
> *And why shouldn't we? Or more precisely, why should we have to? They belong to us. We've paid our taxes and our water bills, maintained our homes, made some improvements, put up with the stench of the sewer plants. Now the NLDC says we have to go. We have to make room for people who will better fit into a "hip little city."*

*We have no objection to a hotel, conference center or wellness
clinic. We are happy to see that Fort Trumbull will be open as a state
park. We welcome Pfizer. But not at the expense of the people who
have invested so much in this neighborhood.*

*Most of the work in mounting and maintaining this campaign
to save our homes has fallen on the shoulders of myself and
Kathleen Mitchell. We have learned that in the esoteric language of
redevelopment, "hip" means "higher-income people." "In the way of
progress" means "we want your homes."*

Where is the justice in forcing senior citizens out of their homes?

*Let us keep our homes. Ask yourself this: "What would I do if
it were my home or that of my parents or my children?" Those who
wanted to go (and some who didn't) have gone from Fort Trumbull.
You can safely assume that the rest of us want to stay. Please
support us.*

Susette's letter was published under the title: "No room for
New Londoners." Seeing her byline in the newspaper emboldened Susette.

The opposite page carried an essay by Fred Paxton titled
"Little 'social justice' in strong-arm tactics." In it he artfully
used Claire's words against her. He took her slogan statement—
"Economic development and social justice are two sides of the
same coin"—and listed all the injustices being committed as a
result of the NLDC's plan to complement Pfizer's global research
center. "This means the disappearance of landmarks, among as
many as 26 small businesses and 115 homes," Paxton wrote. "Why
can't they be part of the plan? As it is, their lives have been up in
the air for almost two years."

Paxton's printed bio as a professor at Connecticut College hit
Claire like a slap in the face.

The sudden onslaught persuaded the NLDC to agree to a
meeting with the new coalition.

The first time Susette had approached Matt Dery to join a neighborhood association, he had made it clear he would never join
any group effort to oppose the NLDC. But since then, a lot had

changed. Susette went to see Dery again. She told him about the new coalition and all the smart people who had joined. She explained that the coalition had pressured the NLDC into holding a meeting at St. James Church, where NLDC officials would answer questions. She asked him to attend.

He complained that for years no one had even known their neighborhood existed. No one had known what was beyond the train tracks. "We were in a world by ourselves," he said.

She got the picture. "When the story first came out in the papers that they wanted the fort," she said, "people in the city were like, 'Where the hell is that place?'"

"Nobody ever cared about us," Dery said. "They put the shit plant down here. They don't plow here when it snows. They don't pick up our garbage. This was a forgotten neighborhood."

She nodded.

But after Dery said his piece, he agreed to attend the meeting with her.

December 7, 1999

Fred Paxton donned his reading glasses and plugged in his laptop at St. James Church. Kathleen Mitchell, John and Sarah Steffian, and the Hallquists filed in with prepared questions. They couldn't wait to get at the NLDC. Mayor Beachy had passed along some intelligence: the NLDC had retained a nationally renowned engineering firm—Wallace Roberts & Todd—to suggest options for how to redevelop the ninety-acre peninsula, and the firm had actually advocated keeping the houses in Fort Trumbull. The NLDC eventually replaced that firm with a lesser known one that advocated demolishing all homes.

Admiral David Goebel and four other representatives from the NLDC filed in. After a brief introduction, the coalition began to fire questions at Goebel. One coalition member wanted to know why the NLDC had dismissed the design firm that recommended preserving the homes and integrating them into the redevelopment plan.

"I wouldn't say they were fired," Goebel said. "Their work was done, and they just fell off."

Paxton found Goebel's statement disingenuous. He felt firms of that caliber didn't "fall off."

"This is a conflict of interest," Paxton said. "The NLDC was interested in buying properties with the clear intent of demolition."

Goebel emphasized that the development would serve the best overall interest of the city by increasing tax revenues by $12 million a year. Most of the revenue, he insisted, would come from Pfizer, which would help the city's schools, health care, and art and cultural programs. He sounded like Claire had fed him his lines.

Steffian didn't appreciate Goebel's sidestepping the coalition's core issue: saving homes. He challenged Goebel, saying the homes could easily be integrated into any development design.

Goebel didn't have an answer.

Matt Dery nudged Susette. "Ask Goebel if he's going to do anything to help us save our homes," he said.

"Mr. Goebel," Susette said, "is there anything that you or the NLDC is going to do to help save our homes?"

"In order to complete the development of the area, in order to do that, we must acquire all the homes," said Goebel, adding that the homes he had seen were not in good shape. Speechless, Susette turned to Dery. Goebel's dig hit Dery like a punch in the heart. Only Paxton's fingers' pecking at his laptop keyboard broke the awkward silence.

"He didn't even lie and at least *say* they would try and save our houses," Susette whispered to Dery.

After a distinguished career as an architect and designer, John Steffian had no patience for what Goebel was saying. What did Goebel know about engineering, architecture, and urban design? The guy was a retired admiral, not an urban planner. He was used to giving orders. In this instance, he sounded a lot like an NLDC yes-man, a preprogrammed mouthpiece who would say anything to justify the agency's determination to give Pfizer what it wanted—an entirely new neighborhood.

The next morning's headline read: "NLDC will demolish all the homes in the Fort Trumbull area even though a coalition has asked it to preserve them."

December 15, 1999

Governor Rowland had had it. Nearly six months had passed since the Freedom of Information Commission had ordered the NLDC to turn over documents to the newspaper. And it still had not complied. Meanwhile, the NLDC's battle with holdout home-owners in Fort Trumbull had become a full-blown controversy with no signs of slowing down. Protest letters and essays had become routine on the newspaper's editorial page. The public sentiment seemed to be tilting in favor of the property own-ers. The media seemed headed that way too. Worst of all, time had clearly demonstrated that Claire was not someone the state could control.

The governor decided to remind her where the power rested. He issued Claire a letter threatening to withhold state funds from the NLDC if it didn't comply with the freedom-of-information law. The governor made sure the press got a copy of the letter.

Claire issued a written statement, promising to comply.

When John Steffian completed his alternative design for the Fort Trumbull peninsula, the coalition distributed copies to the media, along with a press release. Steffian also sent his plans to the NLDC. The renderings showed a way to integrate the exist-ing historic neighborhood into the new development in such a way that the old would complement the new. Steffian's plan also preserved the elements important to Pfizer, including waterfront access and new amenities appealing in a corporate campus.

No one at the NLDC cared to see Steffian's design—not Claire, not Goebel, not Percy. A staffer merely stuffed the plan in a file cabinet.

Chastised by the governor, Claire had her lawyers withdraw the freedom-of-information appeal. Still smarting from the defeat, she wrote to publisher Reid MacCluggage. "I have reflected on how the newspaper and the development effort can move in more synchronous ways," she said. "As you probably know, Bill Taylor, retired publisher of the *Boston Globe* and member of the board of the *New York Times*, was a trustee of Connecticut College. I have sought Bill's advice in the past on many issues, including those related to dealing with the press. Bill has graciously agreed to come to New London to a closed meeting with you and the members of the *Day* staff for a discussion on civic journalism if you would like to invite him to come. He has offered five dates."

Claire advised MacCluggage to have no one outside the newspaper staff attend the meeting. "I am hopeful that on behalf of the City of New London and its great past, we can move forward as fellow citizens in the new year," she said. "The *Day* has played a powerful role in the city's past. I am looking forward to its playing an equally powerful role in the city's future."

MacCluggage could not believe Claire had the nerve to contact one of the more respected names in print journalism and ask him to make a presentation to the newspaper without first checking with him.

He wrote her back:

> *I wish you had consulted me before asking Bill Taylor to come to the* Day *for a discussion on civic journalism. I have the highest regard for Mr. Taylor, and you have put me in the position of turning him down. I don't like that. Had you contacted me first to ask whether I would be amenable, I would have explained that the staff and I are already very familiar with the notion of civic journalism. It is apparent you are unaware of the leadership role the* Day *played in the early discussions of the concept nearly a decade ago.*
>
> *Please check with me before you ask someone to make a presentation at the newspaper.*

MacCluggage copied the letter to Bill Taylor.

Claire got the last word: "I have received your letter and regret that you have turned down Bill Taylor's offer," she wrote back, insisting she had been well aware of the *Day*'s previous leadership role in developing civic journalism.

It seemed appropriate to invite Bill Taylor to engage all of you in moving your leadership forward.

You should also know that I asked Bill if he would consider such an opportunity only after discussing this issue with a number of your staff. It appears that the staff at the Day *. . . are quite enthusiastic about this opportunity, which you may wish to discuss with them in some open format. They have reported to me that they do not know why you made the decision not to invite Bill to join you for a closed discussion on this issue which is after all, Reid, every bit as important as FOI [freedom of information].*

22

RUBBER STAMP

As the city's attorney, Tom Londregan saw it as his duty to do everything in his power to get the NLDC's municipal-development plan (MDP) passed in compliance with the law. The law, he believed, allowed for the use of eminent domain. But for him, it went deeper than simple legal analysis. Personally, Londregan believed the development being attempted by Pfizer and the NLDC would help New London.

The city had one more legal hurdle to clear before the city council could vote on whether to approve the NLDC's plan: a public hearing. Judging from the tone of editorials and letters in the newspaper, Londregan expected some real opposition to the plan at the hearing. The threat of eminent domain had become a flash point.

With the public hearing set for early January, Londregan huddled with the city council. In 1998, the council had passed a resolution directing the NLDC to prepare a redevelopment plan. The NLDC's plan called for the Fort Trumbull neighborhood to be razed and redeveloped. To approve the plan, the council had to say yes to eminent domain. "The question is," Londregan said, "do you want to do that?"

Mayor Beachy had consistently made his feelings known. "I don't want to throw anybody out of their home," Beachy said.

But the idea of taking people's homes didn't seem to bother the rest of the council members. They were more concerned about taking the blame if the public and the press reacted neg-

atively. By authorizing the NLDC to use eminent domain, the
city's elected officials could shield themselves from any political
fallout. If things went badly, the blame would fall on the NLDC.
At the same time, the city recognized that using the NLDC meant
relinquishing power to the agency, and the city officials didn't
like that.

"What are our choices?" one council member asked.

There were not many, Londregan explained. The state had
put up the money for the project, so the state called the shots.
And the state had chosen the NLDC as its agent. If the city wanted
$70 million to flow from the state to the city for redevelopment,
the city had to be willing to bow to the NLDC and, if push came
to shove, give the NLDC final say on homes that had to go.

Londregan made a case for why no homes could be left standing: if the NLDC permitted a few scattered homes to stay, no
developer would take the project on. A developer would want a
complete site. If the plan called for a complete site, then some
tough decisions would be required when it came to using eminent domain.

Mathew Greene was the first attorney Claire had hired after taking over the NLDC. A probate judge with a private law practice in
New London, Greene had made friends with all the right people
in the city—politicians, fellow lawyers, and businessmen. Likeable, athletic, and handsome, Greene hadn't been Claire's first
choice to serve as the NLDC's in-house counsel. But he had come
highly recommended, so she obliged.

Greene recognized that eminent domain might be a ticking
time bomb. He also understood why the NLDC wanted to use it
and why City Hall wanted the NLDC to use it. From a legal perspective, Greene didn't see any problems for the NLDC. But from
a personal perspective, he saw Claire as opening herself up to
more and more unfriendly fire. She was already shielding Pfizer
and the governor's office from political heat. Now she would become the shield for City Hall on eminent domain.

Yet it wasn't Greene's responsibility to give Claire personal
advice. Besides, he figured, she probably wouldn't take it anyway.

He respected her even though he believed that patience and humility were not among her virtues. But she was the real deal, unlike one or two other board members whom Greene viewed as second-rate wannabes riding on Claire's coattails.

Claire's approach had Greene hearkening back to something a wise city leader had told him years earlier: "New London politics is about people, not about issues. It's always about people." In a city where everyone seems to be related to someone else in the city, outsiders didn't fare well. Claire was an outsider playing an insider's game. *Dangerous*, Greene thought, *dangerous*.

City Hall officials scheduled two public hearings leading up to the city council's vote on whether to approve the NLDC's municipal-development plan. Kathleen Mitchell and the coalition mobilized hundreds of opponents to attend. When the time came, residents from throughout the city packed the hearings.

Mitchell also did some research on Claire's home. When she had become president of Connecticut College, Claire had moved into the president's residence, a stately white colonial with red shutters located next door to a land conservatory. Additionally, she and her husband had purchased a second home away from New London in an exclusive waterfront community known as Mumford Cove, on Long Island Sound. She had a personal driver and a limousine to shuttle her from place to place.

Compared to the people Claire had been attempting to drive out of Fort Trumbull, she had some pretty upscale living standards. Mitchell figured the time had come to expose all this to the public. She spread the word that while enjoying two expensive homes Claire was busy trying to deprive others of having only one.

At the close of the second public hearing, Claire addressed the issue of owning multiple homes, defending her and her husband's lifestyle. "We were very, very, very modestly paid professors when we came to this area, when I was asked to be president of the college," she said. "When I came to the college, I had a president's house. If we had not purchased a house within eighteen months, we would have had to have paid capital gain [tax] on the little nest egg that we had in our house. So, of course, we bought a house. The house we could find at the time is on Mumford Cove in Groton. So that is the place where David and I go on the weekends. So I hope you, as fellow citizens, would understand that somebody with my kind of job is basically on a 24/7 schedule. I should have a place to go with my family and be a mom and a wife."

Mitchell loved Claire's answer. It gave the impression that her job was more important than everybody else's. Many people in New London didn't own one home, much less two homes. People in Fort Trumbull weren't looking for a weekend getaway; they were merely trying to hold on to four walls and a roof. Claire talked about trying to avoid capital gains taxes; few people in Fort Trumbull ever had to worry about capital gains.

With the city council set to vote on the NLDC plan on January 18, 2000, Mitchell talked with Susette about making a public statement before the vote. Susette felt hesitant; a thousand people were projected to attend the public comment period before the vote.

Mitchell assured her that most of the crowd would be on her side. That didn't change Susette's mind—she felt very uncomfortable about getting up in front of a crowd that size. She agreed to attend, but she made no promises about speaking. Mitchell suggested she bring a picture of her house, reflecting all the renovations.

The New London High School auditorium was packed when Susette arrived with Mitchell and trailed her toward some seats near other members of the coalition. The city council occupied seats on the stage. Susette recognized only one friendly person— Mayor Beachy.

For four hours the council listened as resident after resident addressed it in a public comment period. Mitchell kept tabs; it appeared that more than 90 percent of the residents who spoke were against the NLDC plan. Wanting Susette to have the last word, Mitchell waited until the very end of the meeting before she stood up to approach the microphone.

"C'mon, Susette," she whispered. "Come with me."

Susette looked up at Mitchell, who was smiling and wearing an old, badly wrinkled blouse and white canvas sneakers that displayed her badly swollen ankles. Admiring Mitchell's strength, Susette stood up, clutching a picture of her house. Side by side, they approached a microphone.

"We're coming up to speak together," Mitchell said to the council. "Susette is not used to speaking in public, and I just wanted the company."

Mitchell reminded the council that senior citizens on fixed incomes were being forced out under the NLDC plan. She gave a list of reasons why the council should not accept a plan that allowed for the use of eminent domain. Then she turned to Susette.

"I'm here tonight in regard to the Fort Trumbull neighborhood," Susette said, describing her house and what it meant to her. She held up the picture. "Does this look like a house that needs to be condemned? Does this look like a house that should be torn down?" She paused. "Please vote tonight to not tear down the Fort Trumbull neighborhood." She stepped back and followed Mitchell back to their seats.

At midnight, the city council ended the meeting and went into executive session before voting 6–1 to support the NLDC's plan. Only Mayor Beachy voted no. The way had been cleared for the NLDC to begin carrying out the development plan.

23

HIGHER EDUCATION

Disillusioned." Fred Paxton couldn't think of a better word to describe his feelings after six months of hard work seemed to add up to nothing. The will of the people had been ignored, despite every effort to use the proper channels to communicate with elected officials.

The rest of the Coalition to Save Fort Trumbull Neighborhood felt the same way. Anger filled the room when members gathered to discuss the city council's vote. They had done research, circulated petitions, organized letter-writing campaigns, garnered positive publicity, mobilized citizens, attended public hearings, and demonstrated strong opposition to the NLDC's plan. They had even produced an alternative plan. Nothing had worked. Some wondered what else could be done.

Mitchell lashed out at the coalition. "We have been playing too nice," she shouted. "We are playing by the rules of the politicians and the others in charge. We're not going to get anywhere using these methods."

All along, Mitchell had been pushing for a more aggressive, confrontational approach. John and Sarah Steffian agreed; the coalition needed to play hardball. But some members feared such an approach would alienate them from the rest of the public and the press, both of which were behind the Fort Trumbull residents. The meeting degenerated into an argument and ended without any resolution on the next steps.

Discouraged and convinced the NLDC would get her house,

Susette walked out in silence. The pain in Susette's expression tugged at Paxton. He had pledged to do all he could to help her, yet nothing he had tried seemed to work. He had let her down. He also felt he was taking a big personal risk by opposing Claire. Some colleagues had started to shun him. Some blamed him for undermining the school's reputation.

But unbeknownst to Paxton, while he had been publicly squaring off with Claire over Fort Trumbull, a small group of faculty at the college had been quietly looking into the finances of the school. One of them contacted Paxton and asked him to attend a private meeting with a college administrator who had firsthand knowledge of the school's accounting records.

Paxton reluctantly agreed. When he arrived at the meeting, the faculty administrator distributed some documents. "Here's the financial status of the college," the administrator said.

While Paxton and his colleagues looked at the numbers, the administrator painted the picture for them. It was not pretty. The school's operating budget had shortfalls and warnings of a hiring freeze and possible cutbacks had reached the faculty. Two dining areas had been closed; hours at the athletic center had been cut back; and campus health service fees had gone up nearly tenfold. The school had also inexplicably run out of money while building some dormitories.

The group determined that something had to be done—fast. Talk ultimately turned to Claire. Paxton left the meeting feeling ill. He was in enough hot water with Claire over Fort Trumbull. The other professors understood that Paxton didn't want to be involved. But the others organized a private meeting off campus and invited senior, tenured faculty. The school's finances weren't the only thing driving the organizers. Some faculty had been at odds with Claire on a variety of issues. And personal gripes and personal offenses came into play too. All of this added up to momentum to orchestrate a change at the top.

April 6, 2000

"Damn."

Mayor Beachy tossed aside a legal notice prepared by the city's

Building Division. It indicated the NLDC had obtained permits to demolish a slew of buildings in the Fort Trumbull neighborhood, including the house right next door to Susette's place and three other homes on East Street. The city council had barely voted to support the plan and the NLDC had already moved to exercise its power to knock down the buildings.

Beachy sent an urgent e-mail to the Coalition to Save Fort Trumbull Neighborhood, alerting them to the impending demolitions. "We must stop this project," Beachy wrote. "Step forward and fight."

A chill ran down Susette's spine when she read the e-mail. She called Mitchell, who had already read it. To Mitchell it was a long overdue call to arms.

Reinvigorated by news that the NLDC planned to start knocking down homes, the coalition reconvened to map out ideas to stop it. John Steffian insisted the time had come to take the fight out of the political process and into the courtroom.

Steve and Amy Hallquist agreed. "We have to get real," Steve said. "Real" meant hiring a lawyer and suing the NLDC.

"It's about time," Mitchell said.

But lawyers and lawsuits, other coalition members pointed out, required money, and the coalition didn't have any money.

The Steffians had money, lots of it. And they had no intention of letting money get in the way of saving homes in Fort Trumbull.

Coalition members had another concern: liability. Suing the city or the NLDC could mean repercussions for anyone involved. Everyone agreed that engaging a lawyer probably made sense. But few were eager to become litigants.

Steve and Amy Hallquist volunteered to join the Steffians to search for an attorney.

24

BLURRED VISION

Admiral David Goebel came across as a guy who liked rules and obedience, not exceptions and excuses. That was only natural. He had spent his career in the military, a world that simply didn't work if the rules weren't clear and followed clearly—by everyone.

The deal Jay Levin had cut with the Italian Dramatic Club wasn't something Goebel would go for: exempting the men's club from demolition posed a conflict. The NLDC had a mandate to present a developer with a peninsula free of all buildings, and the NLDC had the power of eminent domain to achieve its mandate. To Goebel it was simple: if the Italian Dramatic Club refused to sell and relocate then it should be subjected to the same treatment as any other holdout in Fort Trumbull. Goebel urged his fellow board members not to make an exception.

Others at the NLDC saw the wisdom in Goebel's position and agreed with him. Attorney Tom Londregan sided with Goebel too. For Londregan it came down to a simple analysis: a secret deal that exempted one building—a private men's club, no less—had legal danger and political controversy written all over it. Londregan suspected a lawsuit over eminent domain might be brewing. A runner, Londregan had found that legal disputes were a lot like races. Reaching the finish line was hard enough, and facing hurdles would only make it harder. The same holds true for lawsuits. Making an exception for the Italian Dramatic Club, Londregan argued, would create an unnecessary legal hurdle for the city and the NLDC.

Besides, Londregan figured, the Italian Dramatic Club wasn't a strong-enough political force to oppose the NLDC. The fallout for forcing the club to move would be little to none.

But Jay Levin had political clout. And Levin had promised the club's president, Aldo Valentini, that no one would touch his club. Claire was caught in the middle. She liked and respected Levin, but she had no idea why he had made such a promise to the club. And she understood where Goebel was coming from. With pressure mounting to take the club down, Claire agreed to revisit the subject with Levin.

A proposed compromise emerged: the NLDC would pay for the club's relocation to another site outside the development-area footprint. That meant either physically moving the building to a new piece of real estate or simply constructing a brand-new building at a new location. Valentini said he'd consider it. He agreed to host a meeting at the club to discuss the particulars with Claire and Levin. Intent on protecting his interests, Valentini decided to call an old friend to advise him during the negotiations.

Judge Angelo Santaniello had unparalleled stature in New London. At age seventy-six, he had been on the bench longer than most attorneys in the city had been practicing law. Besides presiding over hundreds of trials and mediations, Santaniello had a long history of involvement in the Republican Party. Prior to becoming a judge in 1965, he had served as legal counsel to the Connecticut State Senate for the party. Later, Republican governor Thomas Meskill elevated him to the bench of the Superior Court. He then became chief administrative judge of the civil division of the Superior Court for all of Connecticut. If Judge Santaniello called John Rowland, the governor would take the call.

Santaniello also had special standing among Italians in New London, where he had been a pioneer in the legal profession. He had been a friend and a patron of the Italian Dramatic Club. When Aldo Valentini called him asking for help, Santaniello agreed. Valentini told him that the NLDC wanted the club's land and that Claire had floated the idea of paying the club to relocate its building.

"Before you start talking about moving, let's talk about the finances," Santaniello told him. He asked Valentini the value of his building.

Valentini said the NLDC had appraised his building at $170,000.

Santaniello assured him that was nowhere near enough money to build another building like the one the club had. "So you better know where you're heading and what you're going to do before you start doing it," Santaniello advised. Valentini wasn't sure what Santaniello meant, so the judge cut to the bottom line: "They are not going to give you enough money to rebuild and buy the land."

Valentini asked Santaniello to intervene. Santaniello agreed to call Claire.

David Goebel felt his discussions with Jay Levin over the Italian men's club had been progressing toward a favorable resolution. Then Goebel got an unexpected call from Claire, who had heard from Judge Santaniello. She told Goebel to collect all the documents involving negotiations with the club.

Goebel didn't appreciate the judge's sudden intervention. Nonetheless, at Claire's request, he had paperwork and engineering plans put together for the judge, along with a list of available buildings and parcels of land for the men's club to move to or build on. He had all the information delivered to Judge Santaniello.

After Santaniello reviewed the documents, he attended a meeting at the club with Claire, Levin, Valentini, and a couple of others. Santaniello and Levin knew the club well; Claire didn't. When she arrived, a couple of members met her outside. "We can't bring you in the front door," one told her.

"Oh," Claire said, assuming the front door was broken or otherwise impassable. "I don't mind." They led her in through a basement door.

Inside, one of the men leaned toward her. "You know," he said, "you couldn't come in the front door because women never enter that door." Valentini entered the room. "But don't tell him I told you," the man whispered to Claire.

Unfazed, Claire got down to business.

"Where will you find suitable land?" Santaniello asked her.

Claire rattled off a few possibilities.

"What makes you think you could raise this building without it falling apart?" Santaniello asked.

She had no answer.

"Who is going to foot the bill?" Santaniello pushed.

Claire had no answer for that either.

Santaniello figured Claire didn't like having him involved, since power brokers usually don't get along with other power brokers. But Santaniello wasn't in a popularity contest. He wanted to know where the money would come from. Levin indicated he might be able to get $300,000 in federal money.

Santaniello had his doubts. To him, Pfizer represented the most logical source for funds. After all, it was Pfizer that wanted the land cleared. It was Pfizer that had a big financial stake in what transpired next door to its new facility. Yet Pfizer was not at the table. To Santaniello this was a mistake.

Valentini liked the prospect of getting Pfizer money in the mix. The group needed to determine whether Milne would consider financing the preservation of the Italian Dramatic Club. The meeting ended with the group committed to feeling Milne out as a possible source of funding.

Ever since meeting John and Sarah Steffian, Susette had more confidence that she'd be able to keep her home. The Steffians were smart, wealthy, and very generous. Their willingness to engage an attorney had Susette anticipating good news when she arrived at the coalition meeting.

But Steve Hallquist had bad news. He had approached many top lawyers and law firms in the city, and they all said no. None of them wanted to sue the city on behalf of the coalition. Some simply said the case could not be won. Others said they had a conflict of interest due to ties to city officials, Pfizer, or Connecticut College.

Mayor Beachy had a suggestion. He had been privately talking to lawyers in the city too. One had recommended Scott Sawyer, a young lawyer with a solo practice. Beachy said he didn't know Sawyer but that he seemed like someone the coalition should pursue.

"Amy and I know Sawyer," Steve Hallquist said. A year earlier, Sawyer had helped them resolve a simple property-line dispute. "We'll call him."

The private off-campus meeting held by Connecticut College faculty ended up being a planning session to oust Claire as president. She was criticized for everything from finances to her leadership style. Some faculty were so angry they wanted to go directly to the board of trustees with a letter spelling out the school's financial woes and demanding Claire's resignation. Others suggested a less confrontational approach—sending a small group of respected senior faculty to talk with her directly and encourage her to step down voluntarily. This approach would spare Claire any public embarrassment and keep the school's financial woes out of the newspapers.

The more diplomatic approach prevailed. But the half dozen senior faculty who enjoyed good relations with Claire failed to make the kind of headway their colleagues wanted to see. And with only a few weeks remaining before the end of the spring semester, a small group of professors drafted a petition calling on Claire to resign. Mobilized and energized, the leaders of the petition drive needed only two weeks to get 78 of the school's 105 tenured professors to sign it. Before submitting it to the board of trustees, one of the professors tipped off the *Day*. On May 7 the newspaper broke the news of the petition.

The news was stunning. The college president who had used her clout to spearhead an economic revival in New London had suddenly become vulnerable. It was the talk of the town from the Fort Trumbull neighborhood to City Hall. It was hard not to suspect that her extensive time commitment to the city had led to her neglect of the campus.

Two things were clear: the gloves had come off, and Claire

was challenged with a revolt. Her personal secretary, Claudia Shapiro, couldn't believe the faculty had actually gone public against Claire. Shapiro, soft-spoken and in her sixties, had started working for Claire the year she became the president. She found Claire very demanding yet irresistibly likeable. On birthdays and Jewish holidays, Shapiro always discovered a gift from Claire hidden in her desk drawer, usually signed "Aheba, Claire," Hebrew for "Love, Claire."

Shapiro saw sides of Claire that few people saw. She acknowledged that Claire's dominant personality surely had its flaws. "She had a habit of offending people," Shapiro said. "Then people forget the good parts about her and they hold grudges."

But to Shapiro, Claire's qualities far outweighed any imperfections. "She was a workaholic, very driven and very aggressive," she said. "People loved this when she started. But after she made a few mistakes, these same qualities were disdained." And certainly she didn't deserve to be run out, Shapiro felt.

Privately, some professors agreed. "For all the criticism of Claire," one senior professor told Shapiro in confidence, "when a parent brings a child to our campus, all the things we brag about were brought in by Claire."

None of that mattered now. There was blood in the water and the notion of a faculty revolt against a college president immediately attracted national attention. The *Chronicle of Higher Education*, the leading periodical for academia, ran a two-thousand-word story titled "A Promoter of Town-Gown Cooperation Finds Development May Be Her Undoing." It outlined the dispute between the faculty and Claire, quoting professors who had turned solidly against Claire. The *Chronicle* also reported that it had obtained a videotape of Claire speaking at a black Baptist church in New London right around the time she was trying to garner support for the NLDC's plan to demolish the Fort Trumbull neighborhood. In her speech, Claire likened her leadership at the NLDC to the social-justice movements led by Jesus Christ and Martin Luther King Jr.

"Like them," the *Chronicle* reported Claire's saying to the Baptist congregation, "I'm operating outside my specialty. Does that mean I'm going to make mistakes? Yes." But in her speech Claire urged the congregation to support her work. "Jesus is calling us in this city to witness," she said. "You and I are called to be transforming interveners, like the Messiah, like Martin Luther King."

The board of trustees had a huge problem on its hands; its financial woes and the internal battle between Claire and the faculty had oozed into public view.

Shapiro instantly saw the change in Claire. One of the things she most admired about Claire was her physical beauty and her fearlessness about showcasing it through a bold wardrobe. Suddenly, Claire was showing up for work looking terrible, after staying up until four in the morning each night dealing with a crisis. "She had such a vision," Shapiro lamented. "In many ways it may have been unrealistic."

25

TIME IS NOT ON OUR SIDE

Steve Hallquist had secured an appointment with Scott Sawyer. John and Sarah Steffian planned to attend. But other members of the coalition feared that a local lawyer wouldn't have enough firepower to stop the city. "This is bigger than us," said Peter Kreckovic, a local artist who had joined the coalition. "We need outside help."

No one disagreed. Yet no one knew any out-of-town law firms that specialized in personal-property rights. Plus, the cost of landing that kind of firm seemed prohibitive.

Suddenly, someone in the group brought up a public-interest law firm—the Institute for Justice—that handled property-rights cases. Based in Washington, D.C., the firm operated as a nonprofit that did not accept legal fees from its clients.

It had been in the news for helping an elderly widow fend off the State of New Jersey from taking her home. The state had planned to condemn the widow's home and a couple of neighboring properties in order to sell the land to Donald Trump, who planned to convert it into a limousine waiting area and a lawn for one of his Atlantic City casinos. Legal experts had given the widow no chance of prevailing. The case had made national headlines when a Superior Court judge ruled against the state, saying that any public benefit from condemning the properties was far outweighed by the overwhelming private benefit being passed on to Trump. The victory inspired the institute to start a major campaign to revive the public-use requirement in eminent-domain takings, which land-use lawyers and judges had considered a lost cause for decades.

To the coalition, New London's attempt to take land for the benefit of Pfizer sounded a lot like the New Jersey case. Everyone agreed it would be a coup to get the institute engaged in the fight in New London. It all sounded good to Susette. But she had never heard of a law firm that didn't collect legal fees, and she figured the chances of getting the institute to help were probably slim to none.

Hallquist and Steffian insisted they'd press on with trying to retain Scott Sawyer.

"Well, are we going to contact the Institute for Justice?" Peter Kreckovic asked, looking directly at Fred Paxton.

"Why don't you do it, Peter?" Paxton said. Others nodded in agreement.

Shy and self-conscious, Kreckovic doubted he was the right person to contact a Washington law firm. But he feared no one else would get to it. So that afternoon he sat down in front of his manual typewriter. "Dear Sir, I am writing to you on behalf of the Coalition to Save Fort Trumbull Neighborhood," he began, explaining that the state had given millions of dollars to the NLDC to redevelop the neighborhood. "Their plan is to demolish all the houses and commercial buildings to give a clear field to the developers, who can then build high-income condominiums, a hotel and health club on the site. These would support the 220 million dollar research facility being built by Pfizer Pharmaceutical next door."

Efforts by the grassroots organization to seek justice had been ignored. "Demolitions are slated to begin in mid-June," he typed. "We wonder if your organization would be willing to help us."

Three hours later, Kreckovic finished and took the letter to the post office.

Late May 2000

As soon as he had passed the bar exam in Pennsylvania, Scott Bullock had headed to Washington, D.C., in the summer of 1991, to take a job at a start-up legal organization. Bullock's mind had been set on changing the way large masses of people think. He had considered becoming an economist or philosopher, but that, he figured, would limit him to merely speaking and writing. He had something a little more action oriented in mind: using the Constitution as an instrument to alter how others act.

Attorney and entrepreneur Chip Mellor had just founded the Institute for Justice with civil-rights attorney Clint Bolick. Before launching the institute, Mellor had spent five years developing litigation blueprints and strategies for the Pacific Research Institute in San Francisco, where he had become friendly with Milton Friedman. At Pacific, Mellor focused his legal research on property rights, economic liberty, free speech, and school choice. He designed the Institute for Justice to focus primarily on those four issues.

Scott Bullock didn't know Chip Mellor then. But, as a law student, Bullock had interned for Clint Bolick at the Landmark Center for Civil Rights. Bullock jumped at the chance to rejoin Bolick and work alongside Mellor as the third attorney in a nonprofit law practice dedicated to protecting people's rights. It fit his personal philosophy, which was that people ought to be free to do as they wished unless they were harming someone else.

Bullock's view of the world was formed early. Born in Guantánamo Bay, where his father served in the navy shortly after the Cuban missile crisis, Bullock got an early education in personal liberties and what happens when governments suppress them. After his father retired, Bullock moved with his parents and brother back to Pittsburgh, where his larger family had lived for generations. Unlike many Washington lawyers, Bullock didn't come from a high-powered background. He was the first in his family to graduate from college. Most of his relatives worked in Pittsburgh factories. His brother was a mechanic.

But Bullock was influenced early on by the writings of Thomas Paine, Thomas Jefferson, and Milton Friedman, especially Friedman's book *Free to Choose*. At the institute, Bullock started representing private-property owners facing eminent-domain takings by local and state governments. Private law firms thought the institute was wasting its time on eminent-domain cases, taking the view that virtually anything goes when it comes to government taking private property for public use. The institute was determined to change that.

Single, with short hair, wire-rimmed glasses, and a baby face, Bullock sat down at his desk in the firm's Pennsylvania Avenue office in late May 2000 to go through his mail. Facing an etching of Thomas Paine and a picture of jazz musician John Coltrane, he discovered a letter postmarked New London, Connecticut.

Bullock and his partners routinely received letters from strangers around the country seeking help. In any given week, a dozen letters or more might arrive. Few ever got beyond a quick read by Bullock, because most of the letters raised legal questions not suitable for the institute's intervention.

Bullock opened the letter from New London. "Many homeowners in the neighborhood have already sold, unable to deal with the uncertainty in their lives of losing their homes," he read. "But there are some twenty families as well as a number of businesses that are holding out and who are faced with eminent domain."

The story sounded very familiar. Bullock read on. "Many families face considerable financial and emotional damage if eminent domain is used—basically to demolish a working class neighborhood to build more expensive housing," the letter said. "Some of these people have lived in these houses all their lives, and are elderly. Some are in their nineties."

Bullock put the letter down. Well written, it concisely described government abuse of the eminent-domain power. The role of Pfizer and a development agency in seizing homes on behalf of the city intrigued him. Right away Bullock saw the two key elements his firm looked for before accepting a case: a cutting-edge legal issue and outrageous government behavior. Bullock wondered whether the property owners would make sympathetic plaintiffs.

Intrigued, Bullock shared the letter with Mellor, who agreed it had potential and deserved a follow-up phone call.

Peter Kreckovic got nervous when he heard Bullock's voice on his answering machine, saying he had some questions. Kreckovic hadn't really expected a response. Encouraged, he called Bullock and introduced himself. He found Bullock talked more like an activist than a lawyer. The conversation quickly focused on Pfizer and the property owners whose homes were at risk. Kreckovic described Susette and her elderly neighbors.

Bullock liked what he heard. He asked Kreckovic to gather more information and get back to him.

At the end of her nursing shift, Susette paid a visit to a nursing home in the area. Her elderly neighbor Daniel Anton had recently been transferred there from his Fort Trumbull home. The fear of losing his house had led to a rapid decline in his physical health.

Many of Susette's elderly neighbors were succumbing to anxiety attacks about the uncertainty of their future. Susette blamed Claire, who had sent one elderly neighbor, Walter Pasqualini, a letter. "I would like to apologize for any confusion or anxiety that may have occurred regarding NLDC and the potential acquisition of your home," Claire told Pasqualini. "It is not the desire of the NLDC to disrupt the quality of life you enjoy in your home. However, we are moving forward with our plans and as you are aware, our development plans may include the parcel of land that your home is situated on. But again, we are not asking you to move."

Susette peeked in Anton's room. Barely awake, he motioned for her to come in. She clasped his frail hand and glanced at his medical chart. It indicated his vital signs were poor. She figured he had little time left.

"What is going to happen to my home in Fort Trumbull?" he whispered.

"I don't know," she said.

Anton worried about his older brother, Albert, who still resided in the house they had shared together. "Where will my brother go?" he said.

"We're going to try and make it all right," she said. She looked up at the ceiling to keep from crying.

That night she sent an e-mail to her neighbors and to members of the coalition, reporting on her visit with Anton and his question. "I am sorry to say," Susette wrote, "that I don't believe Mr. Anton is going to live long enough to find out."

A few days later Anton died.

June 8, 2000

It was 8 a.m. when Sarah Steffian trailed her husband and Steve and Amy Hallquist into Scott Sawyer's office. The exceedingly tall former college-basketball player led them into a conference room and invited them to sit down.

Determined to retain a lawyer, the group had one overriding question for Sawyer: was he willing to go against the establishment?

Sawyer had just finished bringing a series of environmental lawsuits against the U.S. Coast Guard. But he didn't know enough about the situation in Fort Trumbull to weigh in just yet. The group gave him a brief summary of the dispute. "We're finding resistance from every lawyer we've approached," Steve Hallquist explained. "Nobody wants to touch this."

"Well, let me tell you a little bit about me," Sawyer said. Rather than discuss his professional credentials, Sawyer told the tragic story of his sister's accidental death years earlier. In the fall of 1988, Jill Sawyer, then a college student, and three friends had disappeared one night after visiting a juice bar in New Haven. Five days later, the girls were pronounced dead when the car they had been in was pulled from a river. At the time of the accident, the City of New Haven had been repairing the Chapel Street Bridge, which was closed to traffic. A gap existed between the roadway and the bridge, but the Jersey barriers around the drop-off did not completely block access. In the darkness, the girls had driven through the opening in the barriers and plunged into the water.

Scott Sawyer was a graduate student at the time, and he and his family sued the City of New Haven. Ultimately, the city settled, but not until after seven grueling years of litigation had passed.

The experience inspired him to become a lawyer and open up his own practice.

"I've gone against the current," Sawyer told the group. "I've taken on City Hall. Why don't you tell me the main points of contention here," he said.

John Steffian and Steve Hallquist hit him with a litany of facts. Amy Hallquist raised a series of legal questions. Sawyer took notes: taxpayers, property owners, compensation, and legal standing were his primary concerns. Then the question of legal fees arose.

Sarah Steffian asked to speak with Sawyer in private. The two of them walked away from the group. The Hallquists later realized they were discussing a fee arrangement—attorney fees would come from Sarah and would remain confidential.

Before the group left, Sawyer told them what he told all his clients: "I'm a lawyer who has been a client in a very high-profile case, and I certainly understand that I shouldn't say to anybody 'I know how you feel,'" he said. "I can work with you. But you need to talk to me, and you need to fire me if you're uncomfortable."

After leaving Sawyer's office, Steve and Amy Hallquist met with Sarah and John Steffian to compare notes. They all agreed that Sawyer represented their best hope at bringing a lawsuit, since getting the Institute for Justice looked unlikely. They agreed to retain Sawyer.

"We have fought many battles and lost time and time again," John said. "But by God, we're going to win this time, and we're going to win with you guys." He patted Steve on the back.

Later that night, Sarah wrote Sawyer a letter telling him to forget about issues like taxation and to focus on the most important issue. "Legal action should be taken to contest and stop the eminent domain process," she wrote.

David Goebel checked his e-mail in-box. He saw this: "Dave: Please call Aldo/Judge Santaniello/Jay Levin to tell them that George needs to start the meeting at 4PM at IDC, not 3PM. We're sorry. Our team (besides George, who really isn't available until 4) should gather at NLDC at 3PM to touch heads." The e-mail had come from one of Claire's assistants.

"The judge and Jay have been called," Goebel responded. "The judge will notify Aldo."

The next day, the group assembled at the Italian men's club for a final meeting on the future of the building. Claire thought she had it all figured out. She suggested erecting a monument to Italian heritage and relocating the club to a side street, closer to the waterfront. She even had the perfect spot picked out, right between two quaint houses.

It sounded great to Valentini. Santaniello took a practical approach. "It's always nice to have ideas," he said, "but you have to have money to put them into effect. So where is the money going to come from?"

His question was the perfect cue for Milne. Pfizer officials had advised him to steer clear of the Italian Dramatic Club. Dozens of property owners were being forced out of their homes through eminent domain. If Pfizer financed the relocation or new construction of the Italian club's building, the company would have all sorts of demands for similar treatment. Milne made it clear that Pfizer could not get involved.

Valentini dug in his heels, insisting his club would remain unless someone paid for a new building. He had Jay Levin's word that no one would touch him. Without a commitment from Pfizer, Santaniello knew talking further would be futile. The NLDC had neither the money to move him nor the will to go against Levin's promise.

Everyone at the table realized the club would stay put. Now only a political question remained: how to spin this to the media and the public.

Steve Hallquist had a major concern about suing the city: personal liability. What if the city countersued? Wouldn't personal assets and personal property be put at risk?

Sawyer recommended forming a limited-liability corporation (LLC) to shield them from liability. Rather than suing as individuals, the Steffians and the Hallquists could have the organization sue.

Hallquist liked the concept. "Let's call it the Fort Trumbull Conservancy," he said.

Sawyer explained the group would have to choose officers and establish by-laws. Later, Steve and Amy met privately with John and Sarah to map out the organization.

"Who is going to be what?" Steve asked.

"I'm going to be the president," John said. "Sarah will be the vice president."

Two positions remained: secretary and treasurer. "Which ones do you want to be?" John asked.

"Well, I suck at being a secretary," Steve said. "And Amy's already taking copious notes. So she'll be secretary, and I'll be treasurer."

Normally, a treasurer handled finances and the secretary kept records, but Sarah made it clear that the Fort Trumbull Conservancy would do things a little differently. The treasurer would never see the financial books, and the secretary would never see the legal bills. The money would pass directly from Sarah to the attorney.

More than twenty-five members of the neighborhood coalition joined the Fort Trumbull Conservancy. The by-laws afforded them the chance to vote on the conservancy's decisions and on strategies related to litigation.

With the conservancy in place, on July 18, 2000, Scott Sawyer filed a lawsuit on its behalf seeking to prevent the NLDC from demolishing homes in the Fort Trumbull neighborhood.

Scott Bullock had now been monitoring events in New London for two months through weekly updates from Peter Kreckovic. Bullock had heard enough. The time had come to visit Fort Trumbull and interview the homeowners in search of prospective plaintiffs. He telephoned Susette and confirmed he'd be visiting the area in late August. He told her he wanted to meet with neighborhood residents. Susette volunteered her home as a meeting place.

Bullock asked her to round up as many neighbors as possible. "I've already done that," she said. "I've just been waiting for you to say you are coming."

Bullock liked the sound of that. He had already pegged her as the head fighter, a perfect candidate for the lead plaintiff role. They discussed possible dates and settled on August 28.

"Is it okay if I tell the newspaper that you're coming?" Susette asked.

Bullock paused. The Institute for Justice still had not decided whether to intervene, partly due to the fact that the city had not yet filed any eminent-domain actions. In every potential eminent-domain case, Bullock's first objective was to persuade the municipality not to resort to eminent domain. News that a national law firm was interviewing prospective clients might not be a bad idea, Bullock reasoned. If the city saw a lawsuit coming, perhaps it would change its plans.

"Sure," Bullock said, "I'd be glad to talk to a reporter."

Susette hung up and called Billy Von Winkle. "I've got some news," she told him.

A little while later, he pulled up in his Jaguar. "We're taking a ride," he said.

She hopped in and immediately started talking about Scott Bullock's visit. Eager to sue the city and convinced the Institute for Justice would save the neighborhood, Susette told Von Winkle she couldn't wait to tell the newspaper.

"You gotta be careful," Von Winkle said.

"Why?"

He warned her that the NLDC would punish her if she went too far.

"You know I'm not afraid of those people," she said.

Von Winkle pulled the car over. "Red, you gotta listen to what I'm telling you here. When they offer you the money you better take it. If you don't they'll throw you out and you'll get nothing."

"What are you talking about?"

He detailed the NLDC's strategy for getting rid of all property owners in the fort area, citing information from the NLDC's confidential files.

"Well, how do you know this?" she asked.

"Because I have the documents."

"How in the hell did you get them?"

"I've got my ways."

"Tell me."

"I've been picking up their garbage."

"You've been what?"

"I've been diving every night."

Susette burst out laughing. Von Winkle had been rifling through coffee cups and half-eaten sandwiches to get to hundreds of internal records. "Oh, my God," she said, laughing hysterically. "Those dummies don't even know it?"

Von Winkle laughed.

"Nobody else in the world would ever think of picking through the NLDC's garbage," she said.

"We're never gonna win," he said, the smile disappearing from his face.

"Huh?"

"You know, it's like this, Red," he said. "Pfizer is behind this. The governor is behind this. We're never gonna win."

Susette stopped laughing.

August 28, 2000

Expecting to see boarded-up buildings and dilapidated houses, Scott Bullock navigated his rental car through Fort Trumbull. Instead, he found neat, small houses with seacoast charm: weather vanes, wicker furniture, and porches facing the water.

"This is depressed?" Bullock said to himself. He had grown up in the economically devastated Pittsburgh of the seventies and eighties. The Fort Trumbull neighborhood didn't look depressed to him.

He coasted down East Street and came to a stop across from Susette's house. It was surrounded by flower boxes and white lawn furniture. An American flag waved from one corner of the house. A hand-painted plywood sign leaned against the front steps: "This Land Is Ours! Not Gov. Rowland's. Not NLDC's. Help Us Save Our Homes."

Bullock stepped out of the car and retrieved his briefcase.

"Did you find everything okay?" Up on the porch, Susette

rested her arms on the white railing. Kathleen Mitchell and Steve and Amy Hallquist stood with her.

Bullock climbed the steps and extended his hand. "Hi, I'm Scott Bullock. I'm blown away by the view here," he said.

"This is where we always meet, at Susette's place," Mitchell said.

"This," said Steve, "is ground zero."

Susette pointed to the cranes towering over the tall buildings rising from the Pfizer property next door. "C'mon inside," she said. Nearly twenty neighbors shook Bullock's hand and expressed relief that he had come. The group crowded into a circle of chairs Susette had set up in the kitchen. Peter Kreckovic introduced Bullock and turned the floor over to him.

Bullock started with some brief background on the institute and its interest in the Fort Trumbull dispute. He made it clear that no decision had been made to represent anyone in New London. "I'm here to hear your stories," he said, "and to offer some thoughts that I have on ways of fighting this and things that you need to do to try and organize to fight against this."

He asked the people in the circle to provide their names and addresses, indicate whether they owned or rented, and explain what their interests were in opposing the property takings.

The first man indicated he owned a business in the area. "I don't own the property," he said. "I just rent the property."

Bullock made a note on his pad: "Out of luck." In eminent-domain cases, tenants are powerless unless the owner is dedicated to fighting.

The next man owned a house in an area where the city planned to build a new roadway leading to Pfizer. Bullock dismissed his situation, too. There was little legal basis for opposing instances when a municipality took property for roadways.

Then Susette spoke. She explained that the NLDC planned to take her entire block. Her story ignited the others, who started talking over each other.

"What are they planning to build on this block?" Bullock asked.

"Nothing," Susette said.

"Nothing?" Bullock asked.

"For this block there is no plan," Steve Hallquist said.

"They just want to get rid of it," Susette said.

Bullock had studied a lot of eminent-domain cases. In virtually every case he'd seen, the government planned to take private property for some use. He'd seen disputes over whether the intended use qualified as public use. But he had never come across a situation where a local government had no plan for the land it seized.

There could be a case here, Bullock thought.

"Will you take our case?" Susette asked.

Bullock liked her bluntness. Yet he didn't want to give her false hope. "We are very interested in this," he said. "But there are a lot of things I still have to check out."

Among the top priorities Bullock had was determining the true motives of Susette and her neighbors. They made clear they didn't like the NLDC and its plan to take houses. But how many would stay in the fight once the NLDC started waving more money in front of them? Bullock referred to this point as the plaintiffs' "come to Jesus" moment.

"We don't negotiate property sales for our clients," Bullock explained. "That's just not what we do. We fight to protect people's property."

The members of the group nodded. Bullock liked them already; they reminded him of the people he had grown up with in his working-class neighborhood.

"So if we were to take the case," he said, "we'd want to know that you were committed for the long haul." Promising he would pull out every stop to fight on the homeowners' behalf, Bullock expected in return an ironclad promise that the homeowners would stay in the fight when the pressure was turned up and offers for financial compensation came.

Hallquist and Mitchell liked what they heard. After the meeting broke up, Susette took Bullock on a walk through the neighborhood. She told him something about every house on the street.

"There's Billy Von Winkle's place," she said, pointing to the deli at the top of her street.

"Who is Bill Von Winkle?" Bullock asked. Susette smiled and filled him in. Bullock laughed at the stories, especially the one about putting chicken manure in the City Hall elevator.

"He's a character," she said.

"Can I meet him?" he asked.

She led him to the deli. "I'll wait for you at my place," she said.

Bullock entered the deli. It was empty except for a short, stocky man wearing blue jeans and a partially zipped, hooded sweatshirt and a baseball cap that bore the words "Mayor of Smith Street."

"Are you Bill Von Winkle?"

"That's me. Who are you?"

Bullock introduced himself as a public-interest lawyer from the Institute for Justice.

Von Winkle had known Bullock was in the neighborhood meeting with people. "So what do you think our chances are?" he asked. Bullock outlined a series of legal reasons why the city should be stopped from seizing private property in Fort Trumbull. Confident, but not cocky, Bullock's approach appealed to Von Winkle.

"Why don't you sit down?" he said. Bullock pulled up a chair. Von Winkle told him the neighborhood's history and how he had worked across the street at the old navy facility. In between stories, he told jokes about the people and the places surrounding his deli. The whole time, he looked Bullock right in the eye. It quickly became apparent to Bullock that Von Winkle had spent a good portion of his adult life on these streets.

"So do you think you're going to come help us?" Von Winkle asked.

"Well," Bullock said, "we are looking into the case pretty seriously right now."

Von Winkle explained that he had a lot riding on the outcome. His livelihood rested on all the rental properties he owned in the neighborhood. He had spent years personally renovating outdated buildings to get them in shape for residential occupancy. It angered him that the city could just take away his buildings and his income stream to accommodate a big company's moving into the area. "It's not right," he said.

Bullock detected an edge in Von Winkle's tone, a certain fighter's instinct—an essential ingredient for the kind of plaintiff it would take to endure a bruising legal battle with a city determined to bulldoze the neighborhood.

On the other hand, he was very independent and dangerously unpredictable. Von Winkle had purposely stayed away from the initial neighborhood meeting with Bullock at Susette's house. And he was notorious for doing things on his own. Stunts like his could be a huge liability in a lawsuit.

"By the way, where did you get that hat?" Bullock joked, "Are you the mayor of Smith Street?"

A painful expression swept over Von Winkle's face. "This is Mr. Pasqualini's hat," he said, removing it from his head.

"Who is he?" Bullock asked softly.

Von Winkle explained that he was one of the senior citizens who had died since the NLDC had threatened to take their homes. "He was the mayor of the neighborhood," said Von Winkle. "I wear the hat to pay respect and carry on Mr. P.'s tradition."

Bullock nodded.

"Mr. P. went to his grave worried about eminent domain," said Von Winkle. "People think eminent domain killed Mr. P." Tears welled up in Von Winkle's eyes. He lowered his voice. "What a great guy he was," Von Winkle muttered, running his rough hand across his brow. "I miss him."

Bullock had seen enough. He had come to New London to size up potential plaintiffs. Susette and her home were clearly the flashpoint of the fight. She had the right facts and a tough-as-nails attitude to wage a legal challenge against the city. Von Winkle wore the cap of a dead man who had gone to his grave fearing that his house and neighborhood would be lost to eminent domain. Von Winkle had a score to settle. He would do more than fight to protect his own property: he would fight to avenge a wrong.

Bullock returned to Washington. If the institute took the case, he wanted Von Winkle as a plaintiff alongside Susette.

26

A FIGHT IN THE FORT

The day after Bullock's whirlwind visit to New London, the *Day* reported that a D.C. law firm might help the Fort Trumbull neighborhood residents. The story put the NLDC on notice that it might soon have a lot more to deal with than Scott Sawyer. A lawsuit filed by a national firm promised to drastically slow progress and put a real spotlight on the agency and Pfizer.

Claire and her board had a decision to make. They could treat the news as a warning and reach out to Susette and the other holdouts with a compromise. Or they could try to crush the residents immediately, before the institute had enough time to ramp up and file a suit.

The first option would require the NLDC to spend some money. By offering the holdouts twice the appraised value of their respective properties, the NLDC would probably persuade most of them to drop their opposition. The higher prices would also enable the holdouts to afford housing elsewhere. The second option wouldn't cost anything in the short run. However, this approach came with a much higher risk. If it failed to drive the holdouts out, it would likely trigger a lawsuit that could end up costing the NLDC and the city much more money over the long run.

Claire had been brought to a pressure point. She had fights going on every front. The governor's office had it in for her. She was battling Tom Londregan and City Hall. She had a war going with the press. The Fort Trumbull residents and the conservancy were doing everything possible to portray her as public enemy number one. And the atmosphere on campus had become hostile, with faculty and a contingent of students determined to dislodge her as president.

With this many enemies, the last thing Claire needed was another opponent. It seemed the best course was to modify the plan and ward off a lawsuit from the Institute for Justice.

But Claire liked a quote attributed to Henry Ford: "Obstacles are those frightful things you see when you take your eyes off your goal." Her goal was to turn New London's economic fortunes around, and she had no intention of losing focus now. She opted not to compromise. David Goebel agreed with this approach. The NLDC asked the city council to rescind an earlier motion that had halted acquisition and demolition on Susette's block. The NLDC decided it wanted to act fast. But its request required a vote by the city council in a public meeting, and before that could happen the city had to post the item on an agenda made available to the public beforehand. The notice would tip off the opposition, providing time for the coalition to mobilize a crowd of protestors and news cameras at the meeting.

Faced with this, the city council found a way around the minefield. When the agenda for the September 5 meeting came out, it contained no mention of a vote on the NLDC's request to resume demolition. At the tail end of the meeting, long after the public had gone home, the council added the item to the agenda. With no public opposition present, it voted to authorize the NLDC to demolish properties in Fort Trumbull.

But Mayor Beachy also knew the game. The next morning, he talked to people in the city's permit office. He told them to notify him the minute the NLDC applied for any demolition permits. He also huddled with members of the coalition, and the group organized a list of people with responsibility for calling City Hall on a daily basis to find out if the NLDC had filed any permit requests.

George Milne had a lot more on his mind than the potential of a lawsuit against the NLDC. As a Connecticut College trustee,

Milne had another crisis to deal with. The conflict between Claire and the faculty had gotten personal and ugly. The faculty wanted Claire out, but she had no intention of stepping down. The standoff put Milne in a tough spot. He chaired the Academic Affairs Committee, yet he maintained a strong loyalty to Claire. With the faculty in revolt, it seemed clear that it wasn't a question of if Claire would leave but rather when.

Milne was also facing a career change of his own. Just two months earlier, Pfizer had announced that the Federal Trade Commission had given final clearance for a merger with the Warner-Lambert company.

In conjunction with the merger, Pfizer announced a leadership change in New London. Milne was elevated to executive vice president of Pfizer Global Research and Development.

The $90 billion merger meant that Pfizer instantly had a surplus of real estate and office space throughout the country. Rather than expand, Pfizer now needed to consolidate to maintain efficiency. Suddenly, the company's plans for the New London facility had changed.

Kathleen Mitchell had vowed to take a street fighter's approach to the NLDC. The coalition repeatedly tried to rein her in at board meetings. She decided to use her weekly cable-television show on New London's public-access station to go after Claire. After opening one of her shows in late August with a blistering monologue against Claire and the NLDC, Mitchell opened the phone lines for call-ins. One caller complained about Claire's leadership style at the NLDC. He asked Mitchell what was wrong with Claire.

"Just between you and me, she's a transsexual," Mitchell said.

The statement worked. Within days, the NLDC dispatched a communications specialist and mobilized community leaders to go after Mitchell. The NLDC labeled her remarks "detestable" and demanded a public apology. When the *Day* contacted her for a response, Mitchell defended her statement. "Being a transsexual is . . . it's like foreign to my way of life," she said. "And so is Claire. She's out of touch with everyone. I don't know any other way to explain it. She just seems to be on some other plane. I was so frustrated. I guess it was a way of dismissing her."

When asked if she planned to apologize to Claire, Mitchell balked. "She can wait for a cold day in hell," Mitchell said. "I will never apologize. I'm going to do and say whatever is necessary to prevent what I think is a violation of people's rights."

Primed to demolish homes on Susette's street, some NLDC board members now started having second thoughts. They were taking the homes of senior citizens and lower-income residents who couldn't afford a fight, yet they were allowing an Italian men's club with political ties to remain. "It just doesn't look good," one of the board members insisted.

Claire and Jay Levin didn't seem to have a problem with the double standard. But they didn't have the job of defending it before the city council. That responsibility fell to David Goebel, and it was an announcement he didn't want to make. No matter how he spun it, the NLDC's decision sent a hypocritical message for an organization touting social justice: a politically connected men's club was deemed to be more important than a person's home.

But Goebel's military background had trained him to respect the chain of command. On September 18, he reported to the council that the Italian Dramatic Club would be allowed to remain and that the owners of the club would retain title to the property. Members of the city council didn't get it. The press didn't get it either. The *Day* started asking questions. Nobody involved had a good answer. "I think the NLDC recognized that as the city changes, aspects of the city's heritage have to remain sacrosanct," Jay Levin told the paper.

If the implications hadn't been so serious, Levin's answer would have qualified as comedy. Everyone involved in the decision started backtracking. Justice Angelo Santaniello denied having helped the club. Steve Percy, of the NLDC, became indignant at any suggestion that politics had played a role in the outcome. But politics was the only reason the club had been spared. The building had no more historical value to the city's heritage than

the historic homes and streets in the Fort Trumbull neighborhood did.

Susette didn't know anything about the Italian Dramatic Club
until she read in the newspaper that it had been spared the
wrecking ball. The comments by Levin, Santaniello, and Percy
infuriated her. She called Mitchell.

"I am rippin'!" Susette said. "This is all a political shit show."

Mitchell had read the article. She shared Susette's anger, and
Levin's insistence that the Italian Dramatic Club had special historical significance had her laughing.

"Levin is full of shit," Susette shouted. "There's nothing historic about the IDC. Why can't he see the historic value of the
houses that we live in? Matt Dery's father's house is an original
whaling house." Mitchell agreed. "Unless the IDC is where the
mob bosses from Providence come to meet," Susette said, "it's no
historic landmark."

Mitchell got a kick out of Susette's passion. "Well, what would
you like to do?"

"I want you to write them and tell them they're all full of shit,"
Susette said. "And that I'm not going to stand for it." Mitchell
doubted that would be productive. Susette didn't care. "They're
coming in here and making up this crap about saving a historic
building," Susette said. "But they've already torn down all these
historic homes. Our houses are actually historic. We all know it's
a crock of crap. We all know it's politics. They sit there and say
politics had nothing to do with it. Politics has everything to do
with it in New London."

"I'll write the letter," Mitchell said.

After hanging up, Susette couldn't stop fuming. She walked
two blocks to the men's club. Three cars were parked outside. Otherwise, the place looked abandoned. Tall weeds poked through
cracks in the pavement leading up to the door. She knocked. No
one answered. She opened the door and stepped inside.

Male voices rose from the basement. She slowly made her way
downstairs. Three men were seated at a table, eating cheese and
drinking wine. They turned and gave her a funny look.

"I'm Susette Kelo, and I live on East Street," she said.

The men looked at each other. "This is a men's club," one of the men pointed out. "Women are not allowed in."

"Don't worry, I won't be here long," she said, looking around. She felt like she had walked into a scene from *The Godfather*. "I just want to know what you guys did to make it so you could stay, because I want to stay too."

Caught off guard, the men said nothing.

"We don't want to stop the development," Susette continued. "We just want to keep our homes."

The oldest of the three men looked her in the eye. "We're sorry for you," he said. "But it is better not to fight. It will cost you too much money."

She wondered how much they had paid and to whom to get their way. Again, she asked what they had done to save their club.

"We didn't have anything to do with it," one of the men said. "We're really not sure what happened."

The longer Susette stayed, the friendlier the men became. In the end, they repeated their advice not to fight the NLDC.

By the time Susette returned home, Mitchell had finished a draft letter for her. She read it to her over the phone:

> *We the people who live in the Fort Trumbull neighborhood are heartened by the recent announcement that the City has decided to save the Italian Dramatic Club. We view this as a significant step in preserving the cultural diversity of our historic neighborhood.*
>
> *We call upon the City Council and New London Development Corporation to sit down with us, the residents of Fort Trumbull, in a sincere effort to reach a plan of action that is acceptable to all of us. We cherish this neighborhood and its proud history and we are optimistic that we can allow progress and preserve our historic past.*

Susette wanted to hammer the NLDC. Mitchell suggested using the Italian club decision as a basis to demand equal treatment.

Susette wanted to bash Levin. "He went there and he assured

them that nothing was going to happen to that building," she said.

Mitchell couldn't believe Susette had walked into the Italian men's club unannounced. She encouraged her to avoid accusations in the letter. Susette trusted Mitchell. She had her deliver the letter to her house, and Susette signed it as chairperson of the Fort Trumbull Neighborhood Association and sent it to the city council and the NLDC. "If they're willing to work with the IDC," she said, "maybe they'll work with us."

Mitchell had another idea: a petition. She already had a draft, and she showed it to Susette. It read: "We, the undersigned, support the efforts of the Coalition to Save the Fort Trumbull Neighborhood to amend the Municipal Development Plan to save a majority of the residential neighborhood and business at Fort Trumbull."

By securing signatures from 5 percent of the city's registered voters, the coalition could force the city to hold a referendum on whether the homes in Fort Trumbull should be demolished or preserved.

Susette liked it. She offered her home as headquarters for the petition drive. Mitchell worked with the coalition to organize a vigil on East Street. On the first night, dozens showed up. Clipboards and pencils rested on tables on the sidewalk in front of Susette's house. The next night, even more people showed up. Lines of residents outside Susette's home got longer each night.

Not to be outdone, Claire organized her own petition, titled, "Citizens in Favor of New London Development." Claire and members of the NLDC began soliciting signatures. Pfizer president George Milne put his signature on the petition first.

Claire had more clout than Susette and attracted signatures from influential people who had prestigious titles. But Susette had a groundswell of everyday people behind her and got far more people to sign her petitions. Once she and the coalition had more than enough signatures to satisfy the city's legal requirements, the coalition presented the petitions to the city clerk for certification. The clerk forwarded them to attorney Tom Londregan for review.

27

LINE IN THE SAND

September 28, 2000

When Mayor Beachy gathered with coalition members on Susette's street for a morning prayer vigil, he felt good about the number of signatures on the petitions that had been submitted to City Hall. While the city reviewed the petitions, the coalition kept close tabs on the permit process, and the NLDC still hadn't secured permits to demolish any structures on Susette's block. At the end of the vigil, Fred Paxton's wife, Sylvia, assured the group she had called City Hall first thing that morning. "No houses are coming down today," she reported.

At the end of the prayer service, the group agreed to go elsewhere for coffee. After coffee, the mayor's wife, Sandy, had a hunch. "Let's drive back through the Fort," she told him.

The mayor agreed.

Wearing a sleeveless flannel shirt that showcased his massive arms, Chico Barberi maneuvered the jaws of his excavator toward the corner of a house at the top of East Street. An NLDC official in a hard hat stood behind the excavator, directing Barberi which homes to demolish. Susette, Von Winkle, Matt Dery, and other neighbors stood near the excavator, shouting over the machine at the NLDC official.

"You Nazi," one of them shouted.

"I'm just following orders," the official said.

"That's what Hitler's regime said," one of the homeowners shouted.

Suzanne Dery huddled on her property, crying.

Mayor Beachy couldn't believe his eyes. Less than an hour earlier, the street had been quiet and vacant.

"Beach, I've had it," Sandy seethed. "Stop the car and let me out."

He parked. Sandy got out and instructed him to go home and retrieve the quilt she had been making. She planned to sit on the front steps of the home Barberi was approaching. She wanted the quilt to work on in order to keep her hands from shaking.

Sandy walked past Barberi's machine and plopped down on the doorstep. The mayor sped home. When he returned fifteen minutes later, a larger crowd had gathered on the street. Officials from the city's building department were on the scene. They had failed to alert him that the NLDC had secured demolition permits.

"Damn you," Beachy shouted, his face red and quivering as he crossed the street.

A building official tried to explain that the NLDC had slipped the paperwork in at the last minute.

Beachy didn't want to hear it. He threw his hands in the air and stormed off, taking a position next to his wife. They crossed their legs and sat side by side, blocking the machine's path.

The decision to demolish homes on East Street had made the fight personal for Beachy and his wife. When they had first moved to New London, in the 1970s, they had lived across the street from the demolition site, in officers' quarters at the Naval Undersea Warfare Center. At night, their four sons would take a break from homework, hop the navy base fence, and get a sandwich at the deli on the corner of East Street, two doors up from the houses now facing the wrecking ball.

"There's no way in hell I'm standing by while these guys try to demolish these houses," Beachy said.

Barberi shut off his machine and folded his massive arms, frustrated at being unable to complete his job. Susette and her neighbors continued shouting obscenities at the NLDC official.

Kathleen Mitchell pulled up in her car. She had been listen-

ing to her police scanner and heard a dispatch to East Street.
Mitchell looked at the crowd standing across the street from
Beachy and his wife. Most of the onlookers opposed the NLDC.
Yet no one else dared to sit shoulder to shoulder with Beachy.
Mitchell looked at Susette before crossing the street and taking a
seat next to the mayor and his wife. If it meant getting arrested,
so be it, she thought.

Susette wanted to follow Mitchell, but Von Winkle stopped
her. "You don't want to look like a troublemaker," he said.

Two police officers approached. "Mr. Beachy, Mrs. Beachy,"
one of them began. Neither of the Beachys said a word. The officer advised them that they were trespassing and putting themselves and others in physical danger.

"You might as well arrest us because we're not leaving," Mitchell said.

"Will you walk down here and get in the police car?" the officer asked, looking at the mayor.

Beachy turned to his wife. "Don't walk to the police car," he
told her. "Make them carry you out."

Abundantly overweight, Mitchell didn't feel like getting carried. "I'm not going to let you carry me," Mitchell said, cracking
a smile. She walked to the police car and climbed into the back-
seat.

"We don't want to have to carry you," an officer said to the
mayor.

"We're not leaving voluntarily," he replied.

One officer grabbed Beachy's wrists. Another grabbed his
ankles. Together, they lifted and hauled him to the police car.

Mitchell watched through the rear window of the cruiser as
the officers stuffed their own mayor into the back of another police car. *What have we come to?* Mitchell thought. She had never
imagined the dispute would last this long and be this difficult.
We're fighting the big boys now. This isn't just local politics.

Barberi fired up his excavator and began tearing the house
down. Within fifteen minutes, a house that had stood for a hundred years had been reduced to splinters and rubble.

Susette covered her face with her hands. Tears streamed down her face. Steely-eyed, Von Winkle didn't blink or speak.

Barberi moved his excavator toward the house next door to Susette's.

"The City of New London doesn't care about us," Susette shouted at her neighbors. "They don't give a shit about any of us. They've got a plan, and it doesn't matter what we want or what we do to try and prevent their plan. They are going to do what they want."

The noise of the machine and falling debris drowned out her voice.

Barberi used the excavator jaws to tear off the front quarter of the house. The windows shattered, sending glass flying in every direction. Hysterical, Susette ran into her home and emerged with a broom. Standing only feet from the machine, she frantically swept the glass and debris off her porch while a thick cloud of dust overtook her and the outside of her house.

In the noise and confusion, Barberi didn't realize Susette was within feet of his gnawing machine. He raised the jaws to tug away another part of the house.

"Hey!" the city's fire chief shouted at the NLDC official from the street. "You can't let this happen."

The NLDC official didn't respond.

"Is anyone going to stop this?" the chief yelled.

Everyone looked at him and said nothing.

The chief motioned for Susette to come away from the house.

She ignored him.

Barberi slammed the bucket of his excavator into the side of the house. Shattering glass sprayed Susette, speckling her red hair.

"Hey, Chico, knock it off," the fire chief shouted. Barberi looked over his shoulder, struggling to hear the fire chief above the roar of the machine's engine.

The chief put his index finger and thumb together and ran them across his throat in the motion of a cut. "You have to stop," he yelled. Finally discovering Susette, Barberi killed the engine.

He took out his cell phone and called the police back to the scene.

Von Winkle, Matt Dery, and Tim LeBlanc tried to coax Susette down from her porch. "C'mon, Red," Von Winkle said, "you gotta go."

She kept sweeping, oblivious to the danger. "They're making such a mess." Tears streamed down her face, mixing with the film of dirt on her skin. She appeared to be in shock. No one knew what to do.

"C'mon, Red, I'll take you downtown," Von Winkle said. "We'll have a beer."

Refusing to move, she started wailing.

Barberi had seen enough. He approached Susette. "I'm sorry," he said, his husky voice nearly a whisper. "I didn't know this was going on down here." He turned on the NLDC official. "You never told me this was goin' on down here," he shouted in anger, waving a finger in the official's face. "I can't do any more work with her standing here."

"Susie," LeBlanc said softly, "come on."

The captain of the police department pulled up. The group explained the situation to him. The captain didn't want to arrest Susette. Von Winkle took one more shot at coaxing her down. He approached her on the porch. "Look, you've got the captain of the police department and the chief of the fire department here," he said empathetically. "C'mon, Red. Your house will be okay. We'll come back in a couple hours, and it will all be over."

She dropped her broom and came down from the porch. LeBlanc helped her into the back of Von Winkle's car. Then he called the hospital and explained Susette would be unable to report for her nursing shift that night. Von Winkle took Susette to a bar, where she drank until she couldn't feel the pain anymore.

The next morning, Susette woke up groggy, hoping it had all been a terrible nightmare. She looked out the window. The houses on her street were all gone, replaced by mounds of rock, concrete, busted wood, and dirt. Her neighborhood resembled a war zone. It had not been a bad dream.

She got up, showered, and put on a pot of coffee. Then the doorbell rang. Expecting Von Winkle, she answered. It was Chico Barberi, wearing a tank top. "I'm sorry," he said, handing her a gift basket of perfumed soaps.

She invited him in and offered him a cup of coffee. He followed her through the house to the back porch. They overlooked the piles of debris he had made of her neighbors' homes.

"It's going to be okay, Susette," he said in a low voice.

Too hurt to be mad, Susette just looked away and cried.

In twenty years of demolition work, Barberi had never been face-to-face with a crying homeowner. He put his mug down and wrapped his massive arms around her. Susette buried her face in his shoulder.

Barberi had seen enough.

"I'll never tear your house down," he said. "If it ever comes to that, I'll never do it."

As soon as Barberi left, Susette called Scott Bullock at his Washington law office. Pacing back and forth behind his desk, Bullock grimaced, trying to contain his fury while listening to Susette's account of the demolitions. Legally, he knew the NLDC had the right to destroy the homes; the agency had ownership of the properties. Politically, however, Bullock saw the move as a brutal tactical maneuver to intimidate Susette and the other holdouts.

"What should I do?" Susette asked.

"Try to hang in there," Bullock advised.

"I've about had it, Scott. I can't keep living my life with this threat over my head."

"They were able to do that with those homes," Bullock said, hearing the desperation in her voice. "But that doesn't mean they will be able to do it to yours."

"Okay," she whimpered. "Okay."

As soon as he hung up, Bullock stormed into his law partner Dana Berliner's office and told her what had happened.

Berliner clucked in disbelief. "Why is the city acting so irrationally?" she asked calmly.

"Those bastards tore down those houses to send a message," Bullock ranted. "This was absolutely unnecessary!"

"Legally, the city owned those homes and had a right to tear them down," Berliner reasoned. "But they—"

"But they did it to show the inevitability, to show that this is a done deal," Bullock said, cutting her off, his voice rising. "They did this to show that it's only a matter of time before they get to Susette's house and the rest of them who have the *audacity* to challenge this."

"Well, it's not a done deal," Berliner said.

"Claire takes delight in saying she is engaged in this glorious work of transformation," Bullock said. "The fact that such tyrannical and petty acts could be dressed up in high-minded rhetoric about the greater good is just disgusting. Some of the worst acts in human history were justified as the pursuit of a greater good."

Berliner didn't attempt to slow Bullock down.

"I want to take these people on," Bullock said. "I want to sue those bastards."

Attorney Tom Londregan reviewed the petitions signed by the city residents seeking a referendum on the question of whether the NLDC should demolish homes. It was clear that more than enough people had signed the petitions. But Londregan found a different legal defect: timing. The protestors, he determined, should have filed their petitions within fifteen days of the city's granting the NLDC the power to use eminent domain. The city had made that decision back in January. The time to repeal or put the city council's decision before the city's registered voters had passed. Londregan sent the city clerk a two-page memorandum declaring the petition to save the Fort Trumbull homes invalid.

The same day, Scott Sawyer went to court on behalf of the Fort Trumbull Conservancy and secured a temporary restraining order to stop the NLDC from demolishing any more homes. Two days later, a judge lifted the order. The conservancy had no legal grounds to keep the NLDC from demolishing homes that it already owned.

28

PUT A PRETTY FACE ON IT

Late September 2000

The U.S. Coast Guard had been searching for a site on which to erect its national museum. The NLDC figured there was no better place than New London, home to the Coast Guard Academy, perched on 128 acres on the banks of the Thames River, next door to Connecticut College. The NLDC lobbied the coast guard to make its museum part of the large-scale redevelopment plan in Fort Trumbull—specifically on East Street.

After months of discussions, the NLDC put out word that the coast guard had committed to building in Fort Trumbull and that Rear Admiral Patrick Stillman planned to visit the area. He could not have picked a worse time to inspect possible sites. Piles of busted lumber, twisted house siding, broken bricks and cement, and shredded insulation littered the lots that only days earlier had hosted houses. Temporary orange mesh fencing separated the lots from the sidewalk. Their backs to the fencing, protestors lined the sidewalk all the way to Susette's house, one of the few homes left standing on the block.

With stars and stripes on his uniform jacket, Admiral Stillman approached the protestors, trailed by a uniformed officer. Steve and Amy Hallquist looked him straight in the eye and held up their cardboard sign: "Proverbs 22:16: He that oppresseth the poor to increase his riches and he that giveth to the rich shall surely come to want."

Press photographers snapped shots of the admiral as he walked past Connecticut College students and coalition members telling him not to displace poor homeowners to make way for his museum. The farther Stillman walked down the street, the uglier it got. Susette looked down from her porch. "The coast guard is supposed to save people, not drown them," she said.

Her pink home looked out of place on a street that otherwise looked like it had endured a military bombing. Stillman had heard about Susette's house and her determination to hold on to it. She had made her own sign for the admiral and stuck it near some beautiful mums. Shaped like a Halloween pumpkin, it read: "Cackle, Cackle, Screamie, Screamie, Taking People's Homes Is Awful Meanie."

The admiral didn't like what he saw. The coast guard didn't need to get dragged into a street fight between residents and the NLDC. He penned Susette a letter.

"I understand and can fully appreciate your concerns regarding the future of the land bordered by Smith, Trumbull, East and Walbach Streets," he wrote. "As a property owner, you justifiably have the right to voice your concerns over the matter. If placed in a similar situation, I too would exercise my right to ensure that my viewpoint was made known to the decision-makers with regard to the proposed use of the land."

He said there had been some public confusion concerning the coast guard's intent. He outlined the purpose and scope of the museum, along with the type of site the museum required.

"In closing, and on behalf of the Commandant, I'd like to state that <u>we are not committed to the property bordered by Smith, Trumbull, East and Walbach Streets as the site for the U.S. Coast Guard Museum</u>," he wrote.

Susette faxed a copy to Scott Bullock's law office.

To defuse the impasse with the faculty, Claire and the board of trustees planned to propose a sabbatical for Claire. But too many faculty members wanted Claire gone permanently. Students were clamoring for her removal too. About two hundred of them had marched on campus, chanting: "Hey hey, ho ho, we'd like to know where'd our money go?"

But Claire maintained the criticisms levied at her over school finances were unfounded. "Connecticut College is extremely well-planned and well-managed financially," she told the *Chronicle of Higher Education.*

Yet the college newspaper continued to hammer away at Claire. Front-page stories highlighted the controversy surrounding Claire and the NLDC's attempts to seize homes by eminent domain. Students wrote letters to the editor blasting Claire. "Please feel free to explain to the community how tearing down the Fort Trumbull neighborhood for a hotel that will only be used by Pfizer employees will accomplish any of this [social justice]," one student wrote. "We will not allow you to destroy people's homes and we will not allow you to destroy New London's heritage. We will lead the way to social justice." The editorial-page cartoonist went after Claire, depicting her straddling the back of a collapsed camel. "The camel's back is not broken. In fact it is stronger than ever," read the words coming from Claire's mouth. The paper also ran a color photo on the front page showing Susette on campus, protesting with students.

The scene was surreal to a visiting scholar at Connecticut College who watched as faculty and students tried to push Claire out. "She wasn't a woman that you pushed," the scholar said. "She is a person with passion. When she takes something on she believes she is absolutely right, and she will do whatever she needs to do. There is a fanaticism—'I have a direct marching order from a higher being.'"

Claire's approach didn't surprise the scholar, who had studied leadership. "At the leadership level, transformational leaders end up being unpopular," the scholar said. "Claire falls into that category. She was being attacked from all sides. She never took it to heart. Maybe this is her rough exterior. She was so convinced she was right and on this moralistic quest." Objectively, the scholar saw the paradox of Claire. "She had done a lot of good for that college," the scholar noted. "Even her foes admit that she increased the prestige of the college. And she is brilliant. She is a Renaissance woman."

October 12, 2000

The college's board of trustees could no longer avoid the inevitable. It had to part ways with the president who had brought more publicity and money to the school than any of her predecessors. The trustees convened an emergency meeting with Claire to deal with the details of her departure.

For starters, Claire would receive $551,550 in severance pay. Combined with her annual salary, she'd walk away with $898,410, landing her atop the *Chronicle of Higher Education*'s annual survey of college presidents, ahead of those at the University of Pennsylvania, Princeton, Johns Hopkins, and Yale. The trustees also allowed Claire to go on sabbatical for the spring semester, and they delayed her formal retirement date to June 30, 2001.

From a public-relations standpoint, the trustees agreed to frame Claire's departure only in positive terms, stressing her achievements and the fact that the decision to go was hers.

October 13, 2000

George Milne hated to see Claire's legacy clouded. He considered her a visionary leader who had simply gotten caught up in a perfect storm of events. "The controversy around the NLDC plus the challenges the college was facing all sort of came together and essentially was an unfortunate end to what was a substantial legacy," Milne said.

But Milne didn't let his affection for Claire compromise his awareness of his own responsibilities. He had an ability to compartmentalize, and at the moment his job was to brief the faculty. Behind closed doors he informed them that Claire planned to step down within hours. He insisted the school leadership and faculty needed to figure out how to rebuild.

"Anything that's working in our great nation," Claire had once said, "is working because somebody left skin on the sidewalk."

The quote had often been repeated in defending the NLDC's plans to force the Fort Trumbull residents to leave their homes.

Now it was her turn to fall. Fighting off deep disappointment, Claire stepped to a microphone at a hastily organized press conference on campus at noon. "I thought my work at the college as a change agent was coming to an end," she said, maintaining a smile.

In conjunction with the press conference, the school released a statement to the media. "Claire L. Gaudiani announced today that she will fulfill a long-planned transition by stepping down as President of Connecticut College," it read. "The Board expressed unqualified support for President Gaudiani's leadership."

Almost exactly three years after her status as Connecticut College president helped persuade Governor Rowland to recommend her to be president of the New London Development Corporation, her actions as president of the NLDC had played a key role in the loss of her job at the college. The two-edged sword of popularity had cut both ways and taken an unforgiving toll.

"Sometimes, as a lot of social activists do," Claire reflected, "you run into a buzz saw. But that doesn't make you sorry that you were trying to do good for people who couldn't do more good for themselves. You just take it like it comes. And sometimes you get beaten up."

No one believed in Claire's vision more than Claire. The fact that her vision had helped drive her out of Connecticut College did not deter her, and she held on to her position as president of the NLDC. Three days after enduring the humiliating experience of resigning from the college, Claire, with the rest of the NLDC, faced a monumental decision: whether to finally exercise the power of eminent domain to seize Susette's home and twenty-one other properties that stood in the way of the development plan. As if her ouster at Connecticut College had been ancient history, Claire passionately led the discussion with the NLDC's board of directors. For her the answer was simple: use the power.

Dave Goebel agreed. "We're at a stage in the project where

we have to move forward," he said. "We've talked until we're blue in the face."

A board member introduced Resolution 1016-1. It established the NLDC's designation as the city's development agent and confirmed that the agency's lawfully approved municipal-development plan required the acquisition of Fort Trumbull properties. "Now, therefore, it is resolved that the New London Development Corporation, in the name of the City of New London, acquire certain properties located in the Fort Trumbull Municipal Development Plan Area of New London through the exercise of the power of eminent domain," the resolution read, listing Susette's house, four properties belonging to Von Winkle, four belonging to Matt Dery and his family, and a host of others.

The board voted unanimously in favor of the resolution.

When a member of the NLDC's real-estate-acquisition team called Susette in hope of persuading her to sell at the newly appraised price of $123,000, she told him to forget it.

"For $123,000," he told her, "you could probably get a real nice double-wide."

She bristled at the assumption that she'd desire a trailer home. "You know," she said, "I'm not the double-wide kind of girl." She hung up on the agent.

Goebel wasted no time in sending Susette a certified letter. "To carry out our plans to develop the Fort Trumbull Municipal Development Project, it will be necessary for you to move," Goebel wrote, pointing out that she didn't have to move yet. "When you do move, you will be entitled to relocation payments and other assistance."

As she read the letter, Susette's hands shook. On paper it all sounded so legal, so matter-of-fact, and so unstoppable. Offering counseling, advisory services, and a $15,000 stipend for incidental expenses associated with moving, Goebel promised to provide a list of comparable houses. "From a review of local housing listings, it appears that comparable replacement homes are available in the local market," he said.

Susette laughed. She had an unobstructed water view. She knew she'd never find a home with comparable water views for anything near $123,000.

She finished reading the letter. "Remember, do not move before we have a chance to discuss your eligibility for assistance," Goebel wrote. "This letter is important to you and should be retained."

Desperate, she called Bullock. She didn't bother saying hello. "Are you going to represent us, or what?" she said.

Bullock was eager to say yes, but he had to be honest. He had three major cases pending in other jurisdictions: an eminent-domain case in Pittsburgh, a forfeiture case in New Jersey, and a ballot initiative in Baltimore County. "We're serious about wanting to take the case," he told her. "But we have other serious obligations to cases we've already committed to."

"How serious are you about our case?" she asked.

"Listen, we're very serious. I think we can do it. It's not a question of resources. It's a question of time and people power. We have to be careful not to get overextended."

Susette said nothing. Bullock asked if she was still on the line.

"Well, I'm willing to stick in the fight if you take the case."

"We still need to get approval from our board of directors. But if you are committed to it, we'll fight to the bitter end as we always do once we commit to a case."

Four days later

A stack of case files on his desk, Scott Bullock looked at the clock. It was already after five. He grabbed a cup of coffee and settled in for a late evening at the office. Suddenly his computer notified him he had incoming e-mail. The subject line read: "ED papers served on two." It had come from Amy Hallquist. Bullock opened the message and read:

Hi Scott, I just got a call from Susette Kelo. She stated that two property owners got served ED papers today. They are Billy Von

*Winkle, who owns three buildings, including the Fort Trumbull
Deli, and Rich Beyer, who owns two properties on Goshen.
Looks like things are heating up. Amy.*

The timing could not have been worse. Bullock had a brief
due on one case and was in the middle of difficult negotiations
on another. In a couple more weeks he'd be clear to focus on New
London, but not until then. He clicked REPLY and typed, "I know
it is guesswork, but any idea on when Susette and the other core
people may be served?" He clicked the SEND key.

Hallquist promised to monitor the situation closely.

Bullock had hoped to buy a few more weeks before making
a final decision on whether to take on the City of New London,
but the NLDC's aggressive tactics convinced him he didn't have
three weeks. He e-mailed Hallquist again: "If the owners were offered legal representation by us (without charge of course), how
many do you think from the particular parcels would likely fight
the condemnation? We would take on a case if we thought it had
merit even if there were one property owner willing to fight, but
it is better to have at least a small group."

Hallquist promised to get a head count.

Bullock picked up the phone and called Susette. "All right,
here's the latest," he said. "We may be in a position in a couple
of weeks to announce that we can represent owners who wish to
fight."

Susette shouted.

"Unfortunately, it could be a matter of timing," he continued.

"What do you mean?"

"For instance, if condemnations start next week, we simply
cannot do it due to other commitments."

To Susette it didn't seem fair.

"Hang in there, Susette," Bullock said, promising to e-mail
her and the core members of the Coalition to Save Fort Trumbull
Neighborhood an update in a day or two.

As soon as Susette hung up, Tim LeBlanc showed up at her
house. He said nothing while she checked her answering machine. She had a message from Claire's assistant at the NLDC.

He had identified some properties in the city that had an asking price comparable to what the NLDC was willing to pay Susette for her home. The NLDC wanted to schedule a time to show Susette the homes.

"Oh, my God, Timmy," she shouted. "I can't take this shit much longer."

Bullock needed a better handle on Connecticut's eminent-domain law. He asked his colleague, thirty-three-year-old Dana Berliner, to help him with the research.

Berliner hadn't originally planned to be a lawyer. An expert in blood-vessel disease, her mother taught at UCLA's medical school. Her father taught philosophy of education at California State University and ran the Ayn Rand Institute, named after the novelist who wrote *The Fountainhead*, which libertarians consider a bible. Berliner's exposure to Ayn Rand had influenced her by the time she completed her psychology degree at Yale. Passionate about individual liberties, Berliner entered Yale Law School and set her sights on becoming a prosecutor in order to go after those who infringe on the rights of others.

By the time she obtained her law degree in 1991, however, Berliner figured it made more sense to protect people's rights before violations occurred. Ayn Rand had also had a big influence on those who had formed the Institute for Justice. Berliner moved to Washington and took a position with the institute, where she quickly emerged as one of the firm's most exhaustive legal researchers.

With things unfolding rapidly in Fort Trumbull, Bullock asked her for an update. She had bad news. Unlike in some states, the procedure for taking property by eminent domain in Connecticut was almost impossible to challenge. Under Connecticut law, the condemning authority—in this case, the NLDC—appraised the property to be condemned and filed a statement of compensation with the court. The statement of compensation described the property to be taken, identified all who had a recorded interest in it, and stated the appraised value. When filing the statement of compensation, the condemner deposited the appraised value with the court. A marshal or sheriff then served notice to the property owner.

Bullock wanted to know when and how the homeowners challenged the city's attempt to take their homes. "In most states," he said, "there is a condemnation action filed by the city, and then you raise a defense and you are a defendant."

Not in Connecticut, Berliner explained. "The only thing you can do is file an objection to the amount of compensation being offered in the statement of compensation."

Bullock laughed sarcastically. Under Connecticut law, once a municipality decided to take a person's home, the homeowner could question the amount of compensation, but not the taking itself?

"It gets worse," Berliner said. "Once the statement of compensation is filed, title automatically transfers to the condemning authority." She read directly from the statute: "Upon the recording of such certificate, title to such property in fee simple shall vest in the municipality . . . At any time after such certificate of taking has been recorded, the agency may . . . take whatever action is proposed with regard to such property by the project area redevelopment plan."

The nature of Connecticut's law put property owners at a huge disadvantage. In New London, people were being told to get out, no questions allowed. Bullock insisted this had to be unconstitutional. Under the due-process clause of the Fourteenth Amendment of the U.S. Constitution, a property owner had to be afforded an adequate opportunity to be heard before the government deprived an owner of real estate. People in New London were entitled to some sort of hearing before losing their homes, he felt.

Berliner read Bullock's mind. "There is only one way to challenge the legality or constitutionality of the condemnation," she said.

"What's that?"

"You become the plaintiff and have to file your own lawsuit."

"Wait a minute," said Bullock. "We have to file our own lawsuit in response to this?"

Berliner removed her glasses and smiled. In Connecticut, the statement of compensation filed by a municipality was the equivalent of a lawsuit against a property owner. But there was no provision in the law to challenge or defend against the lawsuit. Susette and her neighbors had one option—they had to file a lawsuit challenging the taking.

Bullock had never encountered a similar situation. Normally he defended homeowners who had been sued by a condemning authority. In those instances, a defendant typically had thirty days to respond. But Susette and her neighbors wouldn't be responding to a suit; they'd be initiating one. He wondered what kind of filing deadline they'd face. Berliner wasn't sure either. Connecticut law didn't contemplate such suits, so it gave no guidance on timing.

"The sooner the better, I guess," Bullock said.

The next day, Bullock composed an e-mail to Susette and key members of the coalition:

Hello all: As promised I want to give you a status report. We have been conducting extensive research on Connecticut law . . . and eminent domain. Also, we have been extremely busy on other cases and will continue to be throughout the next 7–10 days. In fact, I will be out for most of next week.

But with all that being said, I am pleased to report that we are growing increasingly confident that there are several ways of challenging the takings of the remaining properties in Fort Trumbull and we may be in a position in a couple of weeks to announce that we can represent owners who wish to fight it. Unfortunately, it could be a matter of timing. If condemnations start next week, we simply cannot do it due to other case commitments.

But hopefully, within the next weeks we will be able to make an announcement that we will defend Susette and the other "hold-outs" (we prefer to call them "freedom-fighters") who wish to fight once the condemnation papers are filed.

Please, everyone, let's keep this low-key for now and not let it leak, especially to the media. We want to maintain the element of surprise!

Sarah Steffian had no doubt Bullock and the institute would take Susette's case. She forwarded Bullock's e-mail to Fred Paxton with a note: "Impress upon Susette the great importance of not speaking to anyone outside of our group about her plans, the IJ, the lawsuit, or anything else relating to any of it! I know she considers you as someone who is individually sympathetic to her plight . . . I believe that Scott Bullock called Susette yesterday before he sent the e-mail and that shortly thereafter the mailman knew all about it . . . So, short of sitting on her, anything you can do to get her to keep appropriate silence is not only helpful, but downright necessary! Sarah."

Paxton gave Susette a call. She told him not to worry. "I'm not sayin' nothin' to no one," she said.

29

A DEMANDING BEAST

The NLDC had blown through millions of dollars in state money and had almost nothing to show for it. The state would not approve more funding without first seeing some investment by other stakeholders. If the NLDC didn't come up with some quick cash, it would have trouble paying the salaries of those responsible for carrying out the eminent-domain takings.

Claire organized a stakeholder campaign. She set a goal to raise $750,000 from private investors. She targeted businesses that would benefit financially from the NLDC's development plan. Sure enough, banks, construction contractors, law firms, and wealthy individuals with ties to NLDC board members pledged five- and six-figure donations.

Still short, Claire turned to Pfizer. It pledged $75,000. On October 30, Claire issued a press release: "We are extremely fortunate to have Pfizer as a partner in moving New London forward," she said. "Beyond their presence as a leading member of the New London business community, their substantial involvement in the Stakeholders Campaign is further evidence of their commitment to the future of New London."

With its capital campaign completed, the NLDC instructed its law firm to initiate eminent-domain takings against all remaining holdouts in Fort Trumbull.

*　　*　　*

Ultimately, the decision whether to take the case of the Fort Trumbull property owners fell to Chip Mellor, the forty-nine-year-old founder and president of the Institute for Justice. The concept behind the Institute for Justice was the notion of entrepreneurial lawyering at no charge to the clients. There were no contingency-fee cases either. All of the institute's funding came from private donors. To Mellor, litigation was always about much more than winning a single case. In his world, cases had to be platforms for a cause that went beyond any one individual.

When he had formed the institute, in 1991 and at age forty, he developed a simple formula for selecting cases: (1) sympathetic clients; (2) outrageous facts; and (3) evil villains. Based on the reports Bullock had been giving him about New London, Mellor concluded the situation there satisfied all three criteria. He had high hopes that his organization could help the residents of Fort Trumbull and that the fight could end up helping many others around the country. But Mellor agreed with Bullock that one more visit to Fort Trumbull was necessary to sort out which property owners were truly committed to the fight.

November 16, 2000

Eager for Bullock to arrive, Susette worked with Amy Hallquist to arrange interviews for him with ten prospective plaintiffs. The meetings were scheduled thirty minutes apart. Susette put herself and Von Winkle first and second on the list.

Seated across from Susette at her kitchen table, Bullock began by assuring her there would be no legal fees.

She laughed. "That's good, because I don't have any money."

Instead of money, Bullock explained, he expected some other things from Susette. "We're different types of lawyers," he told her. "We don't follow the typical way lawyers do things."

She asked him to explain.

He started with a simple example. When filing lawsuits, the institute always wrote an introduction to each complaint, a sort of short story saying what the case was about. Lawyers, as a rule, didn't write complaints that way. Courts, after all, didn't require a story; they were about reviewing facts and the laws that govern them.

But the institute wanted the press to read its lawsuits, too. If crafted properly, lawsuits could be the basis for changing public policy. If a lawsuit in New London led to better protections against eminent-domain abuse on a nationwide basis, the institute would rather have that than money.

Susette nodded, only half grasping it.

Bullock offered another distinction between his firm and others. Usually when a case involves multiple plaintiffs, the group's lawyer simply lists them alphabetically on the complaint. This means that individuals whose last names began with the letters "A," "B," and "C" were more likely to be lead plaintiffs than those whose names began with "R," "S," and "T."

"We refuse to do that," Bullock explained. "We pick the person who we think will be the primary spokesperson for the case, the person who we think really represents what this fight is all about."

Bullock grinned at Susette and raised his eyebrows.

She didn't flinch.

In Bullock's assessment, Susette had the most dedication and determination among the holdouts. She had led the fight from day one. She had consistently turned down financial offers to sell. Her home had been the gathering place for opposition meetings, rallies, and vigils. She had the stuff to turn a legal dispute into a real national cause. Bullock asked her if she would agree to have her name listed first on the suit.

She said yes.

"You have to be willing to be the public face of this battle and work with the media and not be afraid to have your picture in the newspaper and in our publications," he said.

She explained she had no experience with the press. She felt uncomfortable talking to reporters.

Not to worry, Bullock told her. His firm employed highly skilled media professionals. They would teach Susette the rules of the game, such as how to speak to the media, how to behave in front of the camera, and other useful tips.

"The media can be a demanding beast," Bullock said.

Convincing Von Winkle would be a little more difficult but no less important. Von Winkle owned more property than anyone else in the neighborhood. Without him on board, Bullock figured, it would be too easy for the city to squeeze Susette and any other plaintiffs.

Knowing he needed to make a strong pitch, Bullock walked into Von Winkle's deli and told him he planned to file a lawsuit against the city and wage a high-profile campaign that would put a national spotlight on the injustices being carried out by the NLDC. All the institute's resources would be behind the Fort Trumbull property owners. "Are you interested in being a plaintiff?" he asked.

Von Winkle paused. By claiming ownership of Von Winkle's properties, the NLDC also claimed it was entitled to all the rental proceeds generated by the tenants. "What happens if I lose my rental income during the litigation?" he asked. "If that happens I won't have any income."

"We will fight and do all we can to protect your interests to the greatest extent of our ability," Bullock assured him. "We won't let you be financially ruined during the course of the litigation."

Von Winkle had other concerns. If successful, Bullock's strategy would thrust the homeowners into the spotlight. "I'm not good at speaking to the media," Von Winkle said.

"Don't worry. We won't put you up front. Susette will be the lead plaintiff in the case. Inevitably, she will get more attention as a result."

"That's good, Bull."

Bullock smiled. No one had ever called him that before.

Von Winkle agreed to join the suit.

"Look, I want to be sure I'm clear about our expectation here," Bullock said. "We want people who are going to hang in there and fight this and not sell a couple of months into the battle."

"I won't let you down, Bull," he said with a grin. "I'll stick with you."

With Von Winkle on board, Bullock picked up another plaintiff, Von Winkle's friend Rich Beyer. Though he didn't reside in New London, Beyer owned a business and two buildings in the Fort Trumbull neighborhood. A highly skilled, thirty-one-year-old building contractor, Beyer had renovated one of the buildings and converted it into rental apartments. He had been in the process of renovating the second building when the NLDC padlocked the front door, confiscated his tools and building materials, and tried to force him out after he refused the agency's take-it-or-leave-it offer. The heavy-handed tactics motivated Beyer to stand and fight beside the neighborhood's residents as a matter of principle.

Bullock couldn't have scripted a more suitable plaintiff than Beyer, a self-employed, hardworking guy dedicated to supporting his young family and minding his own business. But his business had been threatened by the NLDC's quest for his property.

Before leaving New London, Bullock lined up the rest of the plaintiffs.

Matt and Sue Dery agreed to join the suit. As the titleholder to the family home, Dery's elderly mother, Wilhelmina, would appear on the complaint. She had never lived elsewhere, and she had no interest in moving. Matt agreed to be her advocate in the fight.

Another elderly couple, Pasquale and Margherita Cristofaro, also pledged to sign on to the suit. They had moved to the neighborhood decades earlier—after losing their previous home to the city's eminent domain. Their son Michael agreed to speak on behalf of his parents in the lawsuit.

James and Laura Guretsky, a younger couple living on Susette's block, also signed on.

So did Byron Athenian, a mechanic with a wheelchair-bound

granddaughter, who lived a block from Susette. He and his mother had a modest home near the Italian Dramatic Club.

Between them, the group owned fifteen of the twenty-two Fort Trumbull properties targeted by the NLDC. They were largely a lunch-pail group—a carpenter, an auto mechanic, a nurse, a self-employed businessman, and some senior citizens hoping to spend their final days in the homes they had occupied for decades. Most of them had dirt under their nails at the end of the workday.

Convinced the institute had to take the case, Bullock returned to Washington and put together a final proposal to submit to his firm's board of directors for approval.

30

WOLVES AT THE DOOR

November 22, 2000

A s a cold wind whipped off the water, Susette trudged up the front steps to her house. The sun had already set, though it was barely past 5 p.m. It had been a long day at the hospital. With aching feet and a sore back, she planned to spend the evening prepping food for the following day's Thanksgiving dinner.

Reaching for the doorknob, she spotted a paper taped to her door. She yanked it down and started reading. "The CITY OF NEW LONDON, acting by the NEW LONDON DEVELOPMENT CORPORATION (the 'Condemner'), has filed with the Clerk of the Superior Court for the Judicial District of New London at New London a Statement of Compensation relative to the taking of the property described in that statement."

Time had run out. Her property had been condemned. The notice made it clear that she no longer owned her property; the NLDC did. "Upon receipt of such return of notice," she read, "the Clerk of the Superior Court shall issue a Certificate of Taking. Upon the recording of the Certificate of Taking, title to the premises described therein shall vest in the municipality."

For the first time, she felt the city had invaded her home. Sometime earlier that day, she realized, a stranger had come on her property and affixed a notice to her door informing her that her home was no longer hers.

She rushed inside and called Von Winkle. He had also received condemnation papers. Others had, too. The elderly were scared. Von Winkle was ready to fight. So was Susette.

"What should we do?" she asked.

"Call up Bull," Von Winkle said.

She hung up and called Bullock's office. He was working late. Breathless with anxiety, she described the condemnation notice.

"Tell me what it says," Bullock said.

While she read, Bullock faced the oversized quote above his desk: " 'For the coming of that day shall I fight, I and . . . my chosen friends. For the freedom of Man. For his rights. For his life. For his honor.'—Ayn Rand."

Susette finished reading. "Scott," she said, "the wolves are at our door."

He promised to get right back to her. Furious, he hung up and marched down the hall to Dana Berliner's office.

"Now what?" she said, observing his fury.

"I am so pissed right now," he said and launched into a tirade about the condemnation notices. "To do this the day before Thanksgiving is so outrageous."

Berliner agreed.

"You know," he said, "everyone in the nation is going to recognize how outrageous this is."

"It will only increase the sympathy that most people will have for the property owners," Berliner said.

"The NLDC doesn't even have the decency to treat them with respect."

"Obviously not," she said.

"This has to stop! It has to stop!" he said. "I want to spread the word to as many people as possible about how wrong this is. This is a perfect example of the human toll of eminent-domain abuse."

Bullock and Berliner spent most of Thanksgiving weekend working. Both single, both determined, and both workaholics, they formulated a game plan for getting the condemnation actions dismissed and saving the homes. They listed the immediate tasks:

- Draft the legal complaint.
- Develop a background paper on the case, discussing the case history and the plaintiffs' background.
- Generate a media advisory.
- Produce a news release for distribution on the day the lawsuit would be filed.
- Plan an event in New London to accompany the filing.

All of it added up to filing a precedent-setting lawsuit against the City of New London and the NLDC. They had a lot to do and very little time. They focused first on the complaint.

"This could possibly have a number of causes of action," Bullock said.

They started with the obvious. Under the Fifth Amendment, the government must have a public use or purpose when taking private property under eminent domain. Susette and her neighbors were convinced their properties were being taken to accommodate Pfizer or some other private party. Bullock and Berliner agreed.

"Plaintiffs' property is slated for redevelopment not for public use, but rather as a health club, office space, and yet unnamed and unspecified development projects," Bullock typed under the heading "FIRST COUNT" in the complaint. "Plaintiffs challenge this abuse of eminent domain authority as a violation of the Connecticut and United States Constitutions."

They decided to point the finger at Pfizer in the complaint. "The development was to enhance the new Pfizer facility that was being built next to the Fort Trumbull neighborhood," Bullock added. "Under the Connecticut and United States Constitution, private property may only be taken through eminent domain for 'public use.'"

Bullock wanted to include another claim: equal protection. The right to own, use, and possess property is protected under the U.S. Constitution. In addition to requiring a legitimate or compelling reason for depriving someone of property rights, the equal-protection clause protected against discriminatory treatment. The city had deprived Susette and her neighbors of their property, while allowing the Italian Dramatic Club to keep its property. The city, in Bullock's eyes, had treated similarly situated people differently. Under some circumstances, unequal treatment was actually permissible, but the government had to show a rational basis for discriminatory treatment.

"By permitting one property owner in the plan (the Italian Dramatic Club) to retain title and possession," Bullock typed, "while denying the ability of Plaintiffs to retain title and possession of their property, Defendants treat similarly situated people differently."

Berliner pointed out that the court took equal-protection claims more seriously when race or ethnicity was the basis for discrimination. The Fort Trumbull homeowners had not faced discrimination based on skin color or ethnicity; they simply lacked political connections to the NLDC's decision makers.

Bullock insisted the claim was still worth raising. "It points out how absurd the NLDC's decision rationale was," he said. "This is a blatant example of them doing favors for those in power and neglecting those without political clout or influence."

Berliner agreed.

Bullock wasn't through. He insisted on a third count against the city based on the fact that taking homes wasn't necessary for the NLDC to complete its municipal-development plan. The city had identified Susette's block as Parcel 4-A. Besides Susette's home, all of Von Winkle's properties and the Derys' properties were within Parcel 4-A. Unlike most of the other parcels within the ninety-acre development area, Parcel 4-A had not been designated for any specific construction. As a result, Bullock reasoned, it wasn't even necessary for the NLDC to take it.

Berliner looked at him like he was nuts. "Necessity has been so watered down by the courts that it is not taken seriously anymore," she said.

Bullock knew she was right. In recent years, courts had given greater and greater latitude to municipalities in condemning private property for public use. "But in this case," Bullock argued, "the takings are truly unnecessary. The NLDC doesn't even know what it's going to do with Parcel 4-A."

Berliner went along.

By the time Bullock and Berliner finished, they had drafted a twenty-four-page complaint alleging eight violations of law. The complaint asked the court to declare the actions by the city and the NLDC unconstitutional and illegal and to dismiss the condemnation papers filed against the homeowners.

Strangers had started showing up at Susette's doorstep to offer support and express admiration for her stand. So she didn't think much of it when she got home from work early one night and discovered a woman on her porch. Approaching her steps, Susette walked past the woman's car without noticing the placard inside the front windshield. It read: "MARSHAL."

"Can I help you?" Susette said.

"Yes. I'm here to serve you with papers for condemnation."

"Well, I'm not accepting them."

"What do you mean you're not accepting them?"

"I'm not taking your damn papers."

The marshal stared at her.

"Now get off my porch."

The marshal didn't budge.

"Get off my porch before I throw you off."

She left without leaving the papers.

"Don't ever come on my property again," Susette said.

December 8, 2000

Dave Goebel got a simple message from the NLDC's lawyers: "The takings have now been completed."

On paper that was true. All the appropriate and necessary legal documents had been filed with the court and served on the property owners. Technically, the NLDC now owned all the remaining homes in Fort Trumbull. But the holdouts still had possession. It fell to Goebel to get them out.

He didn't waste any time. That afternoon, he dashed off a letter to Susette. "On December 8, 2000, the NLDC acquired title to the Premises now occupied by you and which Premises is part of the Fort Trumbull Municipal Development Project," he began. "NLDC hereby gives you notice that you are required to quit possession of the Premises now occupied by you ninety (90) days after the date hereof, being no later than March 9, 2001."

Goebel gave Susette a reason to comply. Now that the NLDC owned her home, it planned to start charging her $450 per month in rent until she got out. "Occupancy payments shall be paid to the 'NLDC,'" he wrote, telling her she would also be responsible for all utilities, maintenance, and insurance payments. "You should maintain liability insurance in the amount of $100,000 naming New London Development Corporation, as additional insured. In the event that we do not receive a Certificate, NLDC may elect to purchase the necessary insurance and bill you."

Goebel's tone stoked Susette's defiance. She called Mitchell and ranted. "He's not getting a dime from me," Susette said. "And I'm not leavin' either."

Claire continued to focus on money and image. In her aggressive push to remake New London, the NLDC had spent $28.7 million in state money in three years. Earmarked for the Fort Trumbull municipal-development project, the money had not resulted in any construction in the fort neighborhood. With some demolitions complete and the takings of homes in the works, the NLDC needed more money, and it needed it fast.

The governor had put the brakes on more state funding, and the NLDC had already tapped its private contributors through fund-raisers. The NLDC had one option left: borrow. The NLDC applied for a $2 million commercial loan from Webster Bank.

But lending millions to the NLDC carried risks. The agency was virtually broke and had no income stream. The bank wanted security. Once again, the NLDC turned to Pfizer, which guaranteed the loan by promising to pay the bank back if the NLDC defaulted.

On December 13 the bank loaned the money to the NLDC.

The Institute for Justice had an unlikely secret weapon in thirty-five-year-old John Kramer. When the institute had opened its doors for business in the early 1990s, Kramer worked at a small public-relations firm in Washington. The institute found him through a headhunter and offered him a PR position. He was quickly elevated to vice president of communications.

Few law firms employed PR specialists, but the institute put a premium on shaping the message and mission behind its legal initiatives. It argued cases not only in courts of law but also in the court of public opinion. That meant Kramer had a responsibility every bit as important as the lawyers' work, and the attorneys worked closely with the PR people to craft a lawsuit's message.

The first time Bullock and Berliner briefed Kramer on the Fort Trumbull dispute, he felt a bond with the plaintiffs. The youngest of nine children, Kramer had lost his father at age two. Fatherlessness left him feeling a bit isolated and taught him to stand up for himself and be his own advocate at a very early age. By the time he reached college he had his heart set on being an advocate, a protector.

The Fort Trumbull situation kept Kramer up at night, wondering how to launch the lawsuit in a way that would galvanize public opinion on the side of the homeowners. He planned on a big announcement to accompany the suit's filing. But he didn't want a press conference from the courthouse steps—that would be too much of a cliché. Instead, he wanted a backdrop with real meaning, something that symbolized the struggle to protect homes.

Finally it came to him: Susette's pink house. It was ground zero for the battle. It was the gathering place for advocates, plaintiffs, and protestors. It was the home of the lead plaintiff. It was where the institute should unveil the lawsuit.

By announcing the case from Susette's front steps, Bullock could introduce the national media to her and her neighbors and illustrate that Susette's home was not dilapidated and run-down, as the NLDC wanted people to think. If Kramer did his job right, Susette's pink house would become a national symbol for the fight against eminent-domain abuse. He spent days preparing an agenda for the announcement and a press advisory inviting national media to attend.

With the complaint polished and the PR plan in place, Bullock caught an evening flight to go to New London.

December 20, 2000

Bundled in winter coats and scarves, a spirited group of supporters huddled in the street outside Susette's house. Inside, Susette and the plaintiffs waited for news that the suit had been filed. Bullock paced the floor, his cell phone in hand. Just before noon, the call from the courthouse finally came. *Kelo v. City of New London* had officially been filed.

Bullock and Kramer burst into action. From the institute's Washington office, Kramer disseminated a press release to media outlets throughout the United States. In New London, Bullock led Susette to her living-room picture window overlooking the street. Press photographers and television cameras looked up at her. Showtime had arrived.

"Are you holding up all right?" Bullock asked.

"I'm okay," she said softly.

"Listen," he said, trying to reassure her. "This is the beginning . . . the first step."

Overwhelmed, she took a deep breath. This wasn't what she had had in mind when she left her husband and a country home for a quiet place on the shore. She looked Bullock in the eye. "This is what we have to do," she said, turning and following him onto the porch. The cheering crowd hoisted signs and placards. "Take Claire's Home for Social Justice," one read. Another said: "New London Destroying Our Constitution."

As the other plaintiffs filed in around Susette, Bullock stepped forward to address the media and the neighborhood supporters. "It's great to be in New London and announce what must have been one of the worst-kept secrets in town," he said. "We are very pleased to announce that *this morning* the Institute for Justice, along with property owners and local counsel Scott Sawyer, filed a lawsuit that aims to end eminent-domain abuse in New London, Connecticut."

The crowd applauded.

"We asked the court to declare that what the city and the NLDC are doing is illegal and unconstitutional," Bullock continued. "We will do everything in our power to keep these people in this wonderful neighborhood."

Standing behind Bullock, Susette stared expressionlessly at the audience of supporters.

"As you all know, the City of New London and the NLDC want these people out because they have decided that someone else can make better use of this land than Susette Kelo or Matt Dery or Bill Von Winkle," Bullock said. "The plan is to take these properties, evict the residents, and bulldoze the properties. In other words, developers get the land, the taxpayers of New London and Connecticut get the bill, and these fine people get the boot."

Supporters yelled and waved their signs. Bullock called out the NLDC and the city. "You let the IDC stay," he said. "You know who wants to stay. They're not interested in taking the money and heading out of town. Do the right thing and let them stay."

With the press seeking reaction to the suit, the NLDC put out a simple statement, saying it couldn't comment publicly on a suit it hadn't seen. Privately, though, the agency was reeling. An NLDC spokesman sent an e-mail to Claire's top aide, reporting that press activity had been heavy following the press conference. "I did brief interviews with Ch. 61 and 30 and Connecticut public radio—no problems—stuck with the script," he wrote. "I'm putting Claire in touch with the *New York Times* as we speak."

The spokesman tried not to sound worried. But he foresaw a problem. "My only concern with this is just how we explain that this is not taking private land for private development," he wrote. "Are the jobs created and tax benefits alone enough of a public benefit?"

As soon as the press conference broke up at Susette's, the plaintiffs and their supporters headed up the street for a celebratory party at Von Winkle's deli. Susette entered with Bullock. The place erupted in cheers. "Now we're fighting back," one of the neighbors shouted, prompting more cheers.

Von Winkle had printed new menus especially for the occasion.

"Here you go, Red," he said, handing her one.

Entrees

Fort Flambé—You'll demolish this sizzling mix of ethnic ingredients.

Pfizer Fettuccini—The heart and soul of our menu. This dish defines our reason for being.

Eminent Domainicotti—This dish originated in the Fort Trumbull neighborhood, but is rapidly spreading across town.

(All dinners include your choice of garlic croissant or our famous Viagra vegetables.)

Grinders

(available on a Rowland Roll—soft, plump & ruthless)

Claire Combo—A manic combination which is all over the place. (This baby is a crazy mix of just about everything.)

NLDC/Pfizer Combo—These two have a natural affinity for each other, as classic as Peanut Butter & Jelly.

Social Justice Salami—Names can be deceiving; this baby packs a wallop you won't forget.

Percy Patties—Fresh turkey burgers marinated in rum and basted with gin (served dry, with an olive and a cute little umbrella).

Soups

Adm. Goebbels Goulash—Served ice cold in a jack-boot.

Laughing hysterically, Susette handed the menu to Bullock. He was grinning broadly. The small print at the bottom of the menu caught his eye: "Enter our weekly drawing for up to $15,000 in relocation expenses. You can't win if you don't leave." The offer had an asterisk, directing readers to even smaller print:

*Offer may be altered or withdrawn without notice. We will never,
ever put anything in writing. We reserve the right to negotiate in
bad faith through the newspaper. All FOI disclosure requirements
will be met (not really). Any resemblance between the NLDC and a
legitimate enterprise is purely coincidental. The fact that not one
NLDC employee has any construction experience shall not be held
against us. Pfizer has the final say over all transactions, as they are
the ones who will eventually take title to this land.*

Bullock smiled and looked at Von Winkle. None of his clients had ever produced anything so innovative and humorous before.

"If I'm ever in a fight, I want you on my side," Bullock said, patting Von Winkle on the back. "Can I keep this?" Von Winkle wanted him to keep it. After all, glory days had returned to the Fort Trumbull Deli. The place was packed. Food and drink were in demand. And everyone had a smile and a story to tell. The plaintiffs smelled victory.

Bullock looked around. He couldn't help thinking this was going to be a fun, unpredictable adventure representing the Fort Trumbull neighbors.

As the party wound down, Steve Hallquist cornered Von Winkle. Ever since filing their own suit with the Steffians, Steve and Amy had been trying to persuade Von Winkle to turn over the documents he had lifted from the NLDC's Dumpster. But he had steadily resisted. Steve hoped Bullock's presence would change things.

"Bill, look, we need that stuff. We need it badly. Anything that you have may be very important to the case."

"You think so?"

"I really do. And what's to lose? You're a plaintiff now. Give Bullock the ammo. Don't hold back the bullets."

Von Winkle led Steve and Amy to the basement and retrieved two black plastic trash bags stuffed with documents. The Hallquists took the bags to Scott Sawyer's office. Days later, Sawyer shipped them to Bullock in Washington.

31

SOME DEVIOUS WAY

No one at the NLDC wanted to admit it, but the lawsuit had the agency very worried. Some wondered whether the agency should modify the municipal-development plan. The project called for redeveloping ninety acres of real estate. Combined, the plaintiffs' land amounted to just 1.54 acres—less than 2 percent of the total area in question. Scaling down the project by an acre and a half seemed worth discussing if it averted a protracted, expensive legal battle that might bring the rest of the development to a screeching halt. Meanwhile, the city council had started getting antsy over the delays. It wanted to see timetables and immediate progress.

Something had to be done, but Goebel had a problem. He was trying to close a development contract with Corcoran Jennison, a Boston-based construction firm that was planning to implement the NLDC's development plan. Any substantial changes to the plan might require approval from the city council and potentially could trigger another round of public hearings. Besides delaying the deal with Corcoran Jennison, this approach might also provide an opening for opponents to shoot down the plan altogether.

In an e-mail to one of the NLDC's top aides, Goebel wrote that reducing the scope of the project to exclude the plaintiffs' land "would be a major change, driving the entire plan, or at least parts of it, back into the public arena. This would be very delaying to the Corcoran Jennison development."

Instead, Goebel wanted to send something to the city council that would appease it while keeping its members beholden to the original commitment. "The resolution that we send over should read that way in some devious way," he said to an NLDC aide. "We need to pre-brief our most friendly councilors on this eventually, i.e., that failure to go with the commitment will drive the major change."

What is the Institute for Justice? Tom Londregan wondered. He had never heard of the outfit until he got word that the institute had sued the city. Before a copy of the suit reached his desk, Londregan started getting phone calls. Reporters from outside New London suddenly wanted to know why the city was trying to force people from their homes.

Londregan wanted to know what the hell was going on. He believed in arguing cases before judges and juries, not in the court of public opinion. Apparently, the opposing lawyers were holding press conferences and issuing press releases. They had changed the rules—and he didn't like it one bit. His firm employed lawyers, paralegals, and secretaries, not PR specialists.

After three years on offense, the city had suddenly been forced into a defensive posture. Rather than simply answering a lawsuit, Londregan and the NLDC had to answer to the national media. Irked, Londregan decided right away he didn't care for the institute's brand of justice. Convinced the city had the right to take the homes for economic development, and determined to prove it, Londregan planned to play hardball in defending the city's interests.

Christmas was barely over when Billy Von Winkle received a certified letter from the NLDC reminding him that it now owned his properties and that it expected all of Von Winkle's tenants to start turning their rent payments over to the NLDC.

A few days later, Von Winkle got another surprise. The NLDC had entered one of his apartment buildings, forced the tenants out, and padlocked the doors to prevent them from reentering. Some of the tenants hadn't even had a chance to grab their shoes before being forced outside into the cold.

Von Winkle called Bullock and told him what was going on. Besides being outraged at how his tenants had been manhandled, Von Winkle complained about the immediate loss of income. "Bull, how am I going to live?" he said.

Bullock struggled to control his temper. It seemed the city was out to bankrupt his clients just a few weeks into the lawsuit.

"Is there a way to stop this?" Von Winkle asked.

"We'll do our damndest," Bullock said.

Ever since losing the freedom-of-information battle with the *Day*, Claire had suffered a series of negative portrayals in the press. No matter what she said or did, her public image kept getting worse. And the NLDC's credibility kept sinking.

Claire blamed a lot of this on Reid MacCluggage. As the *Day*'s publisher, MacCluggage didn't write the stories, but in Claire's eyes he was Darth Vader, a dark, powerful figure working behind the scenes to destroy the NLDC's vision for the city. When a feature writer for the *Day*'s primary competitor, the *Hartford Courant*, Connecticut's largest newspaper, called with a request to follow her around for a cover story in the paper's Sunday magazine, Claire figured she finally had a chance for an unbiased story.

Jane Dee arrived at the president's residence at Connecticut College for the first time on a cold January day a few weeks after the lawsuit was filed by Susette and her neighbors. But Dee hadn't come to talk legalese. She had come to check out Claire and all the talk she had heard about her eye-catching wardrobe, her seductive mannerisms, and her controversial style. She entered the house and waited for Claire.

"Excuse how I'm dressed," Claire said, appearing suddenly and removing a stylish winter parka. "I didn't feel like dressing like a college president today."

Dee had trouble taking her eyes off Claire, mesmerized by her intensity and flair. Dee also had trouble getting a word in; Claire totally dominated the dialogue, and Dee felt she had to interrupt just to ask questions. Claire had a lot to say, occasionally lowering her voice, reclining in her chair, and running her fingers through her hair as she talked. It reinforced for Dee what she had read in one of Claire's essays while preparing for the interview: "The imaginative, even seductive, engagement of people in a fresh way of seeing the world is the first step of vision setting."

By the end of the interview, Dee wanted to spend a lot more time with Claire, and Claire agreed. She also consented to have a photographer tag along. But driving to her office after leaving Claire's house, Dee felt uneasy; she suspected the Claire she had met was the one Claire wanted her to meet. She also wondered about Claire's motives for agreeing to spend time with her. Dee figured that Claire thought she could control the narrative.

The following morning, Dee showed up at Susette's house for a scheduled interview. She brought along a photographer. Billy Von Winkle did his part to set the tone in the neighborhood, papering the windows of his deli with wanted posters featuring sexy pictures of Claire. Dee and her photographer stopped to look.

"Wanted . . . but not by us," one of the posters read. "This subject is armed with a giant rolodex and should be considered dangerous . . . has been known to hang out at drug factories, gyms and schools."

Another one read: "This subject is wanted in Connecticut for fraternizing with devious people including Governor Rowland, for violating Freedom of Information laws, for stealing people's homes, and for pretending to be a social justice authority. Subject is adept at disguises. If spotted, do not approach subject for God sakes!"

A final sign with an oversized shot of Claire's face said: "WANTED for theft, grand larceny, and attempting to pull the wool over innocent people's eyes. Claire Gaudiani has used the following aliases: Dr. Gaudiani, Claire, Martin Luther King, Jesus, Mom and Claire Lois Gaudiani Burnett."

Dee's photographer snapped shots of Von Winkle's posters for inclusion in the story.

The mood inside Susette's house was raucous. Inside, Dee found Steve and Amy Hallquist and Connecticut College students who were vehemently opposed to Claire. Seated around the kitchen table with Susette, the group railed against the NLDC and its tactics. When Dee mentioned Claire, no one had a kind word to say.

The students belittled her approach. "The trend in America is to save what's left of our communities," one of them said. "And Claire's out there knocking them down. It's a mess, just a mess."

Steve compared her to a cult leader carrying out community cleansing.

Amy took issue with her revealing wardrobe.

"She's a ho," someone blurted out.

The provocative quotes about Claire were still on Dee's mind a few days later when she attended a speech that Claire gave to a local chamber of commerce.

"Good morning," Claire began.

"Good morning," a man in the audience responded.

"I love responsive men," Claire told the audience.

Dee couldn't believe it. After the speech, she asked Claire about her seductive style. Claire dismissed the criticism as noise from her adversaries, pointing out that people's obsession with her attire amused her. "It's not like I'm disabled and dragging a bad leg," she said. "So I don't let it bother me."

The one item that stuck with Dee after her visit with Susette was Susette's insistence that Pfizer was behind Claire's push to clear the neighborhood. Dee got close enough to Claire to get an interview with her low-profile husband, David Burnett, who worked under Milne at Pfizer. He looked and sounded more like a professor than a corporate guy. "Pfizer wants a nice place to operate," he said candidly. "We don't want to be surrounded by tenements."

On the day Dee spoke to Burnett, a photographer snapped photos of Claire. Dee's story was quickly taking shape.

In addition to Von Winkle's rental-property crisis, Bullock and Berliner had another problem. Back on December 7, two weeks before the institute had filed its lawsuit, the NLDC had applied for permits to demolish six of the fifteen properties owned by the plaintiffs. The law required the NLDC to wait sixty days before exercising the permits. As of February 5, 2001, the NLDC would be free to start demolishing. All of Von Winkle's properties—including the deli—were on the demolition schedule.

The lawsuit alleged the NLDC had acted unlawfully when taking title to the plaintiffs' properties. With the case headed for trial, Bullock figured, the NLDC surely had to suspend any demolition plans until a judge sorted out the legal questions.

In early January, Bullock telephoned the NLDC's in-house lawyer, Mathew Greene, and asked the agency to hold off on the demolitions until after the case was resolved. Greene said he'd get back to him.

When NLDC president Dave Goebel learned of Bullock's request, he approached it as he would an enemy. He didn't want to give any assurance that his agency wouldn't demolish the houses. He hoped that might force the issue.

Greene informed Bullock that the NLDC would not take up the issue of whether to delay the home demolitions until its next board of directors meeting, on February 13.

That would be eight days too late, Bullock insisted. The mandatory sixty-day waiting period to exercise the demolition permits would expire on February 5. What was there to stop the NLDC from demolishing the properties that day?

Bullock asked Greene if the NLDC would at least agree to hold off any demolitions until the agency's next board meeting. Greene checked and came back with the same answer: no.

Incensed, Bullock huddled with Berliner. "These people are so arrogant they won't even agree to stop demolitions until the court hears the case," he said.

Bullock and Berliner decided to hit back. First, they helped Von Winkle write and submit a tough op-ed piece to the *Hartford Courant* titled: "Eminent Domain Abuse Puts Owners, Tenants Out In The Cold." The piece ran on January 29. In it, Von Winkle hammered the NLDC:

> *Earlier this month, a tenant in my New London apartment building found himself being locked inside: Someone was padlocking his door from the outside.*

I wish I could say this was a prank, but it was a deliberate act by my town's government and a private development corporation to make property owners like me give up what is rightfully ours. . . .

The NLDC claims the right to collect any rent these properties generate. In the middle of January, it forced my tenants out into the street in their stocking feet. This is no exaggeration. This is what happens when government power gets out of control.

The essay had its desired effect, thoroughly embarrassing the NLDC and the City of New London and sparking an outrage among readers across the state.

The day after Von Winkle's piece ran, Bullock and Berliner asked the court to intervene. They filed a motion for a temporary restraining order to prevent the NLDC from taking any action to demolish or alter buildings or homes on the plaintiffs' properties until the court conducted a hearing. They also filed a motion for a temporary injunction to prevent the NLDC from evicting any plaintiffs or demolishing any plaintiffs' homes pending the outcome of the trial. Both motions stressed the urgency of a ruling before the fast-approaching February 5 expiration date on the NLDC's demolition permits.

Bullock and Berliner's motions ended up on the desk of Judge Robert A. Martin at the New London Superior Court. A New London native, Martin had the administrative responsibility for assigning cases to fellow judges. He knew some of the plaintiffs personally. The judge also knew some of the defendants and most of the lawyers involved in the case.

Until the case was assigned, Martin had hoped things would remain low-key. Martin called a conference with all the lawyers in his chambers at noon on February 5, 2001, the same day the sixty-day waiting period would expire.

At first relieved that a conference had been scheduled, Bullock then immediately recognized a major concern. The judge planned to take up the demolition matter twelve hours *after* the NLDC's ninety-day waiting period for exercising demolition permits expired. Nothing was in place to stop the NLDC from bulldozing houses at midnight on the eve of the hearing. He called Berliner and Kramer to his office.

"The legal protection for the homes ends at midnight," he explained. "For twelve hours the homes have no legal protection."

An analysis of the homes with pending demolition permits showed that all of them were occupied except for one being renovated by Rich Beyer. Bullock felt confident that the occupied homes were not at risk. The empty house, however, presented the NLDC with a big, easy target for a knockdown.

"The NLDC is tyrannical enough to do something like that," Bullock told his colleagues.

"The last thing we need right now is for any more of those homes to come down," Berliner said.

"That's right," Bullock said. "If we lose even one home before we present the case that will be a huge psychological blow to them. We have to prevent this at all costs."

The only way to guarantee against an early-morning demolition, it seemed, would be to put a body in the house.

"I'll do it," said Kramer.

Bullock pointed out the house had no heat or electricity, since it was under renovation. "It's going to be pretty cold," he said.

"I'll bring a sleeping bag," Kramer said.

Anticipating a possible standoff with an NLDC bulldozer, Kramer decided to call Stephen Humphries, a reporter at the *Christian Science Monitor* in Boston. Humphries had an interest in eminent domain. If there was going to be drama, Kramer wanted the world to know about it.

Kramer explained the situation and what he'd be doing. "I can't guarantee anything," he said. "But I'm going to do this, and if you're interested in joining me as a reporter, you are welcome to come aboard."

Humphries got approval from his editor and agreed to meet Kramer in New London.

February 4, 2001

Bullock, Kramer and Humphries arrived at Susette's house early in the evening. The plaintiffs had gathered to run through the game plan for standing vigil over Rich Beyer's property until the conclusion of the hearing the following morning. Bullock explained that Kramer and Humphries would go up to Beyer's vacant home around 11:30 p.m. and remain inside until dawn. Then at sunup, the rest of the coalition would surround the house and remain on-site until Judge Martin, they hoped, issued an order blocking any further demolitions until the conclusion of the trial.

While Bullock and Kramer reviewed the logistics, neighbors scurried in and out of Susette's house, dropping off provisions for Kramer and Humphries: homemade brownies, a thermos of hot coffee, and flashlights with extra batteries.

Humphries cornered Susette for an interview for the *Christian Science Monitor.* The more questions he asked, the more emotional she became. When he asked about the possibility that another house would come down in the neighborhood, she broke down.

Kramer spotted Susette wiping tears from her cheeks. He looked at his watch. It was nearly 11:30, time to head over to the empty house. He put on his coat, gloves, and a wool ski cap and called for Humphries. They said good night to Susette, and Beyer led them up the street to the house. From the outside, it appeared in good shape other than some visible signs of damage caused by the NLDC, which had padlocked the front door to keep Beyer out. He had cut off the agency's lock and replaced it with one of his own. After removing it, he ushered Kramer and Humphries inside.

Kramer stepped onto a dirt floor. The stench of cat urine forced him to cover his nose. After Beyer had installed brand-new window casings throughout the house, the NLDC had pried them off with crowbars, enabling stray cats to gain access.

To escape the smell and the dirt, Kramer and Humphries went upstairs, to an uninsulated, open area with nothing but studs and subflooring. They rolled out their sleeping bags on the dusty surface. The temperature outside was subfreezing, and the building had no heat or electricity.

"It's cold as hell," said Beyer, hardly able to take the smell. He was amazed that Kramer was still willing to spend the night in the building. "You need balls the size of watermelons to sleep in this place."

Kramer was determined.

Beyer thanked him profusely and headed home to get a few hours' sleep before getting up early to get ready for his court appearance with Bullock.

Shivering, Kramer got into his sleeping bag and thought of a statement by Thomas Jefferson: "We are not to expect to be translated from despotism to liberty in a featherbed." Suddenly, something dawned on him. Technically, according to Connecticut law, Beyer's house belonged to the NLDC. "We're trespassing," Kramer told Humphries.

"If we get arrested," Humphries said, "my editor will bail me out. But who will take care of you?"

Kramer laughed. "If this is the price to ensure a man's house is free, I'll happily pay it."

Eventually, both men drifted off.

Kramer had drifted into a shallow sleep when pounding on the front door jolted him awake. "You in there?" a man shouted.

It was just after 5:30 in the morning. "This is it," Kramer said to Humphries, hustling out of his sleeping bag. "It's either the police or the demolition crew."

His adrenaline rushing, Kramer hustled down the stairs and opened the front door. Smiling, Matt Dery greeted him with two steaming cups of Dunkin' Donuts coffee and a bag of hot breakfast sandwiches. "I thought you guys could use something warm," he said, his breath visible in the frigid air.

Kramer took a deep breath and thanked Dery for his thoughtfulness.

Before long, the other neighbors and plaintiffs started showing up. By eight, Mayor Beachy had also arrived to stand vigil with the group around the perimeter of the property.

*　　*　　*

Bullock showed up at Judge Martin's chambers expecting to finally meet Tom Londregan. But someone else from his office showed up instead, along with the NLDC's outside attorney, Ed O'Connell, a short, portly fellow who made no effort to veil his disdain for Bullock and Sawyer. Judge Martin welcomed the group into a conference room and asked Bullock to orient him by telling him where each of the plaintiffs' properties was located.

Bullock began with Susette's house, identifying it as being on the corner of East and Trumbull.

"Oh, that pink one?" Martin asked.

Bullock nodded.

"That's Kelo's place?" the judge asked.

Everyone nodded.

"And you've got Cristofaro," Bullock said.

"I know where that place is," Judge Martin said.

"And there's one right behind the Italian Dramatic Club," Bullock said. "That's Byron Athenian's place."

Martin had known Athenian since his adolescent days, and he had once taken a vehicle to Athenian's house to get it repaired. He made it clear he wanted to try to resolve the disputes over demolition, rents, and occupancy without having to litigate each point. Mediation, he explained, was also an option that might avert a trial and enable the homeowners to receive compensation for giving up their homes. He suggested Judge Angelo Santaniello could conduct the mediation.

Bullock politely declined. Santaniello had practiced law with Tom Londregan's brother. And he had been a primary force, along with Jay Levin, in negotiating for the Italian Dramatic Club to stay put while the houses around it were torn down. Bullock didn't trust Santaniello. Besides, his clients wanted no part of mediation for a monetary settlement.

Hardly surprised at Bullock's answer, Judge Martin got to the major points of contention: whether the city was entitled to charge the plaintiffs rent during the litigation and whether the homes would be protected from demolition during any appeals that might be filed after the trial. Bullock had already applied for a preliminary injunction to protect the homes until the end of the trial, and the city and the NLDC agreed that no demolition would take place until the trial judge ruled on the injunction.

Martin looked to O'Connell. The NLDC, O'Connell indicated, was not willing to concede on the rent issue or the demolitions. Bullock said his clients wouldn't concede either.

Convinced both sides were dug in, Martin focused on the one item he could control: insuring a timely, orderly trial schedule. The last thing he wanted was to see both sides in court every other week battling over injunctions, stays of demolition, and a host of other legal challenges that would delay the start of the trial and sap the court's resources and time. He suggested both sides reconvene in his chambers in a couple weeks to work out resolutions to all the pretrial disputes. Until then, the NLDC's lawyers agreed that Beyer's property would be left alone, a promise they had refused to make before Bullock filed his motion.

When Bullock arrived back in Fort Trumbull, Susette and the coalition felt like the cavalry had arrived. He informed them that for now, Beyer's house would remain standing. Although minor and perhaps temporary, the good news felt like a huge victory.

"Thank God," Susette said.

Fulfilled, Kramer didn't bother taking a hot shower or getting into a fresh change of clothes. Instead, he remained in his winter gear for the flight back to Washington. Later that night, he had dinner with his wife and two young children. One of them asked where he had been the previous night. Kramer's answer didn't make sense to his son, who wanted to know why he would bother sleeping in a vacant house.

Kramer referred to his favorite movie, *It's a Wonderful Life*, in which occurs a similar conversation between a father and his inquiring son, George, who didn't understand why his father invested so much time and energy in a profitless bank offering small loans to first-time home buyers. "You know, George," Peter Bailey says, "I feel that in a small way we are doing something important, satisfying a fundamental urge. It's deep in the race for a man to want his own roof and walls and fireplace, and we're helping him get those things in our shabby little office."

"I'm trying to secure that for these good people in New London," Kramer explained. "It's the right to have a home and to be safe and secure within those four walls."

February 21, 2001

Tom Londregan didn't want to give an inch when it came to Scott Bullock's requests. But what Londregan wanted most was a speedy trial. The longer the case dragged out, the longer it would be before the city could start developing the waterfront area. He showed up at Judge Martin's chambers prepared to strike a deal.

With Martin running the meeting, Bullock and Londregan pounded out an agreement. Bullock promised not to amend his complaint and Londregan agreed not to raise any special defenses, both tactics that would have drawn out the trial.

Londregan reluctantly offered to forego the rents, which would have gone to the NLDC not to the city, anyway, in exchange for a commitment from Bullock that the trial could be held within six months. It took another round of negotiations before the NLDC would also agree to Bullock's demand on the rent, but ultimately it did.

Bullock agreed to a shortened discovery period and to complete all depositions by April 27, with a trial date set for May 21.

In return, the city and the NLDC promised to forego any demolitions and abstain from physically ejecting or evicting homeowners or tenants from the properties until the outcome of the trial. The agreement also enabled Von Winkle to continue collecting rent from his tenants.

The compromise was a victory for the homeowners on the main points, while it protected the city's interest in speeding things along. But to the NLDC, it was a major setback. Dave Goebel had been pushing hard to force Susette and her neighbors out. To the NLDC, Susette and her neighbors were breaking the law by refusing to vacate. Now the holdouts had court approval to stay put until the trial ended.

For Goebel, the bad news came at a bad time. The night before Bullock and Londregan reached a pretrial agreement, Goebel had taken a tongue-lashing from the city council. Filling in

for Claire, he had appeared before the council to offer a progress report but had ended up on the defensive. The council felt
the NLDC had gotten too far out in front of the local political
leaders. The harshest criticism had come from some of Claire's
staunchest supporters.

Fed up, Goebel e-mailed Claire:

> *Claire: At Council last night there was a loud cry that we were out
> in front of the City in publishing a strategic plan. Basically, they
> seem to feel that we should do nothing without their prior blessing,
> forgetting that with the exception of the work they have charged us to
> do on the MDP, all else we do as an independent agency.*
>
> *I took a lashing at the Council. I defended the plan from the
> standpoint that the economic development we are involved in is
> intended to provide the funds necessary to raise the standards in the
> community. It all fell on deaf ears.*

Claire responded quickly to Goebel's e-mail, but she had
her mind on other priorities. Ignoring Goebel's concerns about
being hammered by the city council, she asked him to let her
know when the meeting between the developer, Corcoran Jennison, and the state would be held. "We need to take advantage
of the announcement to move forward," she said. "More later,
Claire."

Later in the day, she sent Goebel another e-mail. In just two
days, she reported, the NLDC would make an important announcement. "This should be a simple, laid back but celebratory
announcement," Claire told him. "Even as simple as: 'NLDC is
very pleased to announce that the negotiations underway between Pfizer and CJ [Corcoran Jennison] have reached a decision point. Pfizer will be a partner in the hotel and conference
center. This facility will be used by Pfizer, its staff and visitors. It
will also be available for use by area residents and guests to the
New London area.'"

At the end of the e-mail, she addressed Goebel's earlier complaint: "Sorry about the Council meeting. Don't we always pass

things at the Board level first, and then take things to the Council? Let's talk. Sorry they abused you. Thanks. Claire."

Ten minutes after e-mailing Goebel, Claire e-mailed Peg Curtin, one of her best allies on the city council:

> *I want to check in after the Council's reaction to the strategic plan. I'm a little lost and I know your clear mind will get some clarity for me. What happened Tues night???*
>
> *The staff and maybe Dave could be getting discouraged with the abuse. We are all working hard and need to help and not hurt each other—policy differences are fine to keep confronting, but just whacking—well, Councilors and the NLDC staff both have plenty of other folks who are doing that job. We don't need to whack each other—I must have missed something. Any ideas?*

Before signing off, Claire made sure Curtin knew George Milne was satisfied in general. "I spoke to George many times this week and he is pleased," Claire wrote. "They are taking an even bigger stake in the conference center than they first intended. The next step is the real estate agreement with the State. Hope you are having fun. Love, Claire."

Curtin didn't soften after reading Claire's e-mail. "I don't know what to tell you," she responded. "I am just frustrated at being told that everything is fine and we will have a signed agreement soon. This has gone on for many months saying that. Dave tells us the state is holding things up. I don't get that from the state. I need more info than I'm getting. I don't apologize for what transpired the other night. We are all tired." She didn't bother to sign the e-mail.

After reading Curtin's response, Claire realized Goebel was right; they were losing the support of the city council. This required a quick fix. Flattery had always proven an effective device for soothing the council. Claire e-mailed Goebel.

"Your understanding of the sticking point is correct," Claire told him. "The councilors need some patting. Maybe Chris or whomever you designate should set up some meetings with them in twos for you and me on Sat or Monday so we can walk them through what is going on. We are really going to be in trouble with the state if they go back to [the state officials] complaining."

February 25, 2001

Jane Dee's highly anticipated story on Claire landed right where everyone could see it: on the cover of the *Hartford Courant*'s Sunday magazine. Claire spotted herself at the top of the cover, underneath a caption that read: "Claire Gaudiani had big plans for Connecticut College and New London." A picture of Pfizer appeared below Claire with the words: "Pfizer would come." A picture of Susette's house appeared below Pfizer with the words: "A neglected neighborhood would go." Then Susette's picture appeared at the bottom of the cover, her hand on her temple as if nursing a migraine. The words below Susette said: "It would be wonderful."

That's all Claire had to see to realize the article wasn't going to be flattering. She had clearly read Dee wrong when she had agreed to open up to her. Claire's husband had warned her not to let a journalist get so close. When Claire flipped to the inside pages, it was painfully clear she should have heeded his warning. Dee's story began with big, black letters: "OH, CLAIRE. You're a scholar and visionary . . . if only you could quit leaving skin on the sidewalk."

The two accompanying photos of Claire showcased her beauty. But the words of the story—including some insulting references to her as a "whore" and a "witch"—left her black and blue.

The most damaging revelation in Claire's story came from her husband, David. His admission that Pfizer didn't want to be surrounded by tenements supported the claim made by the Institute for Justice that the city had resorted to eminent domain in order to appease Pfizer's desire to clear the neighborhood. Now a senior Pfizer employee had said as much. With Bullock scheduled to start deposing Pfizer and NLDC officials within weeks, the timing could not have been worse.

None of this surprised Claire's husband. Expecting anything more from a newspaper journalist, he intimated, was pure folly.

To him Claire had been had the moment she agreed to let the reporter into their home.

More than any other story, this one really hurt. Claire had spent days and many hours with Dee. She had opened up about marriage, pregnancy, child rearing, and coping with the pressures of motherhood and running a college and the NLDC in a politically charged atmosphere dominated by men. Claire had thought Dee seemed to get it. Claire struggled to understand where it had all gone wrong.

Jealousy, she determined. That had to be it. Dee must have resented the fact that Claire had it all: professional success, good looks, overachieving children, a marriage of thirty-two years, and an accomplished lifestyle. Yes, that was it . . . jealousy had prompted Dee to turn on her. Jealousy.

32

DISCOVERY

Almost immediately after filing their lawsuit, Bullock and Berliner issued a subpoena to Pfizer seeking all documents pertaining to the Fort Trumbull development. Pfizer didn't readily comply. While working out the pretrial agreement, Judge Martin had invited the attorneys to call him if any further issues arose. He made it clear that legal motions and hearings were not necessary; he'd rather find ways to resolve any disputes quickly and amicably through conferences. Bullock got in touch with him about Pfizer's delay in producing the documents.

In a meeting with Martin, Pfizer's lawyer explained why the company didn't believe it should have to turn over any of its corporate correspondence: the company was not involved in eminent domain; the company was not pursuing eminent-domain actions; none of the land taken via eminent domain was for Pfizer; and the company wasn't involved in the dispute between the homeowners and the NLDC.

Bullock countered that it was obvious that Pfizer wasn't exercising eminent domain—that power was reserved to the government. But it was equally obvious that Pfizer played a major role in the city's redevelopment scheme. Therefore, those Pfizer documents were critical to Bullock. He knew that in any legal case, it was essential to establish a paper trail as it often would yield the most important evidence at trial.

Judge Martin agreed that Pfizer was a relevant party, and ruled that the company would have to comply with the subpoena. For its part, Pfizer insisted on a guarantee that the Institute for Justice wouldn't divulge its documents to anyone. The company's primary concern was the press. The institute had been very active with the media, and Pfizer didn't want its internal correspondence ending up in a press release. Bullock agreed to sign a confidentiality agreement.

Then, once he and Berliner had had a chance to review the Pfizer documents, Bullock wanted to depose an individual from the company. Pfizer's attorney balked at this request.

"Well, we're obviously going to have questions about these documents, and we'll need to talk to someone from Pfizer who can answer them," Bullock said.

It sounded reasonable to Judge Martin. But whom did the institute have in mind?

"Possibly George Milne," Bullock said.

Pfizer's attorney said the company would fight any attempt to produce George Milne for a deposition.

Without much push back from Bullock, Pfizer's lawyer supplied various reasons Milne was not an option. He was a very busy man. He had other commitments. The list went on.

It was clear that any attempt to get Milne under oath would cause Pfizer to draw a line in the sand. Judge Martin didn't want a protracted legal battle over whether Milne could be forced to testify. Bullock didn't either. But Bullock didn't want to back down until he first saw Pfizer's documents and was able to see where the paper trail led.

When word reached Milne that he might be called to be deposed, he was not eager to participate. "That's not a good use of my time," he said. The attorneys assured him that they'd present that argument, along with the fact that he had little to offer.

Milne had no plans to testify, but he held some strong opinions. He disagreed with the way the institute had framed its case. Pfizer, from his standpoint, was being unfairly associated with the NLDC and eminent domain, both by the institute and the media. Yet Milne maintained that the way Pfizer had done things had been nothing but proper; Pfizer had been a catalyst for improvement in New London.

"The Pfizer investment was pivotal in convincing the state to put a tremendous amount of money into New London," Milne later said. "I think we've been pretty clear that these other things had to happen in order for Pfizer to make the investment.

"The state's money was probably an important part of the engine," he continued. "It's a little hard to pull the two apart. In other words, if Pfizer hadn't agreed to make the investment, I'm not sure the state would have made the investment. I have no idea what would have happened at Fort Trumbull, but it certainly wouldn't be the beautiful place it is today if John Rowland and the state hadn't seen this as a showplace. Calamari Junkyard would still be there, and all the rest of that.

"Clearly, the Pfizer involvement was an initiating event."

Dave Goebel wasn't thrilled about the fact that his agency had to turn over documents to the institute. When Bullock arrived at the NLDC's office at a prearranged time to examine the files, Goebel, cold and stern, escorted him into a conference room containing a table lined with files and documents. Bullock pulled out colored note tabs to mark the documents he wanted copied. Goebel took a seat near him, his eyes focused on Bullock.

After an hour passed, Bullock realized Goebel had no intention of leaving the room. Rather than assign a staff person to observe Bullock, Goebel simply stayed. Bullock was long accustomed to being observed while reviewing records belonging to adversarial companies and agencies, but he had never seen a chief executive fill that role.

Going through one file, Bullock discovered a glossy, color architectural rendition of what the area might look like if the existing neighborhood were incorporated into the redevelopment plan. Goebel had momentarily left the room, replaced by another NLDC official.

"Do you know the origin of this?" Bullock asked the official, handing him the drawing. "Have you seen it before?"

A contemptuous smile flashed across the official's face. "Oh, yeah."

"I'd like a copy of it."

The official flung the drawing on the table and shrugged. "You can have it," he said. Bullock picked it up. After the official left the room, he inspected the drawing more carefully and recognized the name of the architect who had drawn it: John Steffian.

After two full days, Bullock had pored through boxes and boxes of files. He also had compiled a list of additional documents he had been unable to locate in the NLDC's records. He handed the list to Goebel, indicating he wanted the NLDC to produce them.

"What are you talking about?" Goebel asked, incredulous.

"Follow-up documents," Bullock said, unsure what had upset Goebel.

"What do you mean *follow-up* documents? You are only here for two days."

"Well," Bullock said, trying not to smile, "the discovery period extends out until the end of April. You have an ongoing obligation to produce these documents during that time period."

"I'll have to talk to the attorneys about that."

Bullock figured Goebel found his presence unnerving.

After Bullock's visit, Goebel e-mailed Corcoran Jennison president Marty Jones to stress the importance of finalizing the development agreement right away. "We [NLDC] . . . feel that concluding the development agreement prior to the start of the Institute lawsuit will go a long way to deflate the argument that property is being taken with no plan in place," he said. "In fact, we feel this is crucial."

After spending nearly two full days examining files at Pfizer's facility, Bullock hadn't turned up any corporate documents that proved that Pfizer was behind the NLDC's efforts to clear the Fort Trumbull area.

Then he came across two letters. The first one had been written by Claire to Milne on December 15, 1997, months before Pfizer announced its decision to build in New London: "Dear George: The directors of the New London Development Corporation are pleased to make the commitments outlined below to enable you to decide to construct a Pfizer Central Research facility in New London," she had written. "The new Pfizer facility will be the center-piece of a concentrated reuse of the area surrounding the former New London Mills."

The letter showed that the promises Claire outlined had been endorsed by Governor Rowland and had ultimately convinced Milne to recommend New London to Pfizer's board of directors. Among other things, Claire had promised a "mixed retail and residential space that will be fully integrated into the surrounding neighborhoods." She had closed her letter with a simple assurance to Milne: "We will work with you to refine this proposal to meet Pfizer's requirements."

The word "requirements" caught Bullock's attention. "Require-ments" has a different implication than "preferences" or "sugges-tions." A requirement is a demand.

The second letter was written by Milne to Claire on March 8, 1999, shortly after Pfizer had begun construction: "We are building a $270 million Global Development Facility [GDF] in New London to open October 1, 2000," he wrote. "This facility will employ more than 2,000 Ph.D.s, M.D.s and other scientists, researchers and clini-cal specialists. Our New London expansion requires the world class redevelopment planned for the adjacent 90 acres in the Fort Trum-bull Municipal Development Plan."

Again Bullock noted the word choice: "requires."

Milne was more explicit than Claire had been, making clear that the redevelopment of the ninety acres around the Pfizer fa-cility was part of the deal. Bullock read on: "The Fort Trumbull area is integral to our corporate facility and to the plan for the revitalization of New London to a world class standard," Milne had written. "The Amended Reuse Plan will provide a waterfront hotel with about 200 rooms, a conference center and physical fitness area, extended-stay residential units and 80 units of housing. We will use the proposed hotel and conference facility as an extension of our facility, committing to 100 of those rooms on a daily basis for visiting international staff and other professionals. In addition we require conference space and are exploring a 'virtual' Pfizer Uni-

versity to keep our researchers up to date on the most recent breakthroughs in biotechnology. The extended-stay housing will provide
for researchers who often stay for periods of up to 3–6 months. Year
round quality housing is also crucial for recruiting top scientists.
The waterfront residential neighborhood envisioned provides a
one-of-a-kind housing option desired by many of our employees."

Bullock's eyes lit up. On corporate letterhead, the president of
Pfizer had told the president of the NLDC that his company saw the
ninety acres around its facility as an extension of Pfizer's research-
and-development headquarters. Milne had committed Pfizer to
occupying one hundred rooms per day in the new hotel. He had
said Pfizer required more conference space outside the footprint of
its own facility. He needed extended-stay housing for visiting scientists and permanent high-end housing for full-time employees. The
specificity of the plan amazed Bullock. It was pretty clear, he concluded, why Pfizer wanted Susette and her neighbors to go away.

"We are prepared," Milne had written, "to enter into agreements with the NLDC and developers to build the type of facilities
we require, but this is not just about Pfizer. The plan developed by
the NLDC is intended to transform New London and is destined,
we believe, to become a model for high impact, high value public/
private partnerships."

For Bullock, the situation was very much about Pfizer. The company had made it a requirement that the state make certain commitments and do things a certain way before it would commit to
building a facility in the city.

When Bullock returned to Washington, he immediately took
Milne's letter to Berliner. "Look what we have here!" Bullock said.

Berliner read it. "This confirms our suspicions," she said. "Pfizer
is the driving force behind the municipal-development plan."

"This document takes it out of the realm of mere suggestion
and into the category of demands," Bullock said. "It wasn't just
Pfizer saying, 'Here's what we'd like and here are our thoughts.' It's
a document that says, 'These are our requirements.' Pfizer required
these things as part of the MDP."

"And all those requirements were put in the MDP," Berliner
said.

"That's right," Bullock said, grinning. "Pfizer was driving this and it was primarily for their private benefit, not the public benefit."

But Bullock and Berliner recognized it would be difficult to link eminent-domain abuse directly to Pfizer since the drug company had never obtained the private properties. That had never been the plan. After all, the company didn't want ownership or even possession of the surrounding neighborhood. It just wanted the area around its facility cleared and redeveloped, a process that would ultimately improve the value of its investment and benefit the company.

Bullock and Berliner began to understand the power and the convenience of the personal relationship between Milne and Claire. The arrangement simultaneously afforded Pfizer both control and cover. Ostensibly, whenever Claire pushed Pfizer's agenda, she was acting in the capacity of an agent for the City of New London, not for Pfizer. Legally, the distinction was critical.

"Pfizer was always one step removed from this process," Bullock said. "The takings were not for Pfizer."

"That's going to make it difficult for us to directly show a private benefit because Pfizer can claim: 'This isn't for Pfizer,'" Berliner said.

"That's right," said Bullock. "And if you accepted the fact that taxes and jobs are a legitimate public use, then of course the city is going to try and benefit Pfizer." He could hear Tom Londregan's defense already. "The city is going to say: 'Of course we did things to please Pfizer. What's good for Pfizer is good for New London.'"

Yet one thing was clear. With documents so clearly tying Milne to the Fort Trumbull development, it was no longer as critical to get him to testify. Bullock preferred to let the documents speak for themselves at trial, convinced that Milne would try to explain away their significance.

This aerial photo of the Fort Trumbull neighborhood was taken in early 2000, prior to the start of demolition by the NLDC. Parcel 4-A and Parcel 3 contain all of the plaintiffs' homes. At the time this photo was taken, the state was in the process of refurbishing Fort Trumbull (shown at the bottom) and converting it into a state park. The Naval Undersea Warfare Center (shown at the right) was still intact. (Photo by Sean D. Elliot, the *Day*, New London, Conn.)

Parcel 3
homes purchased
or taken

Naval Undersea
Warfare Center
prior to demolition

City wastewater
treatment facility

Parcel 4A
homes purchased
or taken

Fort Trumbull
State Park
under construction

Fort Trumbull

As a top aide to Governor John Rowland, Peter Ellef (pictured) hired New London lawyer Jay Levin to help the state redevelop the New London waterfront. (Photo by Skip Weisenburger, the *Day*, New London, Conn.)

While working for the Rowland administration, Jay Levin came up with the plan to use the NLDC as the state's development agent, and he recommended Claire Gaudiani to lead it. (Courtesy of the *Day*, New London, Conn.)

Governor John Rowland was instrumental in getting Claire Gaudiani named president of the NLDC, and he struck the deal with George Milne and Pfizer that promised $75 million in state incentives in exchange for Pfizer's commitment to build in New London. Claire (trailing), Rowland (left), and Milne (right) are seen here shortly after the three of them triumphantly announced their ambitious redevelopment plan. (Photo by Sean D. Elliot, the *Day*, New London, Conn.)

In 1997, Claire Gaudiani, then the president of Connecticut College, privately approached Pfizer executive George Milne and convinced him to join the NLDC's board of directors. Claire and Milne are seen here inspecting signatures on a steel beam during the Pfizer facility's construction. (Photo by Dana Jensen, the *Day*, New London, Conn.)

Raised in poverty by a single mother who was a waitress, Susette Kelo became a teenage mother and had five sons by her twenty-fifth birthday. (Courtesy of Susette Kelo)

After her sons were grown and she'd been through two failed marriages, Susette Kelo bought her first home of her own—a small cottage in the Fort Trumbull section of New London, depicted here. Five months after she moved in, Pfizer announced it would build its headquarters next door. (Painting by Thomas Jennerwein)

When the NLDC threatened to evict Susette Kelo from her home, she led a neighborhood revolt and became the lead plaintiff in a lawsuit against the city. Here she is seen being interviewed on the steps of the U.S. Supreme Court following the oral arguments. (Courtesy of the Institute for Justice)

Following the U.S. Supreme Court's 5–4 ruling against her and her neighbors, Susette Kelo emerged as a national spokesman against eminent domain. Here she is seen talking to the press after testifying before the U.S. Senate. (Courtesy of the Institute for Justice)

Susette Kelo and attorney Scott Bullock teamed up to lead a nationwide push to rewrite laws so they would better protect property owners. Susette and Bullock are seen together here at an anti-eminent-domain rally outside City Hall in New London. (Courtesy of the Institute for Justice)

Attorney Scott Bullock decided to represent the Fort Trumbull property owners after receiving a letter pleading for the Institute for Justice to help those facing condemnation orders. (Courtesy of the Institute for Justice)

Attorney Dana Berliner helped prepare the lawsuit against the City of New London that went all the way to the U.S. Supreme Court. (Courtesy of the Institute for Justice)

John Kramer crafted the media campaign against the City of New London's plan to seize homes by eminent domain. The city and the NLDC were constantly overwhelmed by the national media's relentless focus on their actions. (Courtesy of the Institute for Justice)

Chip Mellor co-founded the Institute for Justice and personally approved the decision to represent Susette Kelo and her neighbors. After losing the Supreme Court case, he spearheaded the public campaign to rewrite state laws to better protect private property owners. (Courtesy of the Institute for Justice)

Tony Basilica, chairman of the City of New London's Democratic Party, feuded with Claire Gaudiani and the Rowland administration over their plans to redevelop the city. (Photo by Dana Jensen, the *Day*, New London, Conn.)

John Markowicz worked alongside Tony Basilica on a committee responsible for figuring out what to do with the real estate that was formerly a navy base. He and Basilica were ultimately forced off the committee when they opposed the state's efforts to acquire the base property. (Courtesy of John Markowicz)

Admiral David Goebel ran the NLDC's day-to-day operations under Claire Gaudiani. (Photo by Skip Weisenburger, the *Day*, New London, Conn.)

After all Fort Trumbull homeowners learned they would lose their homes under the NLDC's development plan, this private men's club received a written assurance from influential lobbyist Jay Levin that its building would be spared. (Courtesy of Sylvia Malizia)

As the mayor of New London, Lloyd Beachy was the only city official who publicly opposed the use of eminent domain. When the NLDC demolished homes, he was arrested and carried off in handcuffs after standing in front of a bulldozer. (Courtesy of Lloyd Beachy)

Reid MacCluggage served as publisher of the *Day*, New London's daily newspaper, when the NLDC announced its plans to redevelop New London. His paper prevailed in a freedom-of-information suit brought against the agency. (Courtesy of Reid MacCluggage)

Stephen Percy served on the NLDC's board of directors and oversaw the agency's effort to acquire real estate in the Fort Trumbull area. (Photo by Dana Jensen, the *Day*, New London, Conn.)

Billy Von Winkle joined forces with Susette Kelo and fought the city's efforts to take his rental properties. (Courtesy of the Institute for Justice)

Connecticut College professor Fred Paxton publicly opposed Claire Gaudiani's efforts to redevelop Fort Trumbull. (Courtesy of Fred Paxton)

Judge Thomas Corradino presided over the trial in *Kelo v. City of New London* and issued a 249-page decision that favored some of the Fort Trumbull property owners. (Used with permission of the State of Connecticut, Judicial Branch, Copyright State of Connecticut, Judicial Branch)

New London City Attorney Tom Londregan fiercely defended the city's right to use eminent domain as a means to clear the Fort Trumbull area for redevelopment. (Courtesy of Tom Londregan)

One of the leading appellate attorneys in Connecticut, Wesley Horton was retained by the City of New London to argue its case before the U.S. Supreme Court. (Courtesy of Wesley Horton)

Houses along East Street in the Fort Trumbull neighborhood prior to the demolitions carried out by the NDLC. (Photo by Sylvia Malizia, courtesy of New London Landmarks)

The NLDC began aggressively demolishing homes along East Street in 2000.
(Courtesy of the Institute for Justice)

The East Street lots where homes once stood. Eight years after the NLDC began
razing the neighborhood, these building lots remain empty. (Photo by Sylvia
Malizia, courtesy of New London Landmarks)

Taken in 2002, after the plaintiffs filed suit against the City of New London, this aerial photo identifies the properties involved in the lawsuit. By this time, all the other homes in the neighborhood had been torn down by the NLDC, along with all but one building at the Naval Undersea Warfare Center. (Photo by Sean D. Elliot, the *Day*, New London, Conn.)

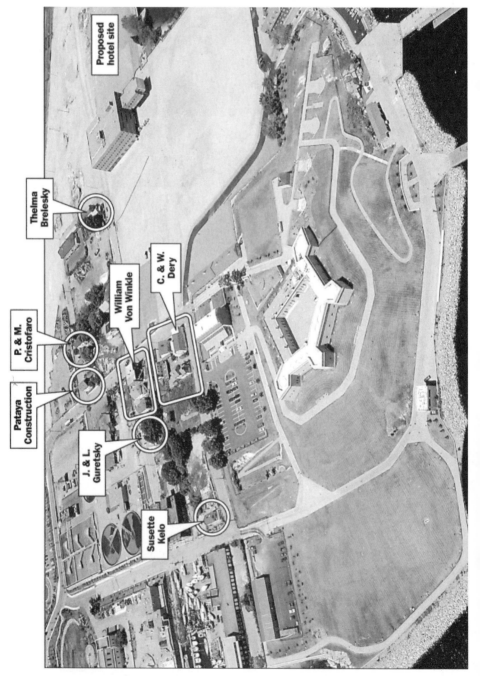

33

GO AHEAD, ASK YOUR QUESTION

June 8, 2001

G iven a choice, Governor Rowland would have stayed as far away from New London as possible. Lawsuits, protests, and nasty brawls playing out like a soap opera on the pages of the city newspaper were not the kinds of things a politician would gravitate toward in an election cycle. But on this day, the governor had to return to New London and its Fort Trumbull neighborhood. Eight months behind schedule, Pfizer was finally ready for the grand opening of its new research facility.

In a carefully crafted statement, Rowland praised Pfizer and lauded the state for its role in bringing the world-class operation to New London. He avoided any mention of the battle being waged by homeowners just one block away. Pfizer officials distanced themselves from the mess too.

For the day, the status quo prevailed. But the governor and Pfizer executives all knew the ticking time bomb next door was about to go off.

July 3, 2001

It was nearly eleven in the morning when Claire Gaudiani sat down in her lawyer's conference room, took an oath to tell the truth, and faced Dana Berliner and Scott Bullock. The two lawyers had decided Berliner would handle the questioning.

After reviewing the rules of a deposition, Berliner suggested they begin with some background on Claire's role as president of the NLDC. "What are your day-to-day responsibilities as president?" she asked.

"I don't have any day-to-day responsibilities," Claire said. "I am a volunteer president."

Berliner moved to Claire's early involvement in the plan to redevelop the Fort Trumbull area. "You were involved in putting together the initial proposal?" Berliner asked.

"You will have to clarify what you mean," Claire said.

"Were you involved in putting together the proposal for the redevelopment of the Fort Trumbull area that was then presented to the City of New London or to Pfizer or the state?"

"The problem is the wording. 'Proposal' is a nonspecific enough word. So you need to focus on what you are asking me so I can answer you."

Berliner knew she was in for a long day.

Claire explained that when she had taken over as the NLDC's president, she had made it a top priority to entice a *Fortune* 500 company to the city. "Pfizer was a wild and crazy possibility that I introduced early," Claire said, "saying, 'Wouldn't it be great if Pfizer would do that?' And I was told Pfizer needs land, but they have two sites already selected, and they are already under way with the decision between the two, so New London will not be considered . . . And then the magic happened."

Claire's word choice intrigued Berliner. Magic is the practice of attempting to produce supernatural effects or control events in nature through the use of charms, spells, or rituals, or the exercise of sleight of hand or conjuring for entertainment. A bilingual professor who frequently spoke to prestigious groups about language, Claire tended to choose her vocabulary carefully. But *Fortune* 500 companies typically bowed to money and other financial incentives, not magic, when making decisions as important as where to construct a world headquarters for research and development. Berliner probed further.

Claire confirmed that she had turned her energies toward getting Pfizer to change its mind. "We began to see what would need to be done in order to get a confirmation from Pfizer that they would turn down the other two sites," Claire said.

"Do you know at approximately what point in the plan it came to the decision that the existing homes and businesses would be moved?"

"I think your question assumes," said Claire, "that all of the properties would move. And that would be incorrect."

Claire's answer surprised Berliner. She asked if Claire interpreted the plan to say that homes and businesses in Fort Trumbull would be incorporated into the development.

Claire chastised Berliner for acting as if she didn't know that there had been extensive discussions about saving the homes in Fort Trumbull. "I worked very hard to try to raise the money to move them," she said. "Tried to get the governor to help me, but he wasn't able to work it out. It is very expensive to move houses."

This was news to Berliner and Bullock.

"You are saying that you attempted to get funding to move the houses of the plaintiffs in this lawsuit—and you weren't successful?" Berliner asked.

"Sure," Claire said. "I am sure you have come to that information before a discussion with me."

"Not exactly," Berliner said.

"If your own plaintiffs haven't told you, you have been misserved. It means you have been headed in, unfortunately, a misinformed direction. I am sure you probably do understand this."

"I have heard something about it," Berliner said. "Getting it from someone who knows all the facts is not the same as hearing about it generally."

"I don't operate at the facts level," Claire said. "I operate at the conceptual level."

Unable to maintain his poker face any longer, Bullock's jaw dropped.

It turned out, Claire insisted, that the cost of relocating the homes was simply prohibitive.

"So is it correct that the barrier to allowing the houses to stay in the MDP area is a financial one?" Berliner asked.

"I would have to characterize it as the major barrier."

Claire's story seemed to be coming out of left field. Nothing in the record supported her account, nor did any of the testimony from anyone previously deposed.

"When did you make these efforts to talk to the governor about getting funding?" Berliner asked.

Claire pointed to an e-mail with George Milne and a directive to "talk to the governor." "That is what we were trying to figure out," Claire said, "to get his advice on which of the state agencies might be able to figure out how to provide funds to move houses."

Bullock looked at the time. He had an appointment with a critical expert witness. Both sides agreed to recess briefly while Bullock and Berliner stepped outside. As soon as they were in private, they burst into laughter.

"This woman is unbelievable," Berliner said.

"She's even worse than what anybody had made her out to be," Bullock said. "She is one of the most insufferable people I've ever met. Her arrogance is breathtaking." Berliner agreed. "With her it is truly a parody of a condescending, elitist academic who knows better than anyone in the room," Bullock said, "and certainly better than the folks in Fort Trumbull."

Berliner still had a long way to go in the deposition. Bullock wished her well.

When the two sides resumed, Berliner asked the court reporter to mark a document as Gaudiani Exhibit 1. Then she handed the document to Claire to examine.

"This is a letter that you sent in March of 1998 to Susette Kelo, one of the property owners in the Fort Trumbull municipal-development-project area. Is that right?" she asked.

"Yes," said Claire.

The letter announced the NLDC's plans to purchase options on properties in the Fort Trumbull neighborhood, and it promised that Susette would not be suddenly forced to move from her property without notice.

"I notice that this letter doesn't mention the possibility of eminent domain. Why not?"

"I have no idea," Claire said.

"In the development stages of the Fort Trumbull concept, did you suggest that it would be necessary to have the power of eminent domain?"

"No."

"Who suggested that?"

"I have no idea."

"Had you ever heard about eminent domain before the Fort Trumbull municipal-development project?"

"I am sure I must have read about it in the newspaper," Claire said. "Not here, but in the *New York Times*."

Berliner had a series of questions about the content of the NLDC's municipal-development plan, including its specific mention of constructing a coast-guard museum on Parcel 2 in the Fort Trumbull neighborhood.

"I'm not aware of that," Claire said, "sorry."

Berliner had trouble understanding how Claire didn't know that the museum was pegged for Parcel 2; it was a major structure in the heart of the plan. "I will represent to you that that is what it said in the actual MDP," Berliner assured her.

"That the coast-guard museum was going to be there?" Claire asked.

"Yes," Berliner said.

"I didn't read the MDP," Claire said.

Berliner loved the answer. The biggest cheerleader for the MDP hadn't read it?

Berliner then asked about the NLDC's plans to construct a hotel and conference center.

Claire pointed out that there were a total of six proposals included in the development plan.

"Okay," Berliner said, unsure of Claire's point.

"I realize this was confusing for you all," Claire said. "Because

Scott was giving talks about taking homes for health clubs, which was drivel. He must have known that, or I assume he did."

"Well, I don't think this is the forum to resolve that issue."

Claire looked at Berliner. "It is probably better to ask me questions based on what I actually know."

Her condescending tone amused Berliner. "Have you been involved in any discussions about the need for office space in the Fort Trumbull MDP area?" she asked.

"Again, I am sorry, the question is misformed for me, the word 'need.'"

Berliner reviewed her notes. They contained questions about the NLDC's decision to exempt the Italian Dramatic Club from eminent domain. She began by referencing an e-mail from Steve Percy to Claire, which said, "We are not pushing Italian Dramatic Club."

"Was that news to you?" Berliner asked.

"I don't remember, my goodness," Claire said. "Sorry."

"Do you recall Jay Levin being involved in the issue of whether the Italian Dramatic Club should be relocated?"

"Yes."

"What do you recall about that?"

"I recall seeing on the wall of the IDC a letter that Jay wrote. I recall Jay at a meeting, I believe, at the IDC. He had many friends in IDC."

Berliner handed Claire a copy of Levin's letter to Aldo Valentini. "Is this the letter that you recall seeing in the IDC?"

"On the wall, yes."

"Did you personally have discussions with Mr. Levin about whether to relocate the IDC?"

"It is too broad a question. I just told you that he was at a meeting that I was at at the IDC, so you really need to relate. I don't understand the question."

"Who else was at the meeting?"

"Quite a crew of us," she said, mentioning Aldo Valentini and George Milne, among others.

"Who called the meeting?"

"I don't remember."

"Do you know if you suggested the meeting?"

"It would be unlikely that I would call a meeting at the IDC. Women go down at the basement level. So I would have been unlikely to call a meeting on their territory."

"What was the purpose of the meeting?"

"Given the letter that Jay had written, which none of us had seen, and having no idea why he wrote it or what he was even talking about in February, we needed to sit and say, 'Let's look at options to move.' And that's exactly what we did."

"Did you discuss with people in the government of the City of New London whether the IDC should be allowed to remain?"

"Your verb doesn't make it possible for me to answer the question," Claire said.

Claire's stubbornness impressed Berliner. She had never deposed anyone who had such an ego. While she tried to figure out what to ask next, Claire kept going. "The verb should . . . You want to know which verb, I guess?"

"Okay," Berliner said.

"'Allowed,'" Claire snapped.

Berliner started a new line of questioning before suddenly pausing to organize her train of thought.

"Go ahead," Claire interrupted. "Ask your question."

It occurred to Berliner that Claire got a kick out of trying to turn the tables on her. Berliner determined not to give her the satisfaction. "Did you discuss the IDC with George Milne?" she asked.

"Well, in order to invite him to the meeting," she said, "I am sure we were going to talk about the status of the IDC."

Berliner kept pressing.

"This was not a big deal," Claire insisted.

"It wasn't a big deal?"

"It just wasn't," Claire said. "It's not a residence, so it has a distinctive—it's just a different entity, and if it could stay and blend, fine. If it couldn't, they were willing to move and were even excited about it. They were going to get air-conditioning."

"Were you involved in getting Justice Santaniello involved in the issue of the IDC?"

"I don't actually remember who asked him to mediate."

Tired of Claire's way, Berliner turned up the heat. Earlier in the deposition, Claire had accused Bullock of deliberately misrepresenting facts about the NLDC's plans to build a health club on land that previously contained homes. "You seemed particularly concerned about the issue of where the health club was going to be and about what you believed to be misstatements about where it was going to be," Berliner said. "Why is that an issue of concern for you?"

"I think it is important to know what you are talking about," Claire said. "The IJ gave the erroneous impression that it is the plan of the NLDC to take poor people's homes for a health club, and that is incorrect, and I have to assume that Scott Bullock knew it to be incorrect."

Berliner asked Claire if she knew that in their answer to the lawsuit, the NLDC had admitted that a health club was going to be on a parcel that contained housing.

Claire had no idea about that.

"Did you know that the answer submitted by the NLDC admitted that the health club was going to be on Parcel 3?" Berliner repeated.

"No. I still don't know it."

"Well, you can check. But I will represent to you that that is true."

Claire didn't want to hear it. "This," she said, "I don't think, is material to what we are discussing."

Berliner cut her off: "I don't have any further questions at this time."

The court reporter noted the time: 3:15 p.m. Berliner and Claire parted without exchanging pleasantries.

Once Bullock and Berliner had deposed all the key players and parties, only one person remained: Jay Levin. As Berliner dialed his phone number on July 16, she wasn't sure whether to consider him a lobbyist for the Italian Dramatic Club, a consultant to Governor Rowland, or simply a fellow attorney. All she knew was that Levin had written a letter to the head of the IDC assuring him that his private club would be preserved. He insisted that everyone in state government—from the governor to the heads of state agencies—had an absolute understanding that the club "is not to be touched by anyone."

When Levin got on the line, Berliner introduced herself. Levin said he was very familiar with the case.

I bet you are, Berliner thought. She referred to Levin's letter to Aldo Valentini and said she wanted to get some more information about it. In particular, she wanted to know whom Levin had talked to in state government to secure the assurance that the state would exempt the IDC from being taken by the city.

Levin said he didn't remember whom he had talked to.

But the letter specifically said that even Governor Rowland knew not to touch the IDC. Very few people have the governor's ear, and even fewer people speak for him, Berliner said.

Levin insisted he spoke to a lot of people.

"We'd like to call you to testify," Berliner told him, and offered a date.

Levin had been the chief architect of the original idea to reactivate the NLDC. He had recommended Claire to lead it. And he had secured the exception for the Italian Dramatic Club. Simply put, he knew where the bodies were buried in this fight.

"I will be unavailable during that week," Levin told Berliner. "I am scheduled to undergo major surgery."

"What about testifying before the surgery?" Berliner asked.

"I am not in a condition to appear at trial because I will be heavily medicated in preparation for that surgery," Levin said.

Berliner pushed for a deposition from Levin; the Institute for Justice could arrange to interview him right away, she said.

"A deposition at this time would be very difficult for me," Levin said. Instead, he offered to submit an affidavit.

The next day, Berliner faxed Levin a letter. "As you know, getting an affidavit introduced in lieu of testimony is difficult," she told him, "but I will send a copy to the defendants in advance of trial and try to get an agreement from them to stipulate to its admissibility given the circumstances." She explained she would be issuing him a subpoena in order to demonstrate to the court a good-faith effort to obtain his live testimony.

She enclosed with her fax an affidavit for Levin to sign. It stated that he had spoken to representatives from state agencies about preserving the Italian Dramatic Club and that he had subsequently met with Gaudiani, Goebel, and Judge Angelo Santaniello at the IDC to argue that the club should not be torn down and that the solution he personally had suggested was the one that had been adopted by the NLDC.

July 19, 2001

After making some minor changes to his affidavit, Levin signed it and had it notarized before faxing it to Berliner, who forwarded it to Londregan with a request that he allow Levin's sworn statement to be introduced as evidence at the trial. Londregan told the institute to forget it.

"If you have a witness, put him on the stand," Londregan said. "We want to cross-examine him. That's the way it goes."

That afternoon, Berliner faxed a note to Levin. "To my dismay, the defendants are not willing to stipulate to your affidavit," she said. "I therefore write to see if it would be possible to take a short trial deposition." She offered to schedule it at a time and location of Levin's choice.

Levin balked. "I would appreciate not being subpoenaed for the deposition," he told Berliner. "As you know I am scheduled for surgery a week from today. I do appreciate your courtesy. I am taking a heavy pain medication and could not proceed in any way that I would be comfortable with."

A lawyer knows the weaknesses of his case better than anyone. Tom Londregan had a few problems to overcome. The biggest one had to do with delegation.

Under both the state and federal constitutions, the City of New London had legal authority to take private property for public use through eminent domain. One safeguard against excessive abuse of this power was that it was held by individuals—in this

case, members of the New London City Council—who were ultimately answerable to voters. But the city council had delegated
the power of eminent domain to the NLDC, a private agency
whose key members had been handpicked by a lobbyist and consultant on contract with the governor's administration. There was
no way around the fact that the city had given the power to take
people's homes to an exclusive group of individuals who were not
answerable or accountable to the public.

Another obstacle Londregan faced had to do with timing.
The NLDC had started the process of acquiring private properties well before it had a preliminary plan, much less a publicly
approved final plan, for what to do with the land.

Yet Londregan still felt he would prevail. The fact that the
city's municipal-development plan included new utilities, roads,
and infrastructure to the Fort Trumbull area—all public benefits—
seemed to bode well for the city. The argument was that Connecticut law didn't allow a couple of holdouts to stop an entire
city from carrying out a comprehensive development plan that
was designed to generate badly needed tax revenue and jobs. The
law did afford people just compensation and fair market value for
their properties—all of which had been flatly rejected by Susette
and her neighbors.

Londregan didn't even take depositions from the plaintiffs.
Why bother? He knew what they were going to give him on the
witness stand: emotionally charged sob stories about being forced
out of their homes against their wills.

Even his own mother couldn't influence his thinking about
the case. She had tried, on account of the Londregan family's
rich historic ties to the Fort Trumbull neighborhood. Half Sicil-
ian and half Irish, Tom had had a grandfather—Timothy Andrew
Lonergan—who was the fourteenth of fifteen children. After five
of Timothy's older brothers immigrated to America and got jobs
with the railroad in New London, he changed his last name to
Londregan out of fear the company wouldn't hire six brothers
from the same family. He got hired by the railroad and settled in
Fort Trumbull around the turn of the century.

Eventually, Timothy Londregan's house was taken by eminent

domain to make way for railroad expansion. Londregan built a new home on Goshen Street, within a block of some of the homes now involved in the lawsuit. Tom's father, who died in 1965, had been raised in the Goshen Street house. The NLDC tore down the second Londregan home to make way for the redevelopment project.

Londregan's mother, who was in her nineties, didn't appreciate Tom's decision to defend the city and the NLDC's actions. "You really shouldn't win this case," she flatly told her son.

"Mom, I'm doing a job for my client," he responded.

Yet it was more than a job for Londregan. His legal position was that cities had to have the right to exercise eminent domain in order to survive. Urban centers took care of the poor and disadvantaged. They had low-income housing, Section 8 housing, affordable housing, senior housing, along with mental-health clinics, homeless shelters, and social programs. And in New London's case, a lot of real estate was tied up by nonprofit organizations, government entities and other buildings that were tax-exempt. Eminent domain gave cities a chance to compete with suburbia. "It's the great equalizer," he said. "We don't have large tracts of land. Urban centers are cut up into little parcels. Where do we acquire large parcels of land to attract large economic engines to enable us to compete with suburbia? We can only get it through eminent domain."

The law might be cold, but Londregan believed it was also clear: the city had the right to use eminent domain to carry out an economic-development plan that benefited the entire city.

34

LIFE IS SHORT

July 23, 2001

First it was calling up the mayor. Then it was speaking at a neighborhood forum. Next Susette had had to speak at a citywide hearing at the high school gymnasium, followed by a speech to the press from her front porch. Each time the audiences, venues, and circumstances seemed to take on more and more significance. But speaking in public never got any easier. Crowds and cameras didn't fit in Susette's comfort zone.

Even worse, nothing, she imagined, could be more serious than testifying under oath in a courtroom. Her stomach in knots, she skipped breakfast and dressed for the trial, dismissing all of Bullock's repeated assurances that she would do just fine. That was easy for him to say—he was in front of judges all the time. Susette had never testified under oath.

Alone, she drove two miles to the courthouse, arriving just in time for a press conference outside that Kramer had arranged. Susette spotted many of her neighborhood supporters, including Mitchell, the Hallquists, Fred Paxton, and the other coalition members. The sight of so many close friends who had once been strangers when she moved to Fort Trumbull gave her courage.

With the other plaintiffs, she followed Bullock to a microphone as he revved up the small crowd. "We look forward to presenting our case," Bullock told the press. "We look forward to the property owners having their day in court. We are ready!"

Londregan didn't like what he saw. "I was taught in law school to take my papers and file them in the courthouse," he said. "There are lawyers who file their papers with the newspaper first, then the court."

Inside, Judge Thomas J. Corradino reviewed some last-minute paperwork in his chambers. Corradino didn't reside in New London, and unlike most of the judges assigned to the New London District Court, he was a circuit trial judge, bouncing from one judicial district to another every four years. He figured this had something to do with why Judge Martin had assigned the *Kelo* case to him—he had no ties to the city. And from the city's perspective, this was a very big case. All the pretrial publicity had made that abundantly clear.

But to Corradino, every case was big and important to the people involved. He planned to approach this trial just like any other. The son of Italian immigrants, Corradino had been born and raised in the New Haven area, attending Catholic schools until entering college at Yale and then continuing on to Harvard Law School. By the time he obtained his law degree, in the late sixties, he had heard about a new nonprofit agency called the New Haven Legal Assistance Corporation, which was dedicated exclusively to providing legal assistance to the poor. Corradino moved back home and started working for the agency in 1967, defending poor people in criminal-defense matters. He liked it so much he stayed, turning down many opportunities to earn more money at top firms. By the time he got appointed to the bench, in 1986, he had spent eighteen years as a trial lawyer for people who couldn't afford legal representation.

As a judge, he spent most of his time presiding over criminal trials. He then started presiding over civil trials, in 1993. In preparation for the *Kelo* trial, he carefully studied the arguments raised in pretrial filings by the property owners and the city. He had never handled an eminent-domain case, and the issues were unlike any he had previously encountered in his thirty-three-year legal career. Since the entire case rested on the interpretation of state statutes and constitutional rights, there would be no jury. Judges ruled on matters of law; juries heard factual disputes. Ultimately, it would fall to Corradino to decide whether the plaintiffs got to keep their homes or not.

Everyone stood when Corradino entered the courtroom, wearing his trademark bifocals, and took his place behind the bench at ten minutes to ten. Short and slightly overweight with black hair that was turning gray, he resembled the late Italian actor Vincent Gardenia.

"Good morning," he said. "This is the case of *Susette Kelo v. the City of New London.* Could the lawyers identify themselves? That may be a lengthy process in this case."

The audience appreciated his dry humor as eight lawyers stood up: Bullock, Berliner, and Sawyer for the property owners; Londregan for the city; and four lawyers for the NLDC. After some preliminary administrative matters with the attorneys, Corradino asked for opening statements.

"Good morning, Your Honor," Bullock said. "This case is about the abuse of government eminent-domain power. Eminent domain is the ability to throw individuals off their land and out of their homes."

Seated beside Matt Dery and his family, Susette couldn't help feeling intimidated by the formality of the proceedings. She had trouble concentrating as Bullock outlined the two restrictions placed on eminent domain by the Framers: just compensation and the requirement that private land can be taken only for public use.

"In this case the evidence will show that the defendants have exceeded those constitutional limits with potentially a devastating effect on families who live in the historic Fort Trumbull neighborhood," Bullock continued. "In this case we're not really talking about the City of New London because . . . the government who rightfully exercises eminent-domain authority has delegated this power to private parties for primarily private gain. For instance, the proposed future use of the land in the municipal-development plan was determined largely by a private company, Pfizer, to complement the building of their new facility."

Bullock insisted his clients didn't oppose development; they opposed being forced out of their homes by an agency that couldn't even specify what it planned to do with their land.

He wrapped up with a nod to a past Supreme Court justice. "Your Honor, just as Potter Stewart once tellingly observed, property does not have rights, only people do. And while we are debating the finer points of constitutional law in Connecticut, it is important not to forget that there are real people whose lives and livelihood are at stake in this matter, and we will be hearing from them very soon."

Londregan rose and got right to the point. "Your Honor, simply stated the City of New London followed state statutes," he said with some swagger. "What the plaintiffs are really asking this court to do is to design and adopt a different plan than that which was approved by the legislative body of the City of New London."

He argued that the law authorized the city to delegate the power of eminent domain to an agency like the NLDC. And the law didn't require the private land acquired by the city to be used for a public purpose. "There's a specific statute that allows economic development," he said. "And it's not for public end use. It's for a private end use."

In addition, Londregan pointed out that the NLDC had spent $73 million in state money to upgrade the roads, sewers, streetlights, and underground utilities in and around the Fort Trumbull area—all of which resulted in public benefits. He urged the judge to focus narrowly on the development plan. "When the court focuses in on the plan," Londregan said, "and the decision that was made by the legislative body, I'm confident that this court will find that it was reasonably necessary to take the plaintiffs' property. Thank you."

Bullock called Matt Dery to testify first, getting him to explain that his ancestors had come from Italy and had purchased their first home on Walbach Street in 1901. Bullock displayed a photograph of the house.

"Is that still standing?" Bullock asked.

"Yes, it is."

"Is it one of the properties that the city and municipal-development plan seeks from eminent domain in this case?"

"Yes, it is."

"Who lives in this house right now?"

"My parents live there."

"How long has your father lived in that house?"

"He has lived there since he married my mother, fifty-six years."

"And how old is your father now?"

"He'll be eighty-two next month."

"And how long has your mother lived in the house on Walbach Street?"

"She was born in that house in 1918. She lives there currently. And she's never lived anywhere else. That's eighty-three years."

"Your mother has never lived anywhere else?"

"Never. It's her only home."

Dery lived next door to his parents. Bullock asked how he and his parents had learned that the NLDC wanted their homes.

First, Dery said, a real-estate agent approached. When the Dery family declined the offer, the agent said the properties would be taken by eminent domain. Eventually, a sheriff showed up at the door and served them with condemnation papers.

With the judge's permission, Bullock handed Dery a document. "Who is that letter from?"

"David M. Goebel," said Dery, indicating it was a notice telling the Derys to vacate their homes.

"And what, if anything, else does NLDC tell you in that letter?"

"It informs us that we are to make occupancy payments in the amount of $450 per month for the remainder of our stay in the property."

Bullock asked Dery if his parents had a mortgage on their home.

"No. They've been mortgage-free since 1958."

Winding down, Bullock asked Dery why he and his family didn't want to leave the neighborhood, despite the fact that the NLDC had already demolished most of the old homes and buildings.

"It's home to us," he said. "It's home to my parents and my family for a hundred years. Simply put, there is nowhere else I would rather be. My mother has lived there her entire life. She's eighty-three years old. I know she wants to die in that house. I don't think that's asking too much."

Londregan kept his cross-examination brief, focusing almost exclusively on the fact that the Dery buildings went right to the edge of the sidewalk and would be in the way if the city tried to widen the streets to accommodate the new development. Dery agreed but pointed out that the opposite side of the street had no buildings and offered plenty of room for road widening.

The judge thanked Dery for his testimony, and Susette took the stand.

"My name is Susette Kelo, K-e-l-o. I live at 8 East Street, New London, Connecticut," she said.

Under questioning from Bullock, she told the court when she had bought the property and what she had done to improve it.

"Has anyone in the past four years tried to buy your property?"

"Yes, sir, they have."

"Who is that?"

"It would be Suzanne Howard from U.S. Properties."

"Did the subject of eminent domain ever come up during those discussions?"

"Yes. At the first meeting she told me my property would be taken by eminent domain if I didn't sell to her."

Recounting the incident made Susette angry. Suddenly her fears vanished.

"How did you learn that the eminent-domain lawsuit was filed against you?"

"The paperwork was taped to the door of my house when I came home from work."

The more Bullock questioned her, the angrier she became.

"Did the NLDC tell you you had to vacate your house at a particular time?"

"They said I had to move out of my home by March 9th of the year 2001."

"Did they tell you anything about paying an occupancy fee?"

"They said I was going to be required to pay them rent."

When she learned that the Italian men's club would be allowed to stay, Susette testified, she wrote a letter requesting the same treatment. "They said I couldn't stay," she said.

"Who said that?" Bullock asked.

"David Goebel," she testified. "I asked if NLDC was going to do anything to help us keep our homes, and he said absolutely not."

"Do you have any homes between yourself and the Dery property?"

"No, sir, we do not."

"What happened to those homes?"

"They tore them all down."

Bullock asked if she would welcome new houses to replace the demolished ones. She said she would, along with new businesses, parking lots, a museum, and just about anything else the city wanted to build, as long as she could keep her home.

"What, if anything, Mrs. Kelo, finally, do you want to get out of this lawsuit?"

"I just want to be left alone, be able to come home and relax and just be left alone."

Londregan didn't challenge anything Susette said.

Like any trial lawyer, Bullock didn't want any surprise testimony from his witnesses. He also didn't want any angry outbursts. He and Berliner had carefully drilled the homeowners on the need to stick to the facts and to exercise restraint when being cross-examined by the opposing attorneys.

Bullock wasn't too worried. His clients were so nervous about testifying that they were unlikely to lash out. But Billy Von Winkle was the wild card in the bunch. Besides being unpredictable and prone to playing the practical joker, Von Winkle had some personal history with the NLDC's lead attorney, Ed O'Connell, whose firm had established a trust for Von Winkle. Shortly after the trust was set up, O'Connell's firm notified Von Winkle that it could no longer represent him. Von Winkle had never understood why until the night he dug through the NLDC's Dumpster and discovered the original retainer contract signed by O'Connell's law firm and the NLDC. From that moment on, Von Winkle had no love lost for O'Connell and his partners.

Bullock expected O'Connell to challenge Von Winkle aggressively under cross-examination. To prepare him, Bullock had played the role of O'Connell and attacked Von Winkle in a dress rehearsal the night before the trial. In the rehearsal, the tougher Bullock got, the more Von Winkle played around.

"Bill, c'mon," Bullock said at one point, stopping the role-playing. "Listen, you can't do this at the trial tomorrow. We have to act like this is the trial right now. We've got to temporarily turn off the jokes because it is only going to help them. It's not going to help you."

As Von Winkle made his way to the stand in the real trial, Bullock hoped his message from the previous night had gotten through.

"Good afternoon, Mr. Von Winkle," he said.

"Good afternoon, Mr. Bullock."

After a series of factual questions about how many properties he owned in the fort area and how long he had owned them, Bullock asked Von Winkle how much work and money he had invested in his buildings. In all, he had spent seventeen years upgrading his buildings with his own hands, Von Winkle said. He had replaced everything from the roofing and basement floors to the plumbing and electrical wiring. Using his own money, he had even replaced the broken city sidewalks outside his buildings. Von Winkle's direct examination went smoothly.

O'Connell hoped to get him off track. He had carefully scrutinized the deeds to Von Winkle's buildings and discovered a discrepancy that he planned to spring on him.

"I just want to clear up some minor matters," O'Connell began. "The deeds regarding these properties describe you by various middle initials."

Von Winkle hadn't anticipated questions about his deeds.

"For example," O'Connell said, "35 Smith Street describes you as William A. Von Winkle. Is that you?"

"No, it's not."

"It's not?"

"No."

Confused, Judge Corradino looked over his glasses at Von Winkle. Bullock was confused too.

O'Connell continued. "The deed to 31 Smith Street describes a person named William M. Von Winkle," he said. "Is that you?"

"Yes, it is."

O'Connell read the deed to the third building owned by Von Winkle and noted that it, like the first deed, assigned ownership to William A. Von Winkle. "That's not you?" O'Connell asked.

"No."

"Who is that?"

"That would be my father."

"So you own only one of these three buildings. Is that correct?"

Judge Corradino shifted his eyes from O'Connell to Von Winkle. Bullock leaned over to his co-counsel. "Where's he going with this?" he whispered.

Von Winkle didn't know where O'Connell was headed either. But he figured that any confusion over the names on the deeds had been caused by O'Connell's own law firm when it set up the trust. He couldn't swallow the fact that O'Connell had the nerve to try to use this confusion to undermine his standing in front of the judge. Von Winkle had promised Bullock he'd behave on the stand. But he also felt the judge should know O'Connell's role in the mix-up.

"Well," he said, looking at O'Connell with contempt, "your office set up a trust, which, if you went back, you could find it. You'll know exactly who the owner is. That was done three years ago."

Corradino lowered his glasses. Susette and others in the courtroom laughed. Bullock raised his eyebrows and put his hand in front of his face to conceal his smile. But O'Connell didn't appreciate Von Winkle's response.

"Well, if you can answer my question," O'Connell said. "Is it correct that you only own one—"

"Well—" Von Winkle interrupted him.

Corradino cut off Von Winkle. "Wait until he finishes the question."

"What's that, sir?" Von Winkle asked O'Connell.

"That you only own one building, known as 31 Smith Street. Is that correct?"

"I'm not sure who owns anything."

O'Connell didn't know what to do next. "You're not sure whether you own these buildings at all?"

"Well, I believe I own them. I'm not sure."

"Do you collect the rents?"

"Yes, I do."

"Do you turn the rents over to anyone else?"

"No."

"Yet you're not sure that you own the buildings. Is that correct?"

"I'm not sure how you set things up for me, sir, in your office."

Bullock had to laugh. As much as he didn't want Von Winkle to square off with O'Connell, he took some pleasure in seeing his client turn the tables on his adversary.

"I don't think I have any more questions," O'Connell said.

Londregan knew Von Winkle's reputation well. He had no intention of challenging him. That would be like picking a fight with a porcupine: even if you won you got pricked. Rather, Londregan planned a more nonconfrontational approach. He simply wanted to make the point that one of Von Winkle's buildings was so close to the street that it didn't conform to current zoning regulations. And any attempts to widen the road to accommodate increased traffic would conflict with the location of his building, therefore justifying its removal.

"Mr. Von Winkle, how are you?"

"Not bad," he said.

"Do you agree with the opening statement of your attorney

that you're not opposed to the implementation of the municipal-development plan so long as it doesn't take your property?"

"Right, so long as it doesn't take my property."

Londregan directed him to a photograph of his brick building. "Looking at the bottom left-hand corner, am I correct that the foundation of this building comes to the edge of the sidewalk there?"

"Yes, it does," Von Winkle said.

"Do you happen to know about how wide that sidewalk is?"

"Since I paid for it, I should," Von Winkle said, to laughter from the spectators. "Six and a half feet."

"Is it fair to say that the foundation of that building comes right to the edge of the sidewalk?"

"Yes. Six and a half feet to the street."

Londregan had gotten what he wanted.

"Your Honor, I have nothing further."

By the end of the first day, each of the property owners had testified. Bullock and Berliner couldn't have scripted a better start. All of the plaintiffs had said they would not oppose the city's development plan as long as they could keep their homes. And all of them offered compelling testimony about the NLDC's bullying tactics and hostile treatment.

Over the next couple of days, NLDC officials testified that the agency had in fact made changes and modifications to the development plan, including exceptions that allowed some existing buildings to remain, such as the Italian Dramatic Club. The point was clear: although the NLDC wanted a ninety-acre footprint for redevelopment, it wasn't essential for the agency to acquire every parcel of real estate within that footprint to achieve its goals.

Anticipating that Claire would be their most difficult witness, Bullock and Berliner scheduled her toward the end of the NLDC's slate. Accompanied by her college-age son, she entered the courtroom and made her way to the witness stand.

Accustomed to a certain degree of deference, Claire got none from Corradino. He seemed to know little if anything about her or her reputation. Earlier in the trial, he had repeatedly referred to her as "this lady," prompting Londregan to eventually point out that Claire was the president of the NLDC, among other things. To Corradino, she was just another witness.

To Berliner and Bullock, she was the worst kind of bully, disguising her heavy-handed tactics as goodwill for the poor. After her experience taking Claire's deposition, Berliner had compiled an array of questions designed to hem Claire in with yes or no answers.

From the start of her testimony, Claire looked and sounded less certain and less ornery than she had in her deposition. Yet she still managed to turn her answers into commentaries about the loftiness of the NLDC's objectives and the complexity of its work. After one particularly long and evasive answer, Berliner zeroed in.

"Was the answer to my question yes?"

Remaining evasive, Claire continued to lecture.

Corradino had heard enough. "Okay," he said, interrupting Claire, "why don't we do this? Realizing that life is short, when you're asked a question, if you can answer a yes or no, answer yes or no."

Berliner repeated her question to Claire. "So the final answer to my question was yes?"

"I did already say that, yes," Claire said. "I just said it at the end instead of the beginning. That's the way French logic goes. I'm sorry. I will try to use Anglo-American logic."

Berliner asked her about a specific date in the process for producing a development plan.

"What's the relevance of the date?" Claire responded.

Corradino looked at Claire. "You can't object on relevance," he informed her. "They're the ones that object. You try to answer the question."

From the gallery, Kathleen Mitchell couldn't believe what she was thinking and feeling—sympathy for Claire. For three years Claire had been the face of the enemy in Fort Trumbull. Mitchell had spent that entire time trying to bloody that face with a relentless assault through words, slogans, and protests. Through it all she had seen Claire one way: as a cold, calculating power broker. But suddenly, Claire was in an inferior position. Instead of being in charge, she had been forced into a defensive posture, like a pampered house pet being dropped suddenly into a jungle. A lawyer was badgering her, and a judge was telling her what she could and couldn't say. Mitchell almost didn't recognize Claire.

The trial, in many respects, was Claire's swan song. Already gone from Connecticut College, Claire's days as president of the NLDC were now numbered, too. She didn't plan to seek reappointment, and the agency would soon name a new president. A lot had changed since Claire had stood shoulder to shoulder with Governor Rowland and George Milne while leading city officials down the Thames River on a cruise ship to kick off the revitalization of New London.

After Berliner finished with Claire, it fell to Londregan to restore her credibility. It was a strange role reversal. He had never cared for Claire's style, and she'd never cared for his. They had fought bitterly from the early stages of the project. But the lawsuit had given them a common adversary, and now they needed each other.

Berliner and Bullock had characterized Claire and the NLDC as an iron-handed group that ran roughshod over powerless homeowners. Londregan asked leading questions that stressed the agency's strict adherence to a lengthy and complicated governmental process. With little emotion, Claire gave simple yes or no answers. Her only intention in all of this, she testified, was to help turn New London around.

Mitchell glanced across the aisle at Claire's son, intensely watching his mother defend herself. Mitchell had never thought of Claire as a mother. Bruising political fights tended to obscure the fact that the people on the other side were human beings.

When Claire stepped down from the stand, the judge declared a brief recess. Mitchell made her way over to Claire's son and introduced herself. "I feel really bad," Mitchell told him. "Through this whole thing I've made some real unkind references to your mother. I think it's real kind of you to be here."

"I love her," the boy said. "It's been tough for her. I wanted to be here for her."

Mitchell turned and walked away. She didn't see anyone else in the courtroom for Claire.

The national media wasted no time making up its mind about who had the better argument inside the courtroom. In an editorial, the *Wall Street Journal* jumped on the city and Claire for running people out of their homes to make way for a hotel and upscale housing. "Claire Gaudiani justifies the project by saying, 'Anything that's working in our great nation is working because somebody left skin on the sidewalk,'" the *Journal* said. "That kind of thinking quickly leads to government officials acting like bullies rather than servants."

The *Boston Globe* called the NLDC "ruthless" and blasted the city for allowing the agency to abuse the public use clause of the Fifth Amendment. "Is that how the power of eminent domain is supposed to be used?" wrote the *Globe*'s Jeff Jacoby, "to expel families from their homes for the sake of expanding the tax base?"

Londregan and O'Connell didn't like the pounding they were taking from the press. They resented the Institute for Justice for choosing to execute a relentless media campaign rather than limiting its efforts to what went on inside the courtroom.

Judge Corradino paid no attention to what the newspapers said. He didn't care about local politics, personalities, or press coverage. He had one thing on his mind: interpreting the law correctly. He knew one thing: no matter which way he ruled, his decision would probably be appealed.

With that in mind, he determined to write an exhaustive decision, leaving no questions about his reasoning. He dispatched his law clerk to compile approximately ninety previous cases with any relevance to the facts in the *Kelo* case. He took these cases and all the briefs and trial-testimony transcripts from his case to the law library at the New Haven courthouse, where he studied them. It all seemed to boil down to two questions: Did the taking of private property for economic development qualify as a public use? And if it did, was it reasonably necessary for the city to take the plaintiffs' land to accomplish its development goals?

For the first question, Corradino had to examine the Connecticut law and apply the statute to the facts in this case.

For the second question, he relied on expert-witness testimony. The testimony of one expert, Dr. John Mullin, particularly intrigued Corradino. A professor specializing in economic development and urban planning at the University of Massachusetts at Amherst, as well as a Fulbright Scholar and a fellow of the American Institute of Certified Planners, Mullin had been retained by the Institute for Justice to analyze New London's municipal-development plan. Besides publishing more than one hundred articles on planning and development, Mullin had some specific expertise in the redevelopment of old industrial communities in waterfront areas of New England.

In his testimony, Mullin masterfully cut through the NLDC's cumbersome municipal-development plan, reducing it to the essential facts. The plan divided the ninety acres into seven parcels. Only two of the parcels, 3 and 4-A, had homes remaining within them. The plan called for office space and parking facilities on Parcel 3. The four properties within Parcel 3 that belonged to the plaintiffs amounted to less than one acre.

The rest of the properties in the lawsuit—Susette's, Von Winkle's, and the Dery homes—were in Parcel 4-A. The development plan had no specific plans for Parcel 4-A.

Combined, the plaintiffs' properties amounted to less than 2 percent of the ninety-acre footprint of the NLDC's development area. Yet the agency had consistently insisted that it had to obtain and clear every inch in order for its plan to work.

During the trial, Bullock had asked Mullin, "Is it common for land to be entirely cleared for new development?"

"It's very uncommon," Mullin said. "Over the last ten years in New England, I can only remember one instance where this took place, which was Bridgeport, where there is a large degree of housing that was abandoned and where there was a large degree of chemical contamination that caused this to happen. But other than that I can't point to a single large clearance project anywhere in New England." Mullin had based his opinion on over one hundred redevelopment projects he had worked on or studied.

Then Bullock asked him, "Are existing structures, based on your experience with urban waterfront, commonly kept in those areas where new development is undertaken?"

"Increasingly, yes, they are," Mullin testified.

When Bullock asked him if it was necessary to take the four homes on Parcel 3 in order to achieve the development's objectives for that parcel, he said no; the homes could be easily included in the plan. Regarding Parcel 4-A where Susette's house sat, Mullin said the NLDC's plan called for that parcel to be used for "park support." Mullin had never heard that term before, but assumed it referred to parking space for the upgraded state park.

When Londregan and O'Connell had their chance to cross-examine Mullin, they could not turn up anything to contradict or undermine what he had said.

Corradino couldn't ignore Mullin's points. But at the same time, he couldn't ignore a point Londregan had made over and over again. Nearly 50 percent of New London's land base was not on the tax rolls. Only one city in New England—Boston—had more tax-exempt land. But Boston was more than ten times bigger than New London. Without the ability to assemble large tracts of land for economic development, New London was doomed.

His research complete, Corradino retired to his home to pen his decision.

35

SPLITTING THE BABY

March 13, 2002

It was late in the afternoon when Tom Londregan got a call from the courthouse informing him that Judge Corradino had issued his decision and planned to release it the following morning. The clerk invited Londregan to come in that afternoon to receive an advance copy.

Scott Sawyer got the same message. He immediately telephoned Bullock in Washington. Bullock told Sawyer to call him the minute he got his hands on it.

As soon as the courthouse officially closed, Londregan, Sawyer, and Ed O'Connell filed into Judge Martin's chambers. A big cardboard box containing copies of the 249-page decision rested on the desk. "Judge Corradino has given his decision," Judge Martin said, inviting the lawyers to take copies.

"How many do you need, Scott?" Martin asked.

Sawyer asked for three.

"Some of the plaintiffs are going to like it; Kelo will like it. Von Winkle will like it," Martin said. "But Beyer and a couple of others aren't going to like it."

The lawyers knew what that meant—a split decision.

"He split the baby?" Londregan blurted out, dumbfounded.

"He found a way to split the baby," Martin said.

"I gotta read this," Londregan said, flipping through the pages.

"Can I go now?" Sawyer asked.

Martin nodded, and Sawyer hustled out the door.

Londregan kept reading. Corradino had accepted a major part of Londregan's argument—the city's municipal-development plan constituted a public use. However, Corradino concluded that the NLDC had failed to specify its intended use for any of the properties in Parcel 4-A, where Susette and Von Winkle and Dery had their homes. Without a specific use put forth, those parcels could not be taken by eminent domain.

The fact that part of Susette's house stood in the way of a public road that the city wanted to build didn't matter; nor did the fact that the road would be used to get people to a public park. "I lost my best argument," Londregan complained. "The Kelo house is in the roadbed. Her house is in the fifty-foot right-of-way. How could I lose that argument?"

Corradino ignored the right-of-way issue, concluding the city could make road changes without taking homes. He focused instead on the fact that the city had failed to specify what it planned to do with all the land beneath Susette's house and all the other houses on her block. This went to the heart of the matter for Corradino: was it reasonably necessary for the city to take these homes? Not if the city could accomplish its objectives while leaving the homes intact. In the case of Parcel 4-A, the city had failed to say why it was so vital to have those lots.

But the plaintiffs didn't win every argument. Corradino ruled that the city could, in fact, use eminent domain to take the properties of Rich Beyer, Byron Athenian, and the Cristofaro family on Parcel 3. NLDC's plan for that parcel was quite specific and under Connecticut law was justified, the judge determined.

"Ed," Londregan said to O'Connell, "we followed the law. And they haven't said we haven't followed the law. But Judge Corradino found a way to split the baby."

With his decision, Judge Corradino also ordered a halt on all demolitions pending any appeals. The project, for all intents and purposes, was now at a standstill.

*　　*　　*

When he was a block from the courthouse, Scott Sawyer pulled his car to the side of the road and called Bullock to tell him he had the decision.

"Read it to me," Bullock said.

Sawyer cut to the conclusion, reading off the winners and losers. Before Sawyer finished, Bullock had done the numbers: eleven of the fifteen eminent-domain actions had been declared unconstitutional and unlawful, meaning the deeds would revert to the homeowners, who were now entitled to remain on their properties. Even the property owners who had lost, Rich Beyer (who owned two of the disputed properties), Byron Athenian, and the Cristofaro family, were entitled to hold on to their properties free from any fear of eviction or demolition until all appeals were exhausted. Any way you looked at it, Bullock figured, the plaintiffs had won.

Bullock called Susette. "The decision came down," he told her. "And it came out favorably for you and Bill and the Derys."

"You mean we won?" Susette shouted. Unaccustomed to winning, she couldn't believe it was true. "This means I get to keep my house?"

Bullock chuckled and tried to calm her down. Yes, you can stay in your house, he told her. Then he gave her the bad news. "The decision was not favorable for Rich and Byron and the Cristofaros."

Susette didn't get it.

"The East Street–Walbach block won," he explained. "Byron's block lost. In other words, you won, and Byron, Cristofaro, and Rich Beyer lost."

After Susette hung up, she shared the news with Tim LeBlanc, who had just gotten home from work. By now they had been living together in Susette's house for almost three years, wondering the entire time whether they'd get to stay there. Although not married, they might as well have been. They shared expenses; they shared property; and they shared a bed. Time had convinced Susette that LeBlanc was the kind of man she wanted. And now that her home was safe, she felt richer than she'd ever been.

Suddenly, the phone rang. Word had gotten out. All the

plaintiffs were calling one another. Everyone was meeting up at Matt Dery's place to celebrate. Susette and LeBlanc threw on wool sweaters and blue jeans and ran up the street.

One by one, the plaintiffs and other neighbors streamed in. The mood was like Christmas in March. With the night-lights from the nearby Pfizer building visible through the windows, Dery broke out beer and wine for his friends.

"Is it really over?" Susette asked enthusiastically. "I can't believe it. It's over!"

The members of the group raised their glasses. They had reason to toast. More than four years after real-estate agents had descended on their neighborhood and threatened them with eminent domain, the homeowners had done what everyone said couldn't be done: they had beaten City Hall. They had won the right to stay put.

Bitter over what they had been through, they verbally pummeled Claire, recalling how she had once remarked that the people in Fort Trumbull would jump at the chance to sell their homes and move if the NLDC offered them $15,000 in relocation costs because these people had never seen that kind of money.

Susette and Matt Dery rubbed their fingers together while jointly mimicking what Claire had said: "These people have never *seeeeen* $15,000." Their reenactment generated laughs.

Dery reminded the group that Rich Beyer, Byron Athenian, and the Cristofaro family couldn't celebrate. "It's a bittersweet victory," he said. "Everybody didn't win. We have to continue to support the others."

"And we'll be beside them all the way," Susette said. "We stick together in the fort. We won't disband."

That evening—before Londregan and the NLDC attorneys had finished reading the decision—the Institute for Justice cranked out a press release under the heading "Majority of Fort Trumbull Homeowners Win, Others to Appeal." "This is a great day for these property owners and the Constitution," Bullock said. "We are absolutely thrilled that most homeowners' rights were upheld.

And we will, of course, appeal the decisions for the remainder as they remain where they should be—in their homes."

Londregan didn't appreciate getting calls from the press just hours after the judge had handed out advance copies to the attorneys. He thought the attorneys were supposed to hold the information in confidence until the following day, when the judge was going to make the decision available to the public. O'Connell felt the same way. He was sick and tired of the institute and its tactics.

"I'm not used to competing in the media," Londregan said later. "I'm just used to going to court and arguing a case. We are such novices in the media-relations business that we never got our story out to the public."

Still, both lawyers gave statements to the press that night. "I would say the city is pleased with the decision and that the judge has agreed with the city on all legal, substantive, and procedural issues," Londregan said.

O'Connell was more succinct. "The assault on the validity of eminent domain failed."

Besides losing in court, they had also been badly outdone in the PR department.

The next day, Corradino's decision was made available to the public. Mayor Lloyd Beachy immediately appealed to his colleagues on the city council to renounce any thoughts of appealing. "The city can take eminent domain off the table," he told them. "We can say we are not going to appeal."

For Beachy, the choice was clear. The time had come to bury the hatchet and to move forward with the development under the terms that had been laid out by the court. Continuing to wage appeals would only waste the city's time and money. Other members of the city council agreed. The fighting had gone on long enough. Appeals would only lengthen the delay in starting construction. Led by Beachy, the city urged the NLDC not to appeal.

But the NLDC was bitter and wanted to fight on, especially after seeing the supersized photo of Susette and Matt Dery celebrating victory under the banner headline "EMINENTLY THEIR DO-MAIN" on the front page of the morning paper. But the NLDC board members could also see the writing on the wall—City Hall had lost its desire to fight on, and public sentiment had clearly shifted in favor of the homeowners. The court had spoken, and no one had an appetite for more battles. To draw another line in the sand at this stage would be politically risky for an agency whose lifeblood was political support.

The NLDC's board emerged from a two-hour, closed-door meeting with a proposal: it would not appeal Judge Corradino's decision if the property owners also agreed not to appeal.

One day after celebrating their victory, Susette joined Von Winkle at the Dery residence for a conference call with Bullock. Bullock advised rejecting the NLDC's offer.

Susette felt they couldn't leave Rich Beyer, Byron Athenian, and the Cristofaros hanging out to dry.

Von Winkle and Dery agreed that the group should show solidarity and back their neighbors up. "All for one and one for all," they said.

Bullock liked what he heard. The winners seemed more determined than ever to fight for those who had lost.

"They are trying to pit us against each other," Susette said. "I don't trust those sons of bitches for a minute."

Von Winkle and Dery felt there was no reason to believe the NLDC's statements anyway. Bullock agreed. The same day the NLDC had come out with its promise to withhold appeals if the institute did the same, Dave Goebel had told a newspaper columnist: "Yes, we still intend to implement the MDP, and parcel 4-A is part of that plan." He'd also said that if friendly acquisitions couldn't be achieved, eminent domain remained a possibility in the future. "That's not what we want to do," he had told the columnist. "It's never what we wanted to do. But we need to get the plan done." Goebel's statement had convinced Bullock that the NLDC's promise was worthless.

The decision was easy—appeal. "We're either all staying . . . or we're all going," Susette said.

Two weeks later, on April 1, 2002, the Institute for Justice filed its appeal, challenging Judge Corradino's decision that the city could lawfully take the properties of Rich Beyer, Byron Athenian, and the Cristofaro family through eminent domain.

Tom Londregan had a lot on his plate. In addition to challenging the institute's appeal, he intended to file a separate appeal on behalf of the city. Procedurally, the city had a lot of i's to dot and t's to cross before filing anything with the State Supreme Court. For guidance, Londregan turned to Wesley W. Horton, the state's premiere appellate lawyer.

Horton had practically grown up in the state Supreme Court. After graduating from the University of Connecticut's law school, Horton clerked for the Chief Justice of the Connecticut Supreme Court in the early 1970s. Then he signed on with one of the state's top appellate law firms. Over his thirty-year career he had handled hundreds of appeals and argued more than a hundred cases before the state Supreme Court. He had even written the only published book on the Connecticut Constitution and established himself as the state's resident expert on appellate procedure.

Londregan called Horton and told him about the *Kelo* case. "I need you to consult with the city in helping prepare our brief," he said.

Horton told Londregan he needed to disclose something. In 2001 he had worked on an eminent-domain case involving another Connecticut city, Bristol. In that case, Frank Bugryn and his family had owned about thirty acres that the city had wanted for an industrial park. Bugryn, an elderly man, had refused to sell. The land had been in his family since the 1930s and he had personally planted about five hundred trees on the property. In an effort to satisfy a private developer, the city had used eminent domain to condemn Bugryn's property. Bugryn had fought the city and hired Horton to handle his appeal before the Connecticut Supreme Court.

Londregan hadn't realized Horton had previously argued against eminent domain, but this made him want Horton even more. The two lawyers discussed whether there were any ethical constraints prohibiting Horton from consulting for the city, and they concluded there were none. First, the *Kelo* case didn't involve any of the parties or the same towns. So there was no client conflict. Second, Connecticut lawyers were prohibited from representing both sides of the same issue before the same court, but in this instance, the *Kelo* case had originated in a different court than the Bristol case, which was no longer active. Besides, Horton explained, the facts in the two cases were sufficiently different.

For a modest fee, Horton agreed to advise the city through the appeals process before the state's Supreme Court. Relieved, Londregan prepared and filed an appeal challenging Judge Corradino's decision to return property deeds to Susette and the others on her block. And he filed an opposition brief to the institute's appeal to overturn the lower court ruling against Beyer, Athenian, and the Cristofaros.

From the day Susette had telephoned him for help years earlier, Mayor Beachy had been the homeowners' strongest supporter within City Hall. He cheered Judge Corradino's decision. And despite his hopes of averting an appeal, he respected the rights of those homeowners who chose to press their case.

Nonetheless, he wanted to see the city get on with the development project and he saw no reason why the appeal should stand in the way. After all, of the ninety acres in the NLDC's hands, only a couple of acres were affected by the appeal. It made no sense not to start developing the rest—the city needed the revenue and the jobs.

There was only one problem. The Fort Trumbull Conservancy—the nonprofit corporation set up by John and Sarah Steffian and Steve and Amy Hallquist with attorney Scott Sawyer—had separately filed a series of lawsuits to block the city's development plan on environmental grounds. While the Institute for Justice's eminent-domain lawsuit had garnered all the headlines, the conservancy's environmental claims had quietly gone unresolved. Attorney Sawyer and the conservancy continued to push for a court resolution.

Beachy was determined to find a political solution, and he

figured he was the only one with the political capital to make it happen. No one else at City Hall stood a chance of having a productive conversation with conservancy leader John Steffian, but Beachy and Steffian were friends. They had served on historic-preservation commissions and shared a common passion for historic preservation. And they were two of the founding members of the neighborhood coalition that had been organized to fight eminent domain. The two men trusted each other.

With the complete trust of the Fort Trumbull neighborhood and all those opposed to eminent domain, Beachy was the only one who was also capable of getting the city and the NLDC to the table in hope of finding a compromise that would extinguish the conservancy's suits. The city's Boston-based developer, Corcoran Jennison, welcomed Beachy's efforts, and the company's president met directly with him to discuss possible compromises.

Beachy shared the developer's legal opinion that the conservancy's suits were meritless and would end in victory for the city. But the cost in litigation and in lost construction time made it cost-prohibitive to fight. Beachy suggested an idea to Corcoran Jennison: Agree to relocate the homes owned by Beyer, Athenian, and the Cristofaros from Parcel 3 to Parcel 4-A. This would preserve the last of the neighborhood homes and completely clear Parcel 3 for development.

Corcoran Jennison's president, Marty Jones, surprised Beachy with her response. She said that if the conservancy would drop its suits, she would agree to leave the homes intact where they stood on Parcel 3 and simply develop around them. At this point the developer had no interest in quibbling over three homeowners, though the developer did prefer that Parcel 3 should be cleared.

Encouraged by Beachy's progress, the city council passed a resolution authorizing him to negotiate with the conservancy on behalf of the city.

Beachy telephoned conservancy leader John Steffian at home and told him he wanted to come to a compromise that would persuade the conservancy to step away from its lawsuits against the city. After listening to Beachy's reasons, Steffian indicated he understood his position and wanted to help him succeed.

When Steve and Amy Hallquist heard about Beachy's efforts, they were relieved. Like the mayor, they fully supported the Institute for Justice and the homeowners in their eminent-domain fight, but they also didn't want to cripple the city's ability to redevelop the rest of the land.

The Hallquists had another reason for being eager to end their environmental lawsuits: in their hearts, they had come to believe the suits were bogus. At the time the first conservancy suit was filed, the group had been desperate to do anything to slow down the NLDC and the city from rolling over the powerless homeowners in Fort Trumbull. Morally, they had felt it was the right thing to do at the time. But now the homeowners had excellent legal representation and had gotten their day in court. Continuing to push the environmental claims now bordered on pure obstruction, the Hallquists believed. Ethically, they weren't comfortable doing that.

The Hallquists and the Steffians huddled with attorney Sawyer to discuss the next steps. They agreed to meet with the city, the NLDC, and the developer, but not before convening a meeting with all conservancy members to solicit opinions and arrive at a consensus for demands and concessions they would make in the negotiations.

A few nights later, dozens of conservancy members met at the Hallquists' home and voted overwhelmingly to authorize the Steffians and the Hallquists to enter into discussions with the city, the NLDC, the state, and the developer. The group also directed Steve Hallquist to write a letter outlining their two demands: all homeowners in the eminent-domain case should be allowed to stay in their homes, and public access to the waterfront area of the development had to be guaranteed.

Hallquist wrote the letter and had it published in the *Day*.

When Beachy saw Hallquist's letter on behalf of the conservancy, he sensed a resolution was around the corner. At Beachy's urging, all the parties agreed to meet face-to-face to conduct settlement talks.

Steve and Amy Hallquist arrived at Sawyer's law office for a scheduled strategy session with John and Sarah Steffian before going into the talks. But a series of conversations between the two couples caused Steve and Amy to think they and the Steffians weren't on the same page. They felt the Steffians were adding demands to their list of what it would take to drop the conservancy's lawsuits.

"Are we acting in good faith?" Amy asked. "Are we reasonable people who are trying to resolve this issue, or are we obstructing?"

The Steffians had a different view. To them, it was the city and the NLDC that were being disingenuous. From day one the NLDC had said one thing and done another. It simply couldn't be trusted, the Steffians felt.

Amy didn't necessarily disagree. But Beachy was one person who could be trusted, she felt. And any notion of holding out until the city agreed to scrap its municipal-development plan and start over was unrealistic.

But the Steffians were taking a more global perspective. The laws that had permitted the NLDC to get this far simply needed to be changed. The NLDC and the city had played fast and loose with the eminent-domain power. Using the courts to seek justice and stimulate reform was perfectly appropriate.

During a break in the session in Sawyer's office, Steve was talking with John when one of Sawyer's office assistants came in the room to discuss something privately with Sarah. Steve noticed that Sarah had her checkbook with her and figured Sawyer was due for a payment. Steve and Amy had always wondered how much Sawyer was charging the conservancy in legal fees. But during the two-year period since they had retained him, the Hallquists had never been privy to the billing information. Despite being treasurer, Steve didn't see the books, much less process invoices and issue checks. When it came to legal fees, that was between Sawyer and the Steffians. From a couple of feet away, Steve could see Sarah's checkbook ledger, inadvertently left open on the desk. Steve was stunned at what he saw. He told Amy that it appeared the Steffians had paid Sawyer at least $600,000 up to that point.

"I saw a six and six digits," he would later say.

The Hallquists didn't feel strongly one way or the other about the amount; after all, they hadn't had to pay anything. But Steve couldn't help thinking that the case was not that complicated. He had been studying Connecticut Supreme Court decisions handed down in cases that were similar to the suits the conservancy had filed against the city. From his reading, it was clear that all the legal precedents were against them. He couldn't bite his tongue any longer. He told Sarah the lawsuits were fatally flawed and it was only a matter of time before the suits were dismissed. "You'll lose," he said flatly, suggesting they should do what it would take to settle.

Sarah didn't like the implication that she was throwing her money away. But Steve believed just that. "You are going to lose, plain and simple," he said. The tension between the couples was obvious.

"Have you read the cases?" Steve pressed. "There's precedent here. You are going to lose and lose bad."

Sawyer had a different opinion.

Steve didn't want to hear it. "Your opinion doesn't count," he snapped. "There's a friggin' state Supreme Court decision."

Frustrated with Sawyer, Steve told Sarah, "You're throwing your money away. If you really want to change the law you better get a lobbyist because a lawyer isn't going to help you."

September 5, 2002

Mayor Beachy welcomed representatives from the city, the NLDC, Corcoran Jennison, the State of Connecticut, and the Fort Trumbull Conservancy into the chambers at City Hall. Marty Jones, the president of the development company, sat at one end of the table, an attorney at her side. Sawyer sat opposite her on the other side of the table, flanked by the Hallquists on his right and the Steffians on his left. Beachy, Londregan, Goebel, and city officials filled in the seats along the sides.

Beachy made his pitch: the city would take the remaining homes from Parcel 3 and relocate them to Susette's block, which would be preserved. This would allow construction of new office complexes on Parcel 3 and hotel and upscale housing along the waterfront.

The NLDC still couldn't accept the idea that these homes would be permitted to stay. But Jones expressed her opinion that her firm could proceed under Beachy's concept. "Do you see any problem with this approach?" Jones asked a state official.

"No," the official said.

Jones looked back across the table. "We can do this," she said.

Goebel pointed out that the plan didn't call for these properties to stay. Jones dismissed his concern, saying her firm could work around it. Goebel didn't say much more.

We've got ourselves a deal, Beachy thought. In his mind, the biggest hurdle had been crossed and a settlement was in reach. Even Londregan was convinced a compromise was in reach.

But John Steffian was far from convinced. All along, he and his wife had been pushing for a change in the way the city carried out its municipal-development plan. Among other things, they wanted a guarantee that eminent domain would not be used to take homes, whether that came by way of a city ordinance or some other measure. Also, going into the talks the Steffians had repeatedly asked who was ultimately calling the shots. Was it the state, the city, or the NLDC? They still hadn't gotten a straight answer. So the idea that this group was on the cusp of reaching a settlement was ridiculously premature, in their view. Besides, John heard a lot of double-talk. Even before the trial the city and the NLDC had been arguing that it had to tear down homes in the Fort Trumbull neighborhood because they were on a flood plain. But that wasn't true: a seven-story building at the Naval Undersea Warfare Center, known as Building 2, rested on a much lower elevation and was in the flood plain, yet the city had no plans to tear it down. More dishonesty.

John Steffian decided to weigh in. He suggested that in order for the argument to remain consistent, Building 2 should be torn down.

The room suddenly went silent. The building in question was

worth millions and probably the most suitable for reuse in the Fort Trumbull area.

Beachy was floored by Steffian's statement. He knew the city's plan had been a devious one, but Beachy was earnestly trying to cobble together a compromise that would satisfy all sides. He thought he had had Steffian's commitment to that end. Suddenly it felt like the rug had just been yanked out from under his feet.

The Hallquists were even more stunned. Amy jabbed Steve. "How can he do this?" she whispered, convinced there was an effort afoot to derail the settlement.

Seething, Steve froze.

"Say something," she said, kicking Steve under the table.

Steve stood up. "I don't agree with John," he announced.

John paused and turned toward Steve, who faced the others in the room.

"This is not what we agreed to," Hallquist continued. "We're here to negotiate."

Infighting was a bad sign. Beachy sensed trouble.

"Mr. Steffian is speaking for himself," Amy interjected. "This is not a directive from the conservancy, and I personally don't agree with his opinion."

"We need a recess," Steve said.

Beachy buried his face in his hands, sensing any hope of an agreement had just evaporated.

Londregan didn't know what to think. "I thought we had an agreement," he said. All the property owners in the lawsuit were going to be free to continue their legal fight to protect their homes. And the city's developer would be free to commence building on the parcels that were outside the contested area. "Let these projects go forward for the betterment of the city," he said.

But Londregan's offer lacked the certainty that the Steffians and Sawyer were after. "It was an empty promise," Sawyer explained.

The Hallquists and the Steffians exited the room, trailed by Sawyer.

Once outside, Steve started shouting. Amy pulled out the notes from the membership meeting held at her home weeks earlier. "Do you see anywhere in the notes where we were directed to negotiate on the demolition of a building?" she shouted. "No!"

"So why are you bringing this up?" Steve pressed.

John Steffian was just as angry. "City, state, and NLDC officials comported themselves throughout this meeting as if the conservancy's questions did not exist!" Steffian later explained. "By steadfastly refusing to discuss the larger issues of eminent domain, the environment, or alternative plan possibilities, the meeting's focus became increasingly circumscribed, irrelevant, and limited by those officials."

Sawyer figured that if Steffian's suggestion about Building 2 was enough to halt the talks, then the talks hadn't had much substance to begin with. "The others," he later said, "did not want or were unable to have a meaningful discussion, as evidenced by their complete failure to answer the most basic inquiries."

A few minutes after stepping out, the Hallquists walked back inside the chamber.

"It's over," Steve Hallquist announced.

Furious with John Steffian and Scott Sawyer, Beachy blew his top. "They just don't want to resolve this!" he shouted.

36

INTERESTED BYSTANDERS

September 10, 2002

Pfizer executive Dan O'Shea had just gotten to his New London office when he picked up his copy of the *Wall Street Journal*. The above-the-fold headline on page one grabbed his attention: "Needy New London Saw Cure for Its Ills in Pfizer's Arrival." The story opened with an account of eighty-five-year-old Albert Anton, the brother of Daniel Anton, on a pilgrimage back to the Fort Trumbull neighborhood, where he led *Journal* reporter Lucette Lagnado to a pile of rubble. "This is where my house used to be," Anton told the reporter.

O'Shea didn't like what he read next. "Mr. Anton didn't want to move but Pfizer Inc. had other plans for Fort Trumbull. And how one of the world's largest pharmaceutical companies tried—but so far failed—to realize its vision for Mr. Anton's neighborhood is a big reason this city of 25,000 people languishes, divided and anxious for the economic renaissance it was convinced would come."

The lengthy feature story hit Pfizer hard, indicating that the drug company had come to New London with a plan to transform the city. "But redeveloping scores of acres in Fort Trumbull, next to Pfizer's own 24-acre site, would require evicting many longtime residents," the *Journal* reported.

Stung by what he'd read, O'Shea put down the paper in disgust. As the vice president of operations and public affairs for

282

Pfizer's research division, O'Shea had carefully followed all the stories about the development project in the local press. Although he hadn't liked all the controversy, none of it had concerned him too much as long as it was largely confined to the *Day* and other Connecticut papers. After all, investors, shareholders, and Pfizer's corporate executives in New York didn't read the *Day*. But they all read the *Wall Street Journal*. The fact that the nation's leading financial paper had fingered Pfizer as the corporation behind the city's efforts to drive people from their homes in Fort Trumbull had O'Shea steaming.

Smart, shrewd, and cautious, O'Shea had spent four years trying to protect Pfizer from guilt by association with the NLDC and its use of eminent domain. But his task had been made difficult by the close association between George Milne and Claire Gaudiani. Her style and the NLDC's reputation made O'Shea bristle.

When he had first learned that Milne was considering New London as a development site, O'Shea had had serious reservations. In retrospect, however, O'Shea had come to view Milne's decision as a brilliant one. When Pfizer had merged with Warner-Lambert, the company had had to centralize a wide variety of business operations, and the New London site suddenly provided the company great flexibility.

He also took satisfaction in Judge Corradino's conclusion that Pfizer had not directed the NLDC to use eminent domain. But now he had to deal with the *Wall Street Journal*'s suggestion to the contrary.

On a notepad, O'Shea listed his complaints. Then he telephoned one of Pfizer's attorneys, saying they needed to address these issues with the paper's editors. The attorney agreed. O'Shea called the *Journal* and demanded a face-to-face meeting. A few days later he traveled with an attorney to the paper's offices in lower Manhattan. In a meeting with Lucette Lagnado and her editors, O'Shea unloaded, arguing the story was plagued by errors and all kinds of innuendos.

"I didn't like that whenever the NLDC did something our name was attached to it," O'Shea said later. "We had a very specific purpose in mind. The state and the city and the NLDC helped us with our purpose, and we did what we committed to do. Everything else was peripheral and not Pfizer's responsibility. We were interested bystanders."

O'Shea wanted the *Journal* to publish a retraction or a clarification. But the paper declined, standing behind the reporting of Lagnado, a longtime, award-winning journalist. Instead, the paper agreed to publish a letter to the editor from O'Shea.

In his letter, O'Shea said he was "saddened and insulted" by the story and complained that "facts were obscured in favor of innuendo." It was published ten days later. In protest, O'Shea stopped reading the *Journal* and started reading the *New York Times.*

Money. Every time she looked at her checkbook, Susette realized she didn't have enough of it. Her nursing shifts were barely paying her enough for the necessities. LeBlanc had steady work. But as a stonemason in business for himself, he had to hustle just to make enough to pay the bills, too. They knew they needed a little extra income.

Susette had heard that the city was looking to hire a nurse to help children with nutrition and testing for lead poisoning. She and LeBlanc figured it was worth a shot. She applied for the part-time position. When the city received her application, some officials were unsure what to do. They brought the application to Tom Londregan for advice.

Londregan had to smile. He knew what some people in City Hall were thinking—*First she sues us; then she turns around and applies for a job from us?*

Londregan had nothing personal against Susette. They actually shared a couple of traits. Both were tireless professionals, unusually dedicated to serving those in their care—whether a patient or a client. And when it came to defending something they believed in, they were relentless. Neither one of them knew the word "surrender."

"Well," Londregan told those reviewing her application, "if she's qualified, hire her." In late September, the city offered Su-

sette the job as lead and nutrition nurse. She accepted and received a small office next door to the courthouse.

October 21, 2002

Steve and Amy Hallquist knew the time had come to sever
their ties with the conservancy. They no longer agreed with the
direction being taken by Sawyer and the Steffians. "These people
don't know how to put their swords down," Steve told Amy. "They
just hone them constantly." Amy agreed.

Steve submitted a resignation letter to the conservancy and
demanded that the nonprofit corporation remove his name from
all lawsuits and appeals and that it stop using his home address
as its address of record. "I cannot, in good conscience, continue
my relationship with the group," he wrote. "Furthermore, I cannot endorse or be associated with the irreconcilable proposition
recommended by the Conservancy president to have the former
NUWC Building #2 demolished."

Hallquist also withdrew from being represented by Sawyer.
"The strategy he has used to negotiate is incompatible with good
faith negotiations and is patently obstructionist," he wrote. "I do
not feel that lawsuits should be used as bargaining chips. This
kind of leverage is corrupt, fraudulent, and obstruction."

Amy also submitted a letter of resignation, saying the Steffians and Sawyer were taking the conservancy in a direction she
couldn't support.

October 29, 2002

Susette had barely started her evening shift in the emergency
room when the staff got word of an incoming trauma code. Everyone rushed to meet the paramedics who were wheeling in a
man on a stretcher. "I always hate these," Susette said to another
nurse. "I'm always worried it's going to be someone I know."

The victim had lost a lot of blood and sustained severe cranial
and facial injuries in a horrible automobile accident. His pupils

were fixed, and he wasn't breathing on his own. A ventilator mask covered most of his face.

Standing beside the respiratory technician, Susette looked on as doctors cut the victim's clothes off. Something about the man's physical features caught her eye.

"Here's his wallet," one of the technicians said, passing it past Susette to a nurse behind her. At a quick glance, it looked familiar.

Susette bent down and examined the victim's hand, dangling lifelessly from the side of the stretcher. She knew the ring on his ring finger. "Oh, my God," she whispered. Feeling queasy, she stepped toward the nurse who had taken the victim's wallet. "I know who this is," Susette said.

"Who?"

"My husband."

"What?" the nurse said.

"Open the wallet," Susette said.

The nurse removed the victim's driver's license. "It says Timothy LeBlanc."

"Oh, my God!" Susette screamed. "That's him." She sunk to the floor.

The nurse yelled to the doctor, "The victim is Susette's husband."

Another technician called for the shift supervisor. "You need to get down here," she said. "Susette Kelo's husband was just brought in as a trauma code."

In a separate room, Susette's colleagues worked to calm her down. She didn't bother to tell them that she wasn't formally married to LeBlanc. Afraid doctors would soon have to decide whether to remove him from life support, she wanted to be in a position to tell them not to. As a nurse, she knew girlfriends and fiancées didn't have that ability—only spouses did.

Eventually, a surgeon came to see her with an update. LeBlanc had spinal fluid in his nose and ears. Every bone in his face appeared broken. Free air had entered his brain as a result of the skull fracture. The trauma to his face and head had left him unrecognizable. It was unclear whether he would survive.

For the next forty-eight hours, Susette held vigil at LeBlanc's side. When she finally ran home for a change of clothes and a shower, she bumped into Kathleen Mitchell's daughter on the street. "Tell your mother that Timothy was in a car accident," she said.

Soon word spread through the neighborhood that LeBlanc's life was in the balance. Susette had cried so much her eyes were dry. Eventually, LeBlanc started to breathe on his own, and the doctors upgraded his condition. But they informed Susette that even in the best-case scenario LeBlanc would be permanently disabled. His speech would be slow, his memory limited, and his physical mobility severely restricted. Even with an excruciating physical-rehabilitation schedule, LeBlanc would never be the man he had once been.

Matt Dery was the first to check in on Susette. None of the other neighbors wanted to infringe on her privacy at such a sensitive time. "We don't know what to say," Dery told her.

Even Von Winkle stayed away. Whenever he experienced grief, he preferred to be left alone, so he figured he'd leave Susette alone.

When Scott Bullock got the news, he couldn't believe it. He wondered, *What else does this woman have to deal with?*

37

GOD, WHAT HAVE I DONE?

Suing the city was the farthest thing from Byron Athenian's mind when he had first gotten the notice that the NLDC had condemned his house. Self-employed, he had been doing auto-body work for twenty-three years. He had paid $39,000 for his house eleven years earlier and opened up a repair shop in the backyard, earning about $50,000 a year. It was just enough to support his three children and a granddaughter confined to a wheelchair. Just four years shy of paying off his mortgage, Athenian had agreed to join the lawsuit when his respected friend Matt Dery had.

Low profile throughout the case, Athenian first heard about Judge Corradino's ruling when Matt Dery called with the news. "No good," Dery told him before inviting him up for a beer and a celebration with the ones who had won.

Disappointed, yet even-tempered, Athenian had shown up at Dery's house that night and partied with his friends. He had celebrated even harder after they informed him that they planned to appeal on his behalf.

But since then, Athenian had experienced the wrath of the NLDC. He had come home one day and discovered that dump trucks had unloaded tons of dirt on the street right in front of his house. Besides adding four feet in elevation to the roadway just a few steps from his front door, the dust was so overwhelming that it covered the inside of Athenian's house. The first time it rained, the topsoil turned into a mud slide into his basement and first-floor living room. Besides flooding his house and snuffing out his boiler, the mud and water made it virtually impossible to get his granddaughter's wheelchair from the house to the road.

For weeks the city refused to collect Athenian's trash; that was because he no longer had a sidewalk to set it on on pickup days. The NLDC tore down his street sign and put up Jersey barriers around his property, giving it the look of an occupied territory. The agency even detonated dynamite on the neighboring lots it had obtained. The explosions caused the walls to crack inside Athenian's house.

The more the NLDC harassed Athenian, the more the Institute for Justice became determined to win its appeal. To help build public support, the institute funded the formation of a grassroots-activism organization called the Castle Coalition. Dedicated to preserving homes from eminent-domain takings, the coalition launched a Web site and organized a candlelight vigil in the Fort Trumbull neighborhood on the eve of the hearing before the Connecticut Supreme Court.

December 2, 2002

Supporters for the homeowners packed the small courthouse gallery to hear Bullock and Berliner argue their appeal. The plaintiffs sat together, in a show of solidarity. Susette left LeBlanc's bedside at the hospital to attend. There was no way she would miss the opportunity to stand with her neighbors. To her, they were no longer just neighbors locked in a legal fight; they were her family. And with Tim's future uncertain, she needed family more than ever.

The oral arguments were fairly uneventful. Both sides reiterated the cases they had made at the trial court, hoping to get a more favorable ruling this time around.

The real fun took place afterward. Bullock and Berliner took the group out for dinner. Matt Dery chose an Italian restaurant. The neighbors all felt that their attorneys had scored a lot of points before the appeals judges. Everyone felt confident that Beyer, Athenian, and the Cristofaros would end up getting their properties back, enabling the core of the neighborhood's families to remain in place.

The more the group drank, the more it bragged. The dinner was just what Susette needed—a reason to smile.

Mid-December 2002

After nearly two months of hospitalization and rehab, Tim LeBlanc had rung up over $300,000 in medical bills. During that time he had progressed to the developmental stage of a four-year-old. He still had a long way to go and still required full-time care. The hospital recommended a nursing home capable of around-the-clock help and long-term rehabilitation. An administrator explained all this to Susette. She knew she had a big decision to make.

The man she had fallen in love with and lived with for three years was gone. The simple pleasures of life—conversation, walks, meals together, intimacy—were now just a memory. Yet there was no way she could turn her back on LeBlanc now. He needed her.

Susette told the hospital administrator she didn't want LeBlanc in a nursing home. The administrator asked Susette what other option she had in mind. Susette insisted on bringing LeBlanc home to 8 East Street to live with her.

"He is permanently disabled," the administrator pointed out. "He'll be confined to the house. He needs someone to prepare his meals and help him go to the bathroom. The situation requires a full-time nurse."

"What are you, nuts?" Susette countered. "I am a nurse!"

The week before Christmas 2002, the hospital released LeBlanc to Susette's care. LeBlanc was permanently disabled and had no health insurance. Plus his health-care costs were going to continue to mount. This was another headache Susette had to endure.

Fortunately, Susette had complete medical coverage through her employer. If she married LeBlanc right away she could enroll him on her health-care plan with eligibility starting in January, and that would at least cover his future medical bills.

Two days after LeBlanc was discharged, Susette drove him to Maine and married him in a private ceremony. She had been looking forward to becoming LeBlanc's wife one day so that he could take care of her—fulfilling her financial, physical, and emotional needs. None of that was possible now. Ironically, she would resume the role she had played in her previous marriages, taking care of her husband.

Only this time the needs were more acute. She would be more like a mother than a wife to LeBlanc. For starters, she had to deal with the medical bills he had racked up since the accident. After convincing one of the hospitals that had treated LeBlanc to forgive roughly $150,000 in medical bills, Susette set up a payment plan with the other hospital, agreeing to make monthly installments in the range of $100 until the six-figure bill was met.

She set up a room for him at her place, and she arranged for people to be with him when she had to work. No one in the neighborhood spent more time helping LeBlanc than Von Winkle. He wouldn't visit at the hospital, but now that LeBlanc was home, Von Winkle wouldn't leave him alone. He took LeBlanc for car rides, he stayed at his bedside making small talk, and he cleared out space in a nearby building he owned, making way for Susette to store all of LeBlanc's tools. It would be years, if ever, before LeBlanc would be able to use them again.

Susette figured out that Von Winkle had a difficult time expressing love verbally. But he had no trouble showing it. She was the same way. Maybe that was why, she figured, she liked Von Winkle so much. He was tough as nails but had a heart of gold.

Matt and Sue Dery picked up the slack whenever Von Winkle wasn't available to help with LeBlanc. They started bringing him to their home regularly to eat homemade Italian sausages, one of his favorite dishes.

The road to recovery, though, was arduous and had no guarantees. Susette understood the odds. But as long as Billy and Matt and Sue were around, she figured she'd get through it. They had beaten the odds to save their homes. She hoped LeBlanc would be so lucky.

April 2003

Around the time that the Institute for Justice had decided to represent Susette and her neighbors, Dana Berliner had wanted to know how widespread eminent-domain abuses were throughout the country. With the support and encouragement of the institute's founder, Chip Mellor, she had undertaken the first comprehensive study of the problem ever conducted in the United States. After two years of intense research, she generated a report titled: "Public Power, Private Gain." It contained a bombshell. In the previous five years, more than ten thousand private properties in forty-one states had been threatened or taken by eminent domain for private use.

When Mellor saw Berliner's findings, he wanted John Kramer to get them out to the national media. Among other things, Berliner's report showed that what was going on in New London was not unique. It was more like a national epidemic—and no one seemed to be talking about it.

To get the word out, Kramer took a risk. He called *60 Minutes* and asked to speak with the show's legendary creator and executive producer, Don Hewitt. He reached Hewitt's secretary and left a message.

Fifteen minutes later, Kramer's phone rang. It was Hewitt.

"Mr. Hewitt, I know you don't typically take calls from PR people," began Kramer, who went on to say he had something very unusual that might appeal to *60 Minutes*. "Can I give you a thirty-second pitch on it?"

"Go for it," Hewitt said.

Kramer reported that eminent domain was being used nationwide by local governments to take private homes and to give them to developers. And small businesses were being taken to make way for big businesses. "We've documented more than ten thousand cases across the country," he said.

Hewitt asked if the institute had a report to document this.

"I can get you that by FedEx tomorrow," Kramer said.

Hewitt told him to send it. "If it's something we're interested in, we'll call you back."

Two days later, Kramer got a call from Bob Anderson, the producer for reporter Mike Wallace. He said Hewitt had handed him Berliner's report and had said, "I don't know if this is all true, but if it is true, it's a helluva story, and you've got to cover it."

Within a week, Anderson was in the institute's office, and *60 Minutes* had an exclusive.

Over the next five months, Mike Wallace spent time at the institute's office, and he investigated egregious eminent-domain abuses in Ohio and Arizona, cases that involved clients represented by the institute. In the opening episode of the fall season, in September 2003, *60 Minutes* did a blistering report on the widespread abuse of eminent domain throughout the country, featuring interviews with Bullock and Berliner. The segment didn't mention New London, but it had an immediate impact. In one night, more than ten million Americans became acquainted with a topic they had known little about. Almost every major daily paper in the country ended up covering Berliner's study. The coverage was so widespread that the institute received a national award for its expertise in public relations.

March 2, 2004

Scott Bullock was on his computer when he received an e-mail from the Connecticut Supreme Court, informing him that the decision would be posted on the court's Web site the following day. The institute had already prepared two press releases, one anticipating good news and the other anticipating bad news.

The next morning, Bullock and Berliner logged on to the court's Web site and relentlessly clicked the Refresh button until a link to the decision appeared on the computer screen. Together, they scanned the decision very quickly.

Instantly, the crushing shock hit them. It was immediately clear that part of the trial court decision had been affirmed and part of it had been reversed; the court had affirmed Judge

Corradino's decision to let the city's eminent-domain takings against Beyer, Athenian, and the Cristofaros stand. And it had reversed Corradino's decision to let Kelo, Von Winkle, and Dery keep their homes. "They reversed the good part and affirmed the bad part," Bullock said.

Just like that, all of the homeowners were out of luck. The city's municipal-development plan—according to the state's highest court—constituted a public use and therefore gave the government the power to take private property through eminent domain. The fact that a specific use had not been identified for Susette's block didn't matter.

Bullock couldn't believe it. Neither could Berliner.

Groping for something, *anything* positive in the decision, they noted the justices' narrow 4–3 vote margin. The court was sharply divided. Bullock scanned down to the dissenting opinion.

"Look," he said, "the dissent says the court is going further than it has ever gone in the past. It's right in the first paragraph."

Berliner knew what Bullock was thinking: they should appeal the decision to the U.S. Supreme Court. But neither of them had ever argued a case before the nation's highest court. Just the idea seemed overwhelming. Where would they begin?

"The dissenting opinion makes the points we need for a petition to the Supreme Court," Bullock said. "It's right there in the opinion."

Berliner knew one thing: their clients deserved to have the decision appealed. Every one of them was going to be devastated when they got the news, especially Susette, Von Winkle, and the Dery family. The Connecticut Supreme Court had snatched victory away from them.

Bullock and Berliner divided the clients into two call lists. Bullock called Susette first, reaching her on her cell phone at the hospital. When he told her they had lost—all of them—Susette didn't say a word. Bullock would have thought he had lost the connection, but he could still hear all the hospital noise in the background.

"It's an incredibly disappointing ruling," he said softly. "Although it was close, the end result is still that they ruled in favor of the city and the NLDC."

She still said nothing.

He told her they planned to appeal to the U.S. Supreme Court.

That didn't register. All she could hear was that they had lost.

"We will absolutely appeal this," he vowed.

"Yeah, okay," she said, her voice tapering off. "I understand."

Susette didn't bother saying good-bye before hanging up and burying her face in her hands. As a little girl growing up in Maine, she had learned to use socks to protect her hands against frigid winter air when her mother couldn't afford to buy her mittens. It had proven to be a road map for what lay ahead. Throughout her life she had improvised to compensate for what she didn't have. Suddenly she had an invalid husband and was on the verge of having no place to live.

Where would they go? How would she afford to support them? And what if the city came after her for the rent money she would now owe for unlawfully occupying the house for the previous two years?

She couldn't help thinking she should have just gotten out when Pfizer had first come to town. *God, what have I done?* she thought.

When Bullock reached Matt Dery, he was still at work. He had already read the decision online from his office computer. He couldn't believe it. There would be no neighborhood celebration at his house this time. A neighborhood funeral seemed more appropriate.

Billy Von Winkle was in the Fort Trumbull neighborhood when Bullock reached him with the bad news. He didn't take it as badly as the others. Bullock talked up the prospect of going to the U.S. Supreme Court. "The Supreme Court is always a huge long shot," he said. "But we will absolutely appeal this."

"All right, Bull. What are our chances?"

Bullock had to smile. Von Winkle was the businessman in the group, the numbers guy. He had a way of sizing things up and getting right to the bottom line.

Normally, Bullock explained, chances were slim. But in this instance, he figured, the chances were better than normal because the dissenting judges on the Connecticut Supreme Court had plainly stated that the court had made a decision that went far beyond anywhere it had previously gone. That cried out for judicial review.

Von Winkle was up for another round. What did they have to lose?

The power brokers who had been principals behind the idea to remake the Fort Trumbull area were all fading out of the picture. Claire and Milne were still associated with the NLDC, but only from a distance. Both of them had left New London. Claire was teaching at Yale, and Milne had gone off to be a venture capitalist. And Governor John Rowland and his chief of staff, Peter Ellef, were under investigation for their roles in a corruption scandal, so they had more pressing concerns. Even lobbyist Jay Levin had distanced himself from the NLDC, which he had helped revive.

Only Londregan remained to keep the dream alive. And he had succeeded. After the disappointing split decision at the trial stage, the state's highest court had made the victory doubly satisfying by taking away the institute's earlier victory.

Better still, Londregan had been vindicated. The Connecticut Supreme Court had put its stamp of approval on what he had been arguing all along: Economic development was a valid public-use purpose for exercising eminent domain. Cities, especially depressed ones, had to be allowed to take private properties to stimulate private development that would ultimately produce jobs and tax revenue. Tom Londregan could not have been happier with the decision.

He also took personal satisfaction in beating the Institute for Justice. He didn't like their style. He didn't like their approach. And he didn't like their lawyers.

When he found out the institute planned to petition the U.S.

Supreme Court, Londregan called Wes Horton again. Horton explained that the institute had about a one in one hundred chance of having its petition granted.

There were other factors that boded well for the city. The U.S. Supreme Court was more inclined to accept appeals when there was a conflict among the lower courts. In other words, if one state Supreme Court had ruled one way and a different state Supreme Court had ruled another way, the U.S. Supreme Court would have a reason to step in and clear up the matter. The Connecticut decision in the *Kelo* case didn't seem to conflict with any existing decisions from any other state Supreme Courts. The case that most closely resembled *Kelo* had been in Michigan many years earlier and the state Supreme Court there had also ruled against the private property owners.

Londregan asked Horton to walk him through the procedures of the U.S. Supreme Court. Horton explained that once the institute filed its petition with the Supreme Court, the city would have to file a brief in opposition. If the Court accepted the institute's petition, then the city would have to file a second brief on the case and prepare an oral argument.

Londregan asked Horton how much he would charge to write the opposition brief. Horton said he'd do it for $10,000. Londregan explained that the city had very little money. It had already spent a lot more than it wanted to on litigation and other issues stemming from the municipal-development plan. He asked Horton to come down on his price.

Horton had something else in mind. He proposed that the city should pay the full $10,000 for the opposition brief, and if the Court ended up taking the case, he'd do the second brief and the oral argument at no additional charge.

Londregan laughed. "Wes, you're given' me nothin' here," he said. "The Court only takes 1 percent of the petitions. There's a 99 percent chance they won't take the case."

Horton chuckled. But his price remained firm. The price he had quoted was already well below his standard fee. He wouldn't go any lower.

Londregan agreed, satisfied that he had just secured one of the finest appellate lawyers in the Northeast.

Susette started questioning herself. Caring for LeBlanc was proving to be a lot more complicated than she had expected. His physical and mental handicaps were one thing. But as his wife, she also assumed a series of legal obligations that were eating her alive. He owned a house that needed to be sold. It was too far from her work to consider living there. It fell to her to list his house with a real-estate agent. But first she had to repair the place and remove all of LeBlanc's personal property.

Unable to afford construction contractors or professional movers, both tasks fell on her shoulders. It didn't help that LeBlanc was a stonemason and had stored tons of rocks on his property. Worse still, the place was nearly an hour from her house. When she wasn't working one of her two jobs or caring for LeBlanc, she went back and forth between the two houses. The days were all starting to run together.

Despite being physically exhausted, she couldn't sleep. Her anxieties about losing her house kept her mind racing. She felt she had been stupid to think that she could take on City Hall. *Where did it get me?* she thought. *Penniless and soon to be homeless.*

Both the decision to assume responsibility for Tim and the decision to fight the City of New London had been made on impulse. Emotion had won out over reason, reflex over caution.

But her hair-trigger tendency was guided by an instinctive sense of right and wrong. Caring for Tim was simply the right thing to do. Taking people's homes was simply the wrong thing to do. And it would have been wrong to just let the NLDC do it. No matter how much she beat herself up for ending up in such a mess, she couldn't change the way she saw the world.

38

A BEGINNING AND AN END

O nce they made the decision to appeal to the U.S. Supreme Court, Bullock and Berliner now had to convince the Connecticut Supreme Court to grant the homeowners permission to remain in their homes during the appeal process. And once they cleared that hurdle, they then had to deal with the city's desire to collect occupancy fees dating back to 2000. The court prevented this. But by the time Bullock and Berliner got that issue resolved, they didn't have much time until the ninety-day deadline arrived for filing petitions with the Supreme Court.

June 21, 2004

Governor John Rowland wasn't used to being squeezed. But federal prosecutors were ramping up to indict him and his chief of staff, Peter Ellef, on corruption charges. At the same time, state senators were calling for his impeachment and the legislature had subpoenaed him to testify before a committee conducting an inquiry into allegations of graft. If Rowland took the Fifth and refused to testify before the legislature, he'd surely be impeached. On the other hand, if he testified, anything he said could be used against him in the criminal case. Suddenly, fighting for his freedom was more important than fighting for his job.

At 6 p.m., Rowland stepped onto a terrace outside the governor's residence and formally announced his resignation. A year and a half earlier, he had been elected to an unprecedented third term and there had been whispers that he was under consideration for a cabinet position in the Bush administration.

His wife stood beside him as he spoke to the press assembled outside his residence. "I acknowledge that my poor judgment has brought us here," he said. "Tonight is both a beginning and an end for me."

Over a period of years, the Rowland administration had traded favors with construction contractors doing business with the state. Now it was all coming to a head. Connecticut's lieutenant governor, Jodi Rell, would be sworn in as the new governor on July 1.

For most of June, Bullock and Berliner set aside everything but the Fort Trumbull situation—other clients and cases, personal commitments, even sleeping and eating. The legal research they performed for the petition convinced them that their odds of getting a hearing before the Supreme Court were better than average. Nonetheless, they recognized that it had been decades since the Supreme Court had heard an eminent-domain case.

July 19, 2004

Within hours of filing its petition with the Supreme Court, the Institute for Justice hosted a luncheon at its office for the Supreme Court reporters from the *New York Times*, the *Washington Post*, the *Los Angeles Times*, and other influential national publications. Chip Mellor wanted the institute to leave no stone unturned in trying to persuade the Court to hear the homeowners' case. One important ingredient was getting the message out that the case had national implications. Over lunch, Bullock and Berliner briefed the nation's top court reporters on the *Kelo* case.

A couple of days later, Bullock met with an editor from the *Economist* to discuss the case. Then he met with Pete Williams, the legal correspondent for the *NBC Nightly News*. But the institute figured the person it needed to get to most was George Will, one of the most influential writers in the country. His syndicated column appeared in the *Washington Post* and in more than four hundred other newspapers across the country in any given week. And the *Kelo* case presented just the kinds of issues he liked to tackle—a cutting-edge legal dispute with far-reaching legal and political ramifications, not to mention a compelling set of characters.

Immediately after the institute filed its petition with the Supreme Court, it sent a copy to Will, along with a cover letter encouraging him to consider writing about the case. The institute was no stranger to Will. He had spoken at an event commemorating the institute's ten-year anniversary and had championed the institute's cases in his columns on previous occasions.

Shortly after receiving the institute's package, Will agreed to meet Scott Bullock and John Kramer at the Four Seasons Hotel in Georgetown. Over breakfast they discussed the case. Well-versed in the Constitution and the Fifth Amendment, Will asked detailed questions about the *Kelo* case and its broader implications. Bullock consciously tried not to go too far in his pitch. Will wasn't the kind of guy who needed to be told what he should be writing about. He ended the breakfast meeting cordially and made no promises.

As Wes Horton put the finishing touches on his opposition brief to the U.S. Supreme Court on behalf of the City of New London, he felt quite confident that strong legal precedent favored the city. He explained his thinking to Londregan.

A few years earlier Horton had petitioned the Supreme Court on behalf of the Bugryn family in Bristol, Connecticut, Horton had previously told Londregan. In the *Bugryn* case, Horton figured he had had a compelling argument for a hearing: The city of Bristol had used eminent domain to condemn Bugryn's private land purely to satisfy a private developer. The Connecticut Supreme Court had ruled this was okay. And Horton couldn't persuade the U.S. Supreme Court to even consider the case, which enabled the *Bugryn* ruling to stand.

"That puts Ms. Kelo in a very difficult position," said Horton, insisting that the facts in the New London case weren't as egregious as the ones in *Bugryn* had been. "Kelo can't make the argument that the city sold out to the developer," Horton said.

But what about the institute's argument that the city had essentially sold out to Pfizer? Horton wasn't worried about that argument either. "The Pfizer argument is weak for Kelo," he said. "It's promising for the city because Pfizer was there first. Pfizer came in and did all this work without knowing whether the city would do anything. And they weren't saying they were going to leave town if the city didn't take this land."

Horton had another reason to be confident. In his legal research he didn't see the state Supreme Courts disagreeing in their opinions about the public-use clause in the Fifth Amendment. And when there was no conflict among the lower courts, the U.S. Supreme Court was less likely to weigh in.

Londregan had to like what he heard.

July 30, 2004

The minute he saw the decision, Wes Horton became concerned. In *County of Wayne v. Hathcock*, the Michigan Supreme Court had just overturned a prior decision allowing the City of Detroit to bulldoze a neighborhood with more than a thousand residents and six hundred businesses to make way for a more lucrative occupant—a General Motors plant. The Michigan justices had ignored decades of precedent and declared it unconstitutional to take private land through eminent domain and then award it to someone else who could generate more tax revenue for the city.

When the Institute for Justice had filed its appeal to the U.S. Supreme Court less than two weeks earlier, no state Supreme Court had been in direct conflict with the Connecticut Supreme Court's *Kelo* decision. Now one was. And it was a big one. The Michigan court decision unanimously repudiated the Connecticut court's conclusion.

Horton couldn't believe the timing. What were the odds that another state Supreme Court would issue a decision in direct conflict with the Connecticut court right as the U.S. Supreme Court was weighing whether to accept the *Kelo* case?

Horton didn't know the answer. But he figured the chances of the U.S. Supreme Court's taking the *Kelo* case had just jumped from 1 percent to about 10 percent.

Realizing her days in Fort Trumbull were numbered, Susette figured she'd better find a place to go. With Von Winkle's help, she located a small house in Old Lyme, less than a half hour from New London. It lacked what she had in Fort Trumbull—historic value, great water views, and the surrounding close-knit neighborhood. But her only criterion now was affordability. The house in Old Lyme needed a complete makeover, which drove the price down to within her range. Her sons, most of whom were carpenters and tradesmen, promised to remodel the house at no cost.

Susette couldn't bear the thought of abandoning her cottage at 8 East Street. But Von Winkle assured her that she'd be foolish not to secure another place, especially with LeBlanc's medical needs. Pinning hope on the Supreme Court was like going to a casino with the expectation of beating the house.

September 17, 2004

"Despotism in New London." Just the headline made Tom Londregan's blood boil. Syndicated columnist George Will had taken up the cause of the *Kelo* case. "Soon—perhaps on the first Monday in October—the court will announce whether it will appeal a 4 to 3 ruling last March by Connecticut's Supreme Court," Will wrote. "That ruling effectively repeals a crucial portion of the Bill of Rights. If you think the term 'despotism' exaggerates what this repeal permits, consider the life-shattering power wielded by the government of New London, Conn."

Londregan couldn't believe his eyes. One of the most influential political commentators in the country had chimed in on the *Kelo* case right as the Supreme Court was weighing whether to accept it for review. And besides brutalizing New London for running roughshod over its Fort Trumbull residents, Will brought up the Michigan case, saying the conflicting opinions between state Supreme Courts cried out for clarification from the nation's top court.

"In considering whether to take the New London case, the U.S. Supreme Court surely sees, at a minimum, the dangerous emptying of meaning from the Fifth Amendment's 'public use' provision," Will concluded. "If the court refuses to review the Connecticut ruling, its silence will effectively ratify state-level judicial vandalism that is draining the phrase 'public use' of its power to perform the framers' clearly intended function."

Furious, Londregan called Horton, who had also seen Will's column. The timing of Will's piece stymied Horton more than his argument. He couldn't help wondering what had prompted Will to weigh in now. The fact that he had directly called the Supreme Court's attention to the Michigan case in the pages of the *Washington Post* had to have an impact. Now Horton figured that the chances of the *Kelo* case's getting selected had just jumped to about fifty-fifty.

Londregan wanted to give Will a piece of his mind. He pulled out his notepad and ripped off a scathing letter. "What are you talking about?" Londregan began, ripping Will for the way he had gone after the city and ignored the other side of the argument. "You obviously have never read the Municipal Development Plan."

After making all his points, Londregan reviewed what he had written. Satisfied, he crumpled it up and tossed it in the trash. What good would it do to send it? Will was just another voice in the media who didn't get it, he figured.

But Will wasn't just another voice. His column caused a major stir and touched off a slew of stories on national television and radio programs. There were so many requests to talk to the Fort Trumbull homeowners that the institute's John Kramer had to pick and choose which ones the plaintiffs would meet. He lined up Matt Dery on CNN. He sent Susette to appear on National Public Radio. The question on everyone's mind was simple: would the Supreme Court take the case?

September 28, 2004

Scott Bullock picked up the phone in his Washington office and the caller identified herself as a clerk at the Supreme Court. "I just wanted to tell you that the court accepted cert. today in the *Kelo* case," she said.

"What?" Bullock shouted, too shocked to believe what he just heard.

"*Kelo?*" the clerk said, thinking Bullock didn't know what case she was talking about.

"Yes . . . Yes," Bullock said. "Thank you."

He dropped the phone and bolted down the hall to Dana Berliner's office.

She was at her desk doing research. Bullock leaned down and gave her a hug. She had no idea what was happening.

"The Court just accepted *Kelo,*" he whispered in her ear before pulling back to see her reaction.

"Oh . . . my . . . God!" she said.

Bullock roared.

They couldn't wait to call the clients.

Susette was on duty at the hospital when Bullock reached her.

"I have some incredible news, Susette. The Court has agreed to hear the case."

"Are you shittin' me?"

He assured her it was true. And her life was about to change as a result. Hers was the lead name on a historic case before the Supreme Court of the United States.

"I can't believe it," she shouted. "I can't believe it."

As soon as she hung up, Susette started calling the others. The phones were jammed all afternoon. Friends, family, and reporters were trying to reach the plaintiffs for reaction. When her shift ended at 3:30, Susette sped back to her neighborhood. The group had agreed to assemble at the Dery house. It was time to raise the glass again.

Susette didn't bother stopping home to change out of her nursing whites. She couldn't wait to get to Matt's place.

Von Winkle arrived right after she did.

"We're gonna win, right?" she said.

"I think we got 'em now, Red," Von Winkle said, smiling.

"We gotta win. Why else would they take the case if we weren't going to win?"

Neighbors and friends dropped by to congratulate the group. Some visitors even left gifts. One of Matt Dery's friends, a trucker, called all the way from Jackson, Mississippi, to say he had just heard the news on the radio.

Members of the local press showed up to get reactions.

Susette just beamed.

"It's been like a seven-year prostate exam," Dery told a reporter as a photographer snapped pictures.

Susette laughed. Dery liked comparing the struggle to preserve their homes to a never-ending rectal exam. She agreed. But suddenly it was all worth it.

The news came like a kick in the gut. Tom Londregan had never expected the Supreme Court to take up the property owners' appeal. All he could do now was shake his head. He could hear the institute ginning up its press releases now.

But Londregan did see one positive point—the city would get exceptional legal representation at no charge. Wes Horton was on the hook to handle the oral argument and preargument brief at no charge.

Londregan and Ed O'Connell from the NLDC drove up to meet with Horton in his Hartford law office.

"So, Wes," O'Connell said, seated across from him at his desk, "what's it going to be like sitting at counsel table, facing the Supreme Court justices?"

"I don't know," Horton said, smiling. "I've never been there."

Despite having handled hundreds of appeals cases and being admitted to practice before the U.S. Supreme Court since 1975, Horton had never actually argued a case before the highest court.

"Well then, what the hell did we hire you for?" Londregan blurted out.

All three men broke into laughter.

"Tom," Horton said, "the last time a civil case from the Connecticut Supreme Court made it to the U.S. Supreme Court was over thirty years ago. We weren't even lawyers back then."

"This place looks like Beirut," Susette told a feature writer from *People* magazine as she walked her through the neighborhood, pointing out the rubble of all the homes and businesses that had been demolished by the NLDC's wrecking balls.

Back when Bullock had first agreed to represent Susette, he had told her she'd have to get used to working with the media. She had never imagined that would mean talking to a celebrity magazine like *People*, not to mention reporters from the *New York Times*, the *Wall Street Journal*, *USA Today*, the *Washington Post*, ABC's *World News Tonight*, CNN, and *NBC Nightly News with Tom Brokaw*. All had called since the Supreme Court took up her case. Some wanted to know more about the woman whose name appeared on the case. The institute had arranged for a writer and photographer from *People* to spend the day with Susette at her home. On December 13, 2004, the magazine ran pictures of her and her pink house with a story about the case.

Later that week Susette received a personal letter from Steve Forbes, CEO and editor-in-chief of *Forbes* magazine. It read, "Dear Ms. Kelo: You might be interested in one of the editorials on page 25 of the enclosed *Forbes* magazine. Best Wishes. Steve Forbes."

The enclosed editorial, "Don't Junk Property Rights," had been written by Forbes himself and included a photograph of Susette's house. Forbes's essay called on the Supreme Court to do the right thing.

Susette didn't know Forbes's name and she had never read his magazine. But she appreciated his support.

Tom Londregan got almost as many media inquiries as Susette. Only his weren't nearly as flattering. Reporters from around the country were calling his office with questions he felt were unfair, such as, "I hear you're taking an eighty-seven-year-old woman and throwing her out of her house?" which one writer from Texas asked.

Trained to ignore the media and focus on the law, Londregan nevertheless finally agreed to sit down with a television interviewer and tell his side of the case. Tired of sitting back while the Institute for Justice framed the case for the media, Londregan spent over an hour being interviewed.

When he watched the news report a few nights later, he discovered that his entire interview had been reduced to a ten-second sound bite. The reporter had completely ignored all the legal arguments Londregan had used to justify the exercise of eminent domain. Instead, the entire segment focused on plaintiff Byron Athenian and the fact that he and his elderly mother were being driven from their home.

"Oh my God," Londregan said. "This is a nightmare, an absolute nightmare."

Despite all the negative publicity the city faced in the national press, nothing outraged Londregan as much as a short letter-to-the-editor that appeared in his hometown paper, the *Day*. After the NLDC publicly criticized the Institute for Justice for its public-relations efforts, Scott Bullock had submitted a five-paragraph letter to the editor. In it he said his clients could hold their heads high knowing they had fought for the rights of every homeowner in America. "In contrast, New London city councilors, NLDC members and their lawyers should hang their heads in shame at what they have done to Fort Trumbull property owners, the citizens of their city and state, and to the Constitution of the United States," Bullock wrote.

The suggestion that he should hang his head in shame pushed Londregan over the edge. He called up Bullock and ripped into him for what he had written. "That is the most insulting thing anyone has ever said to me in my entire practice of law," Londregan said.

"Are you kidding me?" Bullock asked.

Londregan wasn't kidding. And he let Bullock know he didn't care for his style.

Convinced he was on the right side of the argument and that

lawyers shouldn't be immune to criticism, Bullock didn't care what Londregan thought of him.

Even after he hung up, Londregan couldn't stop fuming. He had heard and seen enough of Bullock. The legal dispute had crossed over into a personal one. More than ever he wanted to beat this guy.

Bullock felt the same way about Londregan.

39

THE SUPREMES

It took Wes Horton thirty years to have a case before the U.S. Supreme Court. The opportunity would probably never come again, and he prepared accordingly. His secretary cleared his calendar for two months prior to the oral argument. His law partners took over all his other cases. And he locked himself away to research, write, and strategize.

A talented tactician with no emotional investment in the consequences of the case, Horton set aside his personal feelings about eminent domain, the city, the homeowners, and the media. He focused on one thing and one thing only: getting five of the nine votes on the Supreme Court. That's all he needed to win, nothing more and nothing less.

Going in, Horton figured he had four votes from the Court's liberal justices: John Paul Stevens, David Souter, Stephen Breyer, and Ruth Bader Ginsburg. He expected they would side with the city's argument that by creating jobs and generating tax revenue from the development, the city would lift the poor. Horton didn't worry about these four justices. Nor did he bother with the Court's three conservative justices, William Rehnquist, Antonin Scalia, and Clarence Thomas—he figured they would vote Bullock's way. That left Sandra Day O'Connor and Anthony Kennedy. In Horton's mind, they were the swing votes. If he could get just one of them to accept his argument, he had the case won. He geared his entire oral argument to appeal to O'Connor and Kennedy.

Studying both justices, Horton determined they were less dogmatic and more likely to ask fact-based questions concerning the New London case. He figured he should do something unusual—prepare a blow-up diagram of the neighborhood and use it to show the justices exactly what the city planned to do in the Fort Trumbull neighborhood.

Along with his visual aid, Horton polished his argument, knowing that legal precedent favored the city. When the U.S. Supreme Court had issued its authoritative decision on eminent domain in 1954, it had affirmed the government's right to take private property for public purposes. The only time it had revisited the issue since then was in 1984, when the Court actually expanded the public-use doctrine to allow Hawaii to condemn and redistribute massive amounts of real estate that had been held by wealthy families prior to Hawaii's joining the Union. O'Connor had written the majority opinion.

Satisfied, Horton tested his case on a group of experienced judges and lawyers who played the role of Supreme Court justices in a mock hearing known as a moot court. The first moot court took place at the University of Connecticut's law school. At one point, as Horton argued that a city's desire to create economic development should justify taking private land under the public-use doctrine, a judge interrupted and asked a hypothetical question: under Horton's theory was it permissible for a city to take property from a small motel and award it to a big hotel capable of generating much more in tax revenue for the city?

It was just the kind of hypothetical question a Supreme Court justice might ask. Horton instinctively answered no, insisting that was probably taking the eminent domain doctrine too far.

In a subsequent moot court before judges and attorneys at Georgetown's law school, Horton got asked the same question. Again Horton answered no. Only this time the judges pressed Horton with follow-up questions. What about if private land was taken from Party A and given to Party B, who promised to build three more hotels on the land, or six, or even a dozen hotels? Certainly that would generate much more tax revenue. Wasn't that a valid public use?

The point was clear. If a city was justified in taking private land to put it to a use that would generate more tax revenue, where did you draw the line between what was permissible and what wasn't?

The more Horton tried to articulate where the line should be drawn, the deeper he dug himself into a hole. Before he knew it, he had spent fifteen minutes trying to answer that one question. He had only thirty minutes for his entire oral argument.

The mock arguments exposed the Achilles' heel of the city's position. Once you expanded the public-use doctrine from taking private land for schools, hospitals, and roads to include economic development, there was no way to draw a boundary on how far a city could go to take people's homes or businesses in the name of economic development. It was a point the institute kept stressing in its arguments. Horton and Londregan knew they had to figure out what to say.

Horton's solution was a practical one—simply change the answer to yes. They should acknowledge right off the bat that it was okay for the city to take land belonging to a small motel and award it to a developer building a big hotel because it would help the city generate more taxes and more jobs.

Londregan bristled, insisting the city wasn't doing anything like taking land from a small motel and giving it to a big hotel. If the Supreme Court asked that question, he wanted Horton to simply say that the question didn't really apply in this instance.

"But I can't tell a justice: 'Your Honor, the question is irrelevant,'" Horton argued. "You have to say either yes or no. And no matter which one you answer, you're going to have a problem. It's sort of like asking 'Are you still beating your wife?'"

Londregan refused to concede the point. "You tell the Supreme Court you don't have to answer that question because we do not have a pure taking from A and giving it to B," Londregan maintained. "We don't have that situation. We have substantial public benefits and public uses."

Horton decided Londregan's answer would end up bogging down the rest of his argument, and he couldn't afford to spend fifteen minutes trying to explain what Londregan was saying. If asked, he planned to simply say yes.

Londregan didn't like it, insisting that answer played right into the Institute for Justice's hands. Horton would be supporting what Bullock had been telling the media and the courts for two years.

"My job is to get five votes," Horton snapped, "not to win the publicity campaign."

Divided over what Horton should say, both men hoped the Supreme Court simply wouldn't ask the question.

Susette had never even been to New York City, never mind to the nation's capital. When Bullock told her she could bring one person with her to observe the oral arguments, she decided to bring LeBlanc. Although his diminished mental faculties wouldn't enable him to understand or appreciate the magnitude of the moment, she felt he deserved to be there. He'd stuck by her through the entire legal struggle. She couldn't see leaving him behind for the best part, even if it meant she'd have to divide her attention between celebrating the moment and looking after him.

The flight to Washington was rowdy. The plaintiffs ended up on the same plane as Londregan and all the City Hall employees and NLDC staff going down to observe the argument. Then both sides ended up at the same restaurant that evening. While people ate, drank, and carried on, Susette couldn't help questioning if what she was experiencing was really happening. In one corner of the restaurant she could see the NLDC and the City Hall folks. All around her sat her neighbors, an unlikely assembly of blue-collar people who had banded together to try to save their homes. She couldn't believe they were all just hours away from squaring off in the U.S. Supreme Court.

February 22, 2005

In the morning Susette flipped on the television in her hotel room. Rallies and protests against eminent-domain abuse were taking place in Philadelphia, St. Louis, Kansas City, Dallas, Minneapolis,

San Diego, and a half dozen other cities across the country, all inspired by her case. She put on the pink blazer she had brought to wear especially for the oral argument. It matched perfectly the shade of paint on her house.

Holding LeBlanc's hand, she approached the Supreme Court building, noting the words "EQUAL JUSTICE UNDER LAW" above the entrance. The massive marble columns and ornate surroundings overwhelmed her. The place seemed more like a cathedral than a courthouse. "Boy, this place is pretty impressive," she whispered.

LeBlanc didn't reply.

The hallway leading to the spectator gallery was packed. Susette figured it must have been similar on the day *Roe v. Wade* was argued. She took her seat toward the front, spotting Bullock, Berliner, and Mellor standing at the counsel table. Bullock made eye contact with her and smiled.

He and Mellor and Berliner had one thing on their mind: convincing the justices that by allowing private homes to be taken for economic development in New London the Supreme Court would be putting private homes and small businesses at risk everywhere in the country. If Bullock could get them to see the long-range ramifications of affirming the Connecticut ruling, five of the justices would have to put a stop to it.

All the small talk ended abruptly when the justices entered the chamber. Two were absent. Chief Justice William Rehnquist was home battling cancer and Justice John Paul Stevens had gotten stranded at an airport. By seniority, Justice Sandra Day O'Connor presided.

"We will now hear argument in the case of *Kelo v. City of New London*," O'Connor said. "Mr. Bullock."

Bullock rose. "Justice O'Connor, and may it please the Court. This case is about whether there are any limits on governments' eminent-domain power under the public-use requirement of the Fifth Amendment. Every home, church, or corner store would produce more tax revenue and jobs if it were a Costco, a shopping mall, or a private office building. But if that's the justification for the use of eminent domain, then any city can take property anywhere within its borders for any private use that might make more money than what is there now."

Justice Ginsburg interrupted him. "Mr. Bullock, you are leaving out that New London was in a depressed economic condition," she said. "The critical fact on the city side, at least, is that this was a depressed community and they wanted to build it up, get more jobs."

"Every city has problems," Bullock said, pointing out that the Connecticut law applied to every city, not just depressed ones. "Every city would like to have more tax revenue."

"But you concede," Ginsburg said, "that on the facts, more than tax revenue was at stake."

"It is a desire to try to improve the economy through tax revenue and jobs. That is certainly the case," Bullock said. "But that cannot be a justification for the use of eminent domain."

Justice O'Connor asked Bullock what standard he proposed to draw a line between when cities could take private land and when they couldn't. Bullock said municipalities should not be able to take land for private uses.

Justice Breyer pointed out that every taking has some public benefit, whether it's increasing jobs or increasing taxes. "That's a fact of the world," Breyer said. "And so given that fact of the world, . . . why shouldn't the law say, okay, virtually every taking is all right, as long as there is some public benefit?"

"Your Honor," Bullock said, "we think that cuts way too broadly."

"Because?"

"Because then every property, every home, every business can then be taken for any private use," Bullock said.

"No," Breyer countered, "it could only be taken if there is a public use, and there almost always is. Now, do you agree with that, or do you not agree with my last empirical statement?"

For most of the remainder of his time, Bullock encountered question after question from the justices, demanding that he tell them where they should draw the line in eminent-domain takings. Even Justice Scalia seemed skeptical of one of Bullock's arguments. "Do you want us to sit here and evaluate the prospects of each condemnation one by one?" he asked.

It all sounded pretty brutal to Susette, like being on a firing line facing seven shooters. Bullock could barely finish answering one justice before another came in with another question. The hypotheticals had Susette's head spinning. What did any of it have to do with her house?

As Wes Horton looked on, he was convinced that his inclination to avoid this same barrage by saying yes to a hypothetical question about hotels was the right move, even if it meant going directly against Londregan's wishes.

Bullock had just three minutes left before a red light would signal his time was up. Convinced he would need to respond to some of Horton's arguments, he asked to reserve his remaining three minutes until after the conclusion of Horton's time.

"Very well," O'Connor said. "Mr. Horton."

Horton took the floor. "There is no principled basis for a Court to make what is really a value judgment about whether a long-term plan to revive an economically depressed city is a public use of higher or lower rank constitutionally," Horton said.

The justices immediately asked him where he would draw the line. Horton said he wouldn't draw one.

Scalia persisted. "I just want to take property from people who are paying less taxes and give it to people who are paying more taxes," he said. "That would be a public use, wouldn't it?"

Before Horton could answer, Justice O'Connor jumped in. "For example, Motel 6 and the city thinks, 'Well, if we had a Ritz-Carlton, we would have higher taxes.' Now, is that okay?"

"Yes, Your Honor. That would be okay."

Bullock couldn't believe his ears. Stunned, he dared not look at Mellor or Berliner. Horton had just conceded the fundamental point of the institute's argument. He had admitted what Bullock had been trying to get the Court to see all along.

Horton's answer appeared to stun O'Connor, too. The expression on her face changed from inquisitive to bewildered.

Londregan bit his lip. The one question he had hoped wouldn't get asked had been asked. And Horton had given the answer he hadn't wanted him to give. To Londregan, it had landed with a thud.

Scalia made sure to drive the point home. "Let me qualify it," he said. "You can take from A to give to B if B pays more taxes?"

"If it's a significant amount," Horton replied.

"I'll accept that," Scalia said. "You can take from A and give to B if B pays significantly more taxes . . . You accept that as a proposition?"

"I do, Your Honor."

Suddenly Bullock figured he didn't need to say much in his three-minute rebuttal. Horton had just made his case for him.

But Horton got the result he wanted. The justices stopped asking him hypothetical questions about what kind of takings were permissible, and he didn't get bogged down trying to justify where to draw the line between when it was okay for a city to take land and when it wasn't. It freed him to stress what he wanted to stress—that New London had no choice but to take land through eminent domain because it had the difficult task of assembling a ninety-acre parcel and the holdouts were right in the middle of the redevelopment-area footprint.

"Well, let's look at the specifics here," O'Connor said. "Pfizer is already in place. That's happened."

"Yes, Your Honor."

"So what are these parcels of the people now before us going to be used for?"

Horton had guessed right—O'Connor wanted to focus on the facts of the case. He pulled out his diagram. "If I may show you, Your Honor," he said, directing her attention to the illustration. "We are out on a peninsula here," he said, pointing. "And here is Pfizer down here, which at the time of the taking was almost completed. They moved in a month afterwards."

"Let's talk about the litigants," O'Connor said.

"They are in Parcel 3," Horton said, pointing to it, "and they are in Parcel 4-A."

"What's planned for 3 and 4-A?" O'Connor asked.

"What's planned for 3 is that it's going to be office space," Horton said. "And the expectation is that it will attract the sorts of offices that will feed on Pfizer. They spent $300 million on the site here . . . Parcel 4-A is for park support or marina support."

Horton finished by talking about compensation, pointing out that the city had tried to compensate the homeowners.

"What this lady wants is not more money," Scalia interjected. "No amount of money is going to satisfy her. She is living in the house . . . and she does not want to move . . . It seems to me that's an objection in principle, and an objection in principle that the public-use requirement of the Constitution seems to be addressed to."

Horton countered that the public doesn't need to actually use the property in order to satisfy the public-use requirement.

"I'm not proposing that the state has to use the property itself," Scalia said. "I'm simply proposing that its use not be a private use which has incidental benefits to the state. That is not enough to justify use of the condemnation power."

Horton tried to cut in.

Scalia kept going. "It's quite different to say you can give it to a private individual simply because that private individual is going to hire more people and pay more taxes. That, it seems to me, just washes out entirely the distinction between private use and public use," he said.

"Well, I don't agree, Your Honor," Horton said, hoping to sum up. "So it seems to me the four words I think that this Court should consider—"

Suddenly, his red light came on, signaling his time was up. "And I'm not going to tell you the four words since my red light is on. Thank you, Your Honor."

His ending drew muffled laughter from the gallery.

Justice O'Connor invited Bullock to make a three-and-a-half-minute rebuttal. Before he could start, Justice Kennedy stopped him. "Mr. Bullock, do you know those four words?" he asked.

The courtroom and the justices laughed loudly.

"I wish I did," Bullock said, smiling.

Horton smiled at Kennedy.

When things quieted down, Bullock wrapped up by harking back to Horton's earlier concession: "I think the key to understanding their argument is the answer to the question, 'Can you take a Motel 6 and give it to a fancier hotel?' Their answer is yes. And that's what's really at stake here."

The smile on Londregan's face quickly evaporated.

"These condemnations are taking place throughout the country," Bullock continued. "A city in California condemns the 99 cents store in order to give it to Costco . . . They did so because they wanted to get the tax revenue, and that's the problem with these types of condemnations . . . The one thing that all poor neighborhoods share in common is that they don't produce much in the way of tax revenue. So you're going to put poor neighborhoods and working-class neighborhoods like the ones that exist in Fort Trumbull in jeopardy if the Court affirms the lower court's decision."

At 11:12, the argument closed. Londregan was still fuming over O'Connor's Motel 6 question. "O'Connor was just wrong," he said. "She did not read the municipal-development plan. It cost us $25,000 for us to print it and present it to the Court. And by that question, it was clear she did not read it. You could not ask that question knowing that we did $18 million in remedial cleanup of an industrial zone, put in a river walk, put in a public park, and upgraded the roads and sewers. These are all public benefits!"

Horton remained convinced he had given the right answer in simply saying yes.

"I'll tell you what I would have said," Londregan said. "'Your Honor, I hope you don't think that's what we're doing in New London. Please read the municipal-development plan, if for no other reason than the fact that it cost us $25,000 to print the damn thing.'"

As soon as the argument ended, Susette led LeBlanc toward the exit. When she emerged from the building, she bumped into Bullock and Kramer on the top step. A sea of reporters and cameras were camped behind a barricade at the bottom of the steps. Susette had never seen so many members of the media.

"Are you ready to talk to them?" Bullock asked.

"You've got to be kidding me," she said, trying to hold on to LeBlanc, who was attempting to walk off.

Bullock wasn't kidding. He wanted to get down there and talk to the press before Horton and Londregan got outside. And he wanted her to join him.

Susette's stomach felt like it was doing somersaults. She let go of LeBlanc's hand. "I didn't know I had to give a talk here," she said. "What am I supposed to say?"

Kramer kept two sticky notes in his desk drawer. One of them read "TRUTH." "Just tell the truth," Kramer told Susette. "Just tell your story. And if one of the reporters asks you a legal question, just direct it to Scott." Kramer didn't bother to tell her the quote on the other sticky note in his drawer: "Mother Teresa said, 'Facing the press is more difficult than bathing a leper.'"

Suddenly, Susette realized LeBlanc was nowhere to be seen. She was afraid for his safety, but was being herded toward the microphones. A couple of members of the conservancy said they'd find him.

"What do I say? What do I say?" Susette asked. Bullock assured her she'd do fine. "Oh, for the love of God," she said, suddenly feeling queasy.

NPR's Nina Totenberg stepped to her right shoulder and pushed a microphone in front of her. Pete Williams from the *NBC Nightly News* approached her left arm and extended his microphone.

"I was very encouraged by today's arguments with the justices," she began, her voice quivering.

Bullock, Berliner, and the rest of the plaintiffs crowded behind her as she answered questions. By the time the last question came—about the City of New London—the city's attorneys had shown up and were awaiting the chance to tell their side. By then, Susette had found her rhythm.

"They have more than enough room to develop everything that they want to develop," Susette said. "We just simply want to keep our homes."

As she stepped away and the press pool turned toward Wes Horton and Tom Londregan, a print journalist approached Susette. "Do you *really* feel confident that the United States Supreme Court is going to side with the homeowners?" he asked.

"Well, why wouldn't they?" she asked, heading off to find LeBlanc.

He was safe. Her friends from the neighborhood had found him.

40

FOR THE TAKINGS

June 23, 2005

Scott Bullock and Dana Berliner hovered over his computer screen, repeatedly hitting the Refresh icon in hope of seeing a new posting about their case on a Supreme Court blog. With only two days remaining in the Court's session, they knew a decision was imminent. Anxious, Bullock had dispatched a paralegal to the Supreme Court to make sure they had a copy of the decision the moment it became available.

Soon after she left, the firm's receptionist informed Bullock that a clerk from the Supreme Court was on the line. Mellor, Kramer, and other staffers rushed into Bullock's office as he took the call.

"I'm calling about the *Kelo* case. I just want to let you know that the Court has issued an opinion and the decision was affirmed."

"Thank you," he said faintly, putting the phone down.

He looked up at his colleagues and said, "We lost."

No one spoke. No one moved. No one wanted to believe it.

A few minutes later Bullock's paralegal returned from the Court with the published decision.

"We know," Bullock told her as she entered the room.

"It was 5–4," she said.

Bullock and Berliner scanned the opinion. "Promoting economic development is a traditional and long accepted function of government," Justice John Paul Stevens had written for the majority. "Clearly, there is no basis for exempting economic development from our traditionally broad understanding of public purpose."

No basis for stopping a city from taking private homes to give to a private developer? Disgusted, Bullock flipped to the dissent, written by O'Connor. "Today the Court abandons this long-held, basic limitation on government power," she had written. "Under the banner of economic development, all private property is now vulnerable to being taken and transferred to another private owner, so long as it might be upgraded."

O'Connor was one of the justices with a reputation for supporting governmental power to take property under eminent domain. But her dissenting opinion made clear that the *Kelo* decision would go down in history as a breathtaking expansion of the power of eminent domain. "The specter of condemnation hangs over all property," the dissent continued. "Nothing is to prevent the state from replacing any Motel 6 with a Ritz-Carlton, any home with a shopping mall or any farm with a factory."

Her dissent was right out of the institute's brief. Bullock shook his head in disbelief. How could the five majority justices possibly vote for a decision that stood for taking a Motel 6 through eminent domain to replace it with a Ritz-Carlton?

Depressed, Bullock telephoned Susette at her home.

"Susette?"

"Yes."

We lost. The decision was 5–4."

Clutching the phone, Susette went silent. Her lips started quivering, and a tear worked its way down her face.

"I'm sorry, Susette," Bullock said, "really sorry."

Without saying a word, she put down the receiver and walked out to her front porch. What would she do now? Moving into the house in Old Lyme was not an option. The work required to remodel the place was much more extensive than she had anticipated when she had purchased the house. And although her sons had offered free labor, Susette couldn't afford the building materials. It could be a year or two before the house was habitable.

The sea breeze caused her thirteen-star American flag, which was mounted to the front of the house, to flutter effortlessly. It was the kind of summer day that people in coastal New England live for. Sunlight and perfect blue sky blanketed the neighborhood.

Now her view and the neighborhood were going to disappear. She had consumed eight years of her life trying to hold on to her home. In the final analysis, five strangers in black robes had taken it away—five people who lived in the kinds of neighborhoods where eminent domain would never be a threat.

Anger suddenly overtook her sadness. She had gone to America's ultimate source of justice and found none. Instead, she had been insulted. The city had the power to take her home, and she was powerless to stop it. But if the city thought she was giving up, it was sadly mistaken. "I know you won, you assholes," she said. "Now come get us out."

If the courts wouldn't help her, she decided, she'd just take matters into her own hands. She went back inside and called Bullock back.

"If the city wants my home, they are going to have to drag me outta here," she told him.

She headed up the street to find Von Winkle and Matt Dery. Folks were starting to gather at Dery's house. None of them could believe the Court's decision. And none of them planned on going anywhere.

Dery insisted they had to find out their legal options. His eighty-seven-year-old mother, Wilhelmina, could not bear the thought of moving out. She had waited eight long years for someone to save her and her family from having to abandon the only home she had ever known. "We may have lost," Dery said. "But now come get us. Try."

Susette insisted she'd press Bullock to come up with a plan.

Von Winkle left to talk to a reporter out on the street. He compared the Supreme Court's decision to getting blindsided in a fight. "A crazy left hook out of nowhere," he said. "It was a hard blow, but it was no knockout. This is the third round of a fifteen-round bout. We're coming out swinging next round. We're not leaving, not by a long shot."

When Susette got back to her house, she already had voice

mails from people from other parts of the country expressing sympathy, support, and fury. A woman from the South thanked her for her courage. Another woman assured her that the nation was behind her.

The calls kept coming from different area codes and time zones. "Ms. Kelo," one caller from Texas said, "it appears that we have something here in Texas that you folks in New London haven't heard of yet. It's called lock-and-load. If you need us, we'll be there."

Another guy, from nearby Rhode Island, said he had an Uzi and a boat. He offered to sail his boat down the river in front of her home and protect her place at gunpoint if necessary. "I'm serious," he said. "I'm ready and I'll be there."

So many calls came in that Susette never broke free to call Bullock back. Soon reporters and photographers were on her doorstep asking for her reaction.

"I'm tough," she told the reporters, fighting back emotion. Her bottom line was that she wasn't prepared to give up. There was too much at stake. "This isn't about me keeping my house anymore," she said. "It's about people's property rights all over the United States. I've gotten a lot of calls today from people who are disgusted—really disgusted." She paused. "I don't know what's going to happen. But I'm not going anywhere!"

A journalist asked what Susette and the others could do. After all, the Supreme Court had ruled.

"We'll fight," she said. "I know we will. We can't quit now."

Vindication. Tom Londregan and the city finally had it. The highest court in the land had endorsed their redevelopment plan and their methods for implementing it, including the use of eminent domain. The margin was razor thin: 5–4. But a win is a win. Wes Horton had done his job and the city didn't even owe him a legal fee, thanks to the deal Londregan had struck with him earlier on. Could things get any better?

With no more courts left to appeal to, Londregan figured the city could finally get on with its development.

* * *

With the mood at his law firm resembling that of a wake, Chip Mellor ducked into his private office and shut the door. For an hour he took no calls and accepted no visitors while he carefully read the decision.

He wasn't altogether surprised. Before the oral arguments he had polled some experts around Washington who were plugged in to the Supreme Court. He had been told privately that the outcome would be 7–2 in favor of the city. "You've got Scalia and Thomas," one source had told him. "But the rest is uphill. You'll be lucky to get Rehnquist."

Yet Rehnquist had voted the institute's way. And so had O'Connor, the justice that Mellor had been told would never end up on their side. Mellor reread her dissent. One paragraph jumped out at him. "Any property may now be taken for the benefit of another private party," O'Connor wrote. "But the fallout from this decision will not be random. The beneficiaries are likely to be those citizens with disproportionate influence and power in the political process, including large corporations and development firms. As for the victims, the government now has license to transfer property from those with fewer resources to those with more."

In his career, Mellor couldn't remember reading a dissenting opinion that cried out for action more than O'Connor's. And judging from the majority opinion, the only way to fix the problem was to get all the states to reform their eminent-domain laws to specifically prohibit taking private property for the purpose of economic development. The Supreme Court's ruling said that "public use" was defined very broadly and that economic development could be considered a public use under the Fifth Amendment. But states remained free to define "public use" more narrowly under their respective state Constitutions.

The more he thought about it, Mellor couldn't accept walking away empty after getting so close to victory. *We can't just take this defeat*, Mellor thought. *We have to rally. We have to figure out how to take this fight to the states.*

At three that afternoon he emerged from his office and called a staff meeting. Mellor faced his troops and complimented them on their herculean effort over the previous four and a half years. He reminded them that their mission was twofold: litigation and public education. In four years' time they had taken a subject that most Americans had known nothing about, eminent domain, and put it on the tongues and minds of people all across the nation. In their journey to the Supreme Court, they had changed things in ways no one had thought possible. "We've come a long way," Mellor said. "And we took a tough blow today. But I can tell you this—it's not over!"

Bullock liked the sound of that. So did Berliner and Kramer.

Mellor knew the institute had to get the states to adopt higher standards to protect against eminent-domain abuse. The question was how to make that happen. "I don't know what the next steps are," he said. "But when I come in tomorrow morning, I will let you know."

That night Mellor didn't sleep much. His mind wouldn't stop racing. Long before he created the Institute for Justice he had read an old NAACP annual report that stressed the importance of the twenty-year public-education campaign that preceded the landmark *Brown v. Board of Education* decision, which desegregated schools. The NAACP report made clear that public education was an essential part of changing public policy. But Mellor saw a more subtle message: big change requires time and a massive groundswell.

While his wife and two children slept, Mellor decided the institute had to launch a nationwide public-outreach campaign aimed at getting every state in the union to pass legislation against abusive eminent-domain practices.

The next morning Mellor looked at the press reports. The *Kelo* decision was on the front page of papers all across the country, including the *New York Times* with a headline reading: "Justices Uphold Taking Property for Development." The press panned the decision. And the public reaction was universal outrage. Unlike *Roe v. Wade*, which had seemed to split the country along pro-life and pro-choice lines, the *Kelo* decision galvanized almost unanimous anger toward the Court. The combination of a hot-button issue, an engaged media, and an outraged public had created a situation that was stoked for a firestorm. All the institute had to do now was strike a match.

Mellor was convinced that his instincts were right. The institute had to launch a national campaign to turn a bad decision into a good outcome. As soon as he got to his office, he again called the entire staff into the conference room. "Next Wednesday, this is what we're going to do," he said. "We're going to hold a news conference at the National Press Club and announce a $3 million campaign to foment eminent-domain reform in as many states as we can across the nation."

He immediately had everyone's attention, especially Kramer's. It was Friday. Wednesday was only five days away.

"I don't know exactly how we're going to do it or what the campaign will be called," Mellor continued. "But that's what we're going to figure out this weekend."

The message was clear. The institute wasn't packing it in and no one was getting the weekend off. Bullock, Berliner, and Kramer were totally on board. Determined to change things for the better, they felt their drive and inspiration bounce right back.

By the end of the weekend the group had decided to infuse money and manpower into the Castle Coalition, and use it to become a grassroots force to pressure states to change their laws. They came up with a name for their new campaign: Hands Off My Home. And they designed a logo: an image of an ominous hand engulfing a home.

With a brand and an image, the staff divided up responsibilities. Kramer took on the PR campaign. Berliner agreed to work on getting a hearing scheduled on Capitol Hill. She had a connection to a lawyer on the Senate Judiciary Committee. Bullock had responsibility for writing legislative testimony. Other staff was assigned to mobilize grassroots organizers in states across the country. Mellor got the job of raising the money to pay for it all.

Having gotten their assignments, everyone went to work.

41

HISS

July 5, 2005

Shoulder to shoulder and clutching wooden stakes attached to signs—"THIS LAND IS YOUR LAND" and "YOUR HOME IS YOUR CASTLE"—hundreds of people from across the country assembled on the steps of the New London City Hall.

Against a backdrop of yellow "DON'T TREAD ON ME" flags, they chanted: "It might be the law, but that doesn't make it right."

The New London City Council was convening for its first public meeting since the Supreme Court handed down the *Kelo* decision. Figuring it was the perfect place and time to kick off its nationwide Hands Off My Home campaign, Bullock and the institute were on hand to lead a rally. Police barricades surrounded City Hall in an attempt to keep the crowd from blocking street traffic. Eminent-domain opponents were everywhere, along with television cameras and reporters. Most protesters were parents and grandparents, working-class people who normally would never show up for an organized rally.

"We're not here because mom and dad are supporting us while we write our thesis on what's wrong with the country," one fifty-six-year-old man from Maine told a reporter. "We're middle-class Americans who have jobs to go to and families to support and we care very deeply about this."

A businessman facing the loss of his auto-body shop in Newark to eminent domain said: "We're here in support of Susette Kelo and anybody who's being abused by this plague of eminent domain across this country."

When Susette ascended the City Hall steps and approached a bank of microphones, the crowd cheered wildly. Overcome by the support, she pursed her lips and started to cry. Losers aren't supposed to get ovations.

"This has never been about money, as some people would have you believe," she said. "There is no amount of money that could replace our homes and our memories. This is where we chose to settle, and this is where we want to stay. This is America, the home of the free, isn't it?"

Her words drew cheers and chants of support. Bullock led the crowd in chants of "Let them stay!"

Inside City Hall, Tom Londregan was starting to think the world outside had gone mad. Earlier in the day, members of the U.S. Senate had expressed alarm at the *Kelo* decision and announced they were introducing federal legislation to give homeowners more protection against eminent domain. The U.S. House of Representatives even passed a resolution formally condemning the *Kelo* decision. And pundits were branding it one of the worst opinions of the century.

"I thought I won," Londregan said. "I thought I won. But nobody cares. America doesn't accept what the Supreme Court said."

Besides being on the front steps of the building, Susette had been in the morning paper with an editorial. "We will not leave our homes. We have not yet begun to fight," she wrote. "I will go on every radio talk show, every television show and tell this horror story about how the New London Development Corporation, the City of New London, and the United States Supreme Court are kicking seven homeowners out of their homes."

Londregan was beside himself. "As a lawyer, what more can I do?" he said, looking back. "I don't know."

The Supreme Court had settled the legal dispute over eminent domain. The burning question now was what to do about the seven underdog holdouts that stubbornly refused to accept the Court's answer. The city and the NLDC wanted to exercise their legal right to evict them, a process that promised to entail physically dragging people out of their homes, including more than one very elderly resident.

Connecticut Governor Jodi Rell didn't want to see it come to that. She also disagreed with the Supreme Court's decision and she didn't think the homeowners should be forced to give up their properties. While her top advisors closely monitored the situation in desperate search of a political solution, Rell let her frustrations be known. Saying she felt like she was fighting five robed justices in Washington, the governor compared the aftermath of the decision to the Boston Tea Party. "Governor Rell strongly believes that the rights of homeowners should not be trampled upon in favor of the advancement of economic-development interests," her spokesman said.

Determined to avert a street confrontation between the city and the Fort Trumbull residents, Governor Rell called for the state legislature to convene a special summer session to take up public concerns about eminent domain. She also called for a statewide moratorium on all eminent-domain actions while the lawmakers deliberated.

At the state's request, the NLDC promptly announced it would honor the moratorium and refrain from commencing eviction actions until the legislature determined whether it would modify the state's laws dealing with eminent domain.

Rell's response was like night and day compared to the attitude of her predecessor, Governor John Rowland. Susette was so thrilled she began publicly praising Governor Rell and privately sending her e-mails expressing her gratitude. For eight years the state had aided and abetted the NLDC in its aggressive tactics toward the residents. Finally, a political leader in Connecticut had stood up and said it was wrong to force these people out.

But Tom Londregan didn't appreciate the governor's actions one bit. To him, she was pandering, not leading. After all, she had been the lieutenant governor when Governor John Rowland had set the redevelopment plan in motion with Claire Gaudiani and Pfizer in 1998. Rell had been part of the administration that had appropriated the $70 million to the NLDC. Either she had been in the loop when all these decisions had gone down, or she had been incredibly aloof while the state had been charting this course and calling the shots in New London on this project. The NLDC, after all, had taken its marching orders from the Rowland administration, not from the city.

To Londregan it was clear: by wringing her hands over the *Kelo* decision, Governor Rell was ignoring the fact that the state had been behind the whole mess. But Londregan wasn't going to let her get away with it. He sent an open letter to the *Hartford Courant* pointing out her hypocrisy:

> *I read with interest Governor Rell's statement that she is fighting five robed justices at the Supreme Court in Washington. The Governor would also be fighting the commissioners of the Department of Environmental Protection, the Office of Policy and Management and the Department of Economic and Community Development, all of whom approved this plan on her watch. She stated that the government took away the rights of property owners without giving them a voice. Governor Rell should remember that she was their voice as an elected official of the executive branch throughout this process. She agreed to invest $70,000,000 of the state taxpayers' monies to acquire Fort Trumbull, clean and remediate its land, reshape, reconstruct and redesign it. She further claimed that in New London the case to take property was not defensible. If that is the case, then why did the executive branch and the legislative branch agree to implement the plan?*

As the institute and the homeowners continued to gain political traction for keeping the homes, the NLDC became impatient. But it couldn't go after the state as Londregan had—that would be akin to biting the hand that fed it. Instead, the agency wanted to do something to undermine the homeowners' overwhelming public support, since that was what was fueling the political momentum.

Dave Goebel and the NLDC's new president, Michael Joplin, decided to make Susette the focal point of their attack. She was the ringleader; her pink house had emerged as the national symbol for eminent-domain opposition. More than anything, the NLDC wanted to bulldoze that damn cottage into a pile of splinters. It gave the agency fits to see the house in so many prominent national publications and as a television-news backdrop to every story about the case. The picture of Susette's quaint, attractive cottage on the water said more than all the legal briefs and oral testimony about what was wrong with the city's justification for using eminent domain. Anyone who looked at that house could see that the argument for tearing it down wasn't based on necessity or blight. It was based on vengeance. And the more the house withstood demolition, the more people started comparing its stature to that of Lincoln's cabin.

To change public opinion, the NLDC went looking for dirt on Susette. When Joplin and Goebel learned she owned a second home in Old Lyme, they pounced. First, the NLDC spread word through the city that Susette owned an out-of-town residence and had lied on her mortgage application. Meanwhile, city council members received copies of Susette's deed and her mortgage, which indicated the house in Old Lyme was her primary residence.

The NLDC did not bother mentioning that Susette had purchased the house in 2004—right after the Connecticut Supreme Court had ruled that the city could seize her home in Fort Trumbull. She had never even moved into the Old Lyme house. Once the U.S. Supreme Court accepted her appeal, she had abandoned any thought of occupying it. She had only purchased it as a last option in case she was evicted. And to qualify for the mortgage, she claimed the Old Lyme house would be her primary residence, which it would have been if the city had taken her home in New London.

None of that mattered to the NLDC now. "Certainly the Institute for Justice has used her as a poster child of someone who is losing her home," Michael Joplin told the press. "While we know she lives part-time in Old Lyme and basically told her bank that that's her full-time residence."

Goebel went harder at Susette. "The part that disturbs me is the lie that is told when she stands in front of the house and claims it as her home and says, 'I'm never going to leave my castle,' when she signed a piece of paper that she is living elsewhere," he said. "I do not like the lie that was told and the lie that the Institute for Justice perpetuated around the country when she clearly didn't live there. If she did, she lied to the mortgage company. Either way, she was not a good woman during that period."

A reporter assigned to do a story on the NLDC's charges went to Susette's house to get her reaction. After Susette confirmed that she never had lived in Old Lyme, the reporter warned her that Goebel had been "very unkind" in his statements about her.

The following morning Susette got the newspaper. When she read the words "she lied" and "not a good woman," Susette stopped reading. It was bad enough that the NLDC was taking her home. Now they were after her dignity and her reputation too.

"That guy is a real jerk," she said.

When Kathleen Mitchell read Goebel's statements, she knew they had to hurt. She called Susette to try to buoy her up.

"I don't give a shit what he says," Susette said.

But Mitchell knew she did care. Beneath Susette's hard-edge exterior she had a compassionate heart. She hadn't gone into nursing to get rich. She hadn't abandoned Tim LeBlanc when an accident turned him from a lover to a patient. And she had never gotten paid a dime to lead the fight in Fort Trumbull. She didn't deserve to be smeared by the agency that resented her for trying to stop them from seizing her home. Mitchell said that Goebel had gone too far.

"I know what he was trying to do," Susette said. "Instead of taking so much time to try and make me look dirty, why not just tell the truth?"

"Let's go get him," Mitchell said.

It was a Sunday afternoon, and Dave Goebel had family and friends over for a backyard cookout. All of a sudden, it sounded like a parade passing by out front. But it wasn't a holiday. Goebel checked to see the source of the commotion. In front of his house he spotted Mitchell and Susette, who was holding a sign that read, "Goebel Minister of Propaganda." Members of the Fort Trumbull coalition and nurses who worked with Susette at the hospital marched behind them on the sidewalk. Pounding on makeshift drums that Mitchell had made out of empty cat-litter containers, many protestors had their own signs: "It's abuse and the abuser lives here" and "'She is not a good woman,' said the man who kicked the woman when she is down."

All together, they started chanting: "Dave is a bad man. Dave is a bad man."

As the crowd swelled, Susette spotted an authentic military Humvee coming down Goebel's street. Painted in camouflage, the oversize vehicle bellowed smoke from the rear exhaust. The driver had on a World War II military helmet and was puffing on a big cigar. It was Billy Von Winkle looking like General George Patton.

The crowd erupted in laughter and cheers as Von Winkle blasted his horn and parked right in front of Goebel's house, revving up the protestors to chant even more loudly.

Susette didn't know how she would have survived the eight-year struggle without Mitchell and Von Winkle. Every time she had felt ready to give up, they had shown up to steady her with their audacity.

Von Winkle hadn't come alone. John Steffian emerged from the passenger seat, carrying his own sign, which quoted the English poet John Milton: "A dismal universal hiss, the sound of public scorn."

Mitchell loved it. Only John Steffian would bring Milton to a street fight in a Humvee operated by a cigar-chomping funny man dressed up like Patton.

"We need to make more noise," one of the protestors shouted.

Cars passing by started honking while people yelled out the windows, "Give them back their houses!" and, "Eminent domain sucks!"

A lazy Sunday afternoon in New London's most upscale neighborhood had turned into an irreverent street exhibition. Since the demonstration remained peaceful and didn't damage property or obstruct traffic, the police let it proceed without interference. Before long, press photographers showed up on Goebel's lawn to record the spectacle, and a reporter knocked on his door, seeking his reaction. "It was a very good lesson for my grandson in constitutional law," he told the reporter.

The retired admiral did not look amused.

42

BLINDSIDED

Rich Beyer was working when he got a call from his tenant in Fort Trumbull, reporting he had received a notice from the NLDC indicating he had to vacate his apartment. "What is this?" the tenant asked.

Beyer dropped what he was doing and drove to the apartment building to examine the document. It was an eviction notice. Beyer's tenants had ninety days to vacate.

Beyer called Von Winkle and asked if his tenants had received eviction notices. Von Winkle checked and confirmed they had not. But the Cristofaro family and Byron Athenian had.

Beyer got the picture. The three property owners on Parcel 3 of the NLDC's development plan had been targeted. But what about Governor Rell's moratorium? Per request of the governor, all eminent-domain actions in the state were supposed to be on hold until the legislature completed its review. The eviction notices strongly indicated to the homeowners that the NLDC no longer cared what the governor or the legislature said.

Beyer was furious. He and Von Winkle agreed it was time to get Bullock involved. Beyer called him.

At first, Bullock thought Beyer had to be mistaken. But when Beyer read Bullock the notice, he realized it was true. On top of serving eviction papers, the NLDC was also demanding monthly occupancy fees and liability insurance during the interim.

Bullock calmly assured Beyer and the others that the institute would fight the evictions. Then he grabbed Berliner and stormed into Kramer's office and blew his stack. "These bastards never cease to amaze me," he said, insisting it was time to drop the hammer on Goebel and Joplin.

The three of them quickly worked up a press release and sent it off to all the Connecticut media. "The NLDC's actions are breathtaking in their arrogance and defiance of the wishes of Governor Rell and Connecticut's legislature," Bullock said. "The NLDC is an unelected, unaccountable body that has been given the government's eminent domain power and is out of control. It is time Connecticut's political leaders at the state and local levels reel in this group."

Joplin and Goebel didn't appreciate the institute's attack. Goebel implied that the moratorium pledge his agency had taken applied only to new condemnation actions—not the ones involved in the Supreme Court case. "There are no new takings," he told the press. "All this was done five years ago, and now the Supreme Court has ruled. The city has been extremely patient waiting for this to go through the court system. Now that this is done, we're implementing the decision."

Joplin echoed Goebel. "Now we've won," he said. "We've reached the end of legal arguments. It's time to move on and push this project forward."

The next day, news of the evictions and the NLDC's decision to break the moratorium splashed across the front pages. Everyone from the New London City Council to the governor was blindsided. They were shocked that the NLDC would take such a drastic step at such a sensitive time.

The news sparked a backlash against City Hall. The city council looked inept. The NLDC looked ruthless. And the governor's wishes looked irrelevant. The Coalition to Save Fort Trumbull Neighborhood issued a statement calling on the city council to disband the NLDC once and for all.

Indeed, the city council appeared ready to do just that. Just twenty-four hours before the NLDC issued its eviction notices, City Hall officials had met with them on the status of negotiations with the homeowners. No one had said boo about resorting to forced eviction. Now the city council had egg on its face. Tired of looking foolish, some members of the council called for a vote of no confidence in the NLDC.

From the governor's mansion, the situation in New London looked like a never-ending train wreck. The longer the standoff continued, the more publicly embarrassing it became. It was bad enough that Tom Londregan had taken the governor to task in the state's largest newspaper. Now the NLDC had squeezed the property owners, validating the perception that the agency was out of control and out of touch.

Governor Rell was at wits' end. But it was hard to know where to direct her anger. She couldn't go after the city; it had nothing to do with the eviction notices going out. And she couldn't just pound on the NLDC. The agency was a creature of the state, set up by her predecessor to serve as a blunt instrument to allow the state to get its way in New London without interference from locally elected officials. The state had passed $70 million through the NLDC to carry out the project. If the state walked away from the NLDC now, it would be kissing a mighty big investment good-bye.

Angry and embarrassed, Governor Rell huddled privately with her legal counsel Kevin Rasch; her chief of staff, Lisa Moody; and Ron Angelo, deputy commissioner of the state's Department of Economic and Community Development, which had more direct contact with and oversight of the NLDC than any other state agency.

The governor felt like telling the city to simply incorporate the holdouts' houses into the development plan or else. But she wasn't sure the city would comply.

Instead, Rell decided to appoint a special mediator in hope of getting the parties to sit down and find a way to resolve the dispute once and for all without resorting to forced evictions. In the meantime, she dispatched her chief counsel, Rasch, to New London to tell the NLDC to rescind the eviction notices at once.

*   *   *

John Kramer was in his office at the institute in Washington when he read online that Goebel and Joplin had denied breaking their moratorium pledge. Smelling blood, Kramer called Bullock on his cell phone in Baltimore, where he had traveled to give a speech. Bullock took the call on a crowded train platform.

"They are now claiming the pledge only applied to new eminent-domain actions," Kramer said, before reading Goebel's exact quote.

"He's lying!" Bullock shouted into the phone, oblivious of the fact that he was surrounded by commuters. "We have to document their lies. I know there are news stories where they are quoted on this."

While Bullock ranted, Kramer did a quick search on his computer and pulled down an Associated Press story from late July that quoted Joplin saying that the NLDC would allow the houses in Fort Trumbull to stand while the legislature took up the eminent-domain issue. "We are going to abide by the moratorium," Joplin told the press at that time.

"We have to do a news release," Bullock said. "We have to destroy whatever shred of credibility these people have left."

Kramer hated to hesitate when he saw an opportunity to bury an adversary. He kept Bullock on the phone and ripped off a release right on the spot. "NLDC LIES CONTINUE: Associated Press Report Impeaches NLDC Claims That Moratorium Promise Now Only Applies to New Takings." As if writing a criminal indictment, Kramer documented one conflicting statement after another by Joplin, attaching dates and putting the most glaring inaccuracies in boldface.

He read the release back to Bullock. Then Bullock dictated a quote for the end. "The NLDC's claim that the moratorium on eminent domain applied only to new cases and not to the homes in New London is a blatant lie," Bullock said. "Now the NLDC is not only breaking its word and defying both Governor M. Jodi Rell and the Connecticut legislature, but it is outright lying to the media and the public."

"Got it," Kramer said. He hung up and sent off the press release, copying the governor's staff.

*   *   *

When NLDC attorney Mathew Greene learned that the governor's chief counsel, Kevin Rasch, was on his way to New London to meet with NLDC officials he figured heads would roll. Greene had weathered many public-relations storms during his seven-year stint as the agency's in-house counsel, but none of them seemed as threatening as this one. The institute was applying intense public pressure on Goebel and Joplin, and the city council had upped its plans from a no-confidence vote to a demand that the NLDC's senior leadership resign. In a matter of forty-eight hours, the city's plans had gone from merely publicly slapping the NLDC's wrist to cutting off its head.

When Rasch arrived at the NLDC's office, he did not mince words. He said that the governor had lost confidence in the agency and that Goebel and Joplin were on thin ice. The governor wanted the eviction notices rescinded immediately.

Goebel and Joplin agreed to comply. Greene also agreed with the decision to rescind.

Following Rasch's visit, Greene met privately with Joplin and suggested a plan to try to fend off the city council's plan to sever ties with the NLDC. Greene still had the trust and respect of the city council, and if there was any way of working out a compromise, Greene had the best chance of facilitating it. "Utilize me," he told Joplin.

Joplin agreed to have Greene see what he could do.

The same day that the NLDC agreed to rescind the evictions, Susette received a letter from Senator Arlen Specter, chairman of the U.S. Senate Judiciary Committee. It read, "Dear Ms. Kelo: On Tuesday September 20, 2005, the Senate Committee on the Judiciary will hold a hearing entitled 'The Kelo Decision: Investigating Takings of Homes and other Private Property.' I invite you to testify at the hearing, which is scheduled to begin at 10:00 a.m. in Room 226 of the Dirksen Senate Office Building." Specter informed her that she would need to provide seventy-five copies of her written testimony and her curriculum vitae for distribution to the committee and the press.

"My God, when is this going to end?" she said out loud.

The demands on her time were overwhelming her. Everyone, it seemed, wanted her attention. Despite the NLDC's doing everything in its power to wipe out her address—tearing down street signs and refusing to recognize the street addresses in the Fort Trumbull area as valid—the mail carrier knew who lived where and continued to deliver mail. In Susette's case, that meant hundreds of letters from supporters around the country. Unsure of her address, many writers put down only sketchy information on the mailing envelopes, hoping it would be enough to reach Susette.

"Mrs. Susette Kelo, Fort Trumbull Neighborhood, New London, CT 06320," read one envelope from a man in Greenville, North Carolina.

"Susette Kelo & Family, New London, CT 06320," wrote a person in Honolulu.

A man from Waterbury wrote, "Mrs. Susette Kelo at the 1893 John Bishop House, Fort Trumbull, New London, Connecticut 06320."

"Susette Kelo, New London, Conn. 06320," a person from Hollywood, California, wrote.

Some mail didn't even have a zip code, like the letter from Savannah, Georgia, addressed to "Ms. Susette Kelo, Eminent Domain Displaced, New London, CT." Somehow, all these letters of support reached her home. Every letter emboldened her to keep on fighting.

With help from Bullock and the institute, Susette got busy preparing her testimony for the Senate Judiciary Committee hearing.

Behind closed doors, Londregan and the city council met to decide what to do about the NLDC. The councilors remained adamant that the agency had to be reined in. A message had to be sent. The best way to do it was to remove the leadership.

Londregan agreed. From the day Claire Gaudiani had been appointed head of the NLDC, the agency had consistently failed to keep the city in the loop on its decisions. This had been going on for years, and it was time to put a stop to it.

Londregan and the city council agreed that the NLDC needed an ultimatum: either the NLDC would remove Goebel and Joplin at once, or the council would dissolve the entire agency.

September 19, 2005

In damage-control mode, the NLDC rescinded its eviction notices. Nonetheless, the city council convened a public meeting at City Hall to vote on whether or not to cut ties with the agency. All the people who had fought to protect the Fort Trumbull neighborhood showed up beforehand for a massive rally to protest eminent domain. The holdout homeowners attended, along with many of the original members of the Save Fort Trumbull Coalition, including Professor Fred Paxton and Steve and Amy Hallquist. The reunion resembled a revival.

Yet times had clearly changed. Instead of a few dozen supporters from New London, hundreds of newcomers had come from outside the city to show solidarity with the holdouts. When the rally ended, they all tried to pack the council chamber. Throngs of people jammed the lobby and the stairwells leading to the chamber, making it impossible for two of the councilors to get to the meeting.

In the chaos, the fire marshal ordered the crowd to clear the building, declaring that the number of people exceeded that permitted by the building's fire code. Other than those in the chamber, everyone else had to evacuate. That didn't sit well with the crowd. Tempers flared. Policemen formed a barricade outside the chamber. Those stuck in the halls and stairwells began shouting.

One councilor emerged from the chamber to assure everyone outside that the meeting would not go on without them.

Nobody believed it. Fort Trumbull holdout Michael Cristofaro, who had received one of the eviction notices, started shouting at the councilor, demanding a chance to address the council.

Emboldened by Cristofaro's fiery words, the crowd began yelling louder.

"You're inciting these people," the councilor said. "Stop yelling!"

Democracy—messy and volatile—had shown up at City Hall and the politicians didn't know how to handle it. The scene around the chamber was teetering on anarchy.

The city council decided to abort the meeting and postpone the vote. Clearly they needed a bigger venue to accommodate the public.

The police ordered everyone to clear the building.

Susette missed all the commotion. She had flown to Washington to get ready for her appearance the following morning before the Senate Judiciary Committee. Her situation was on the minds of many in Washington. And the outrage over the Supreme Court's decision hadn't died down. A group in Los Angeles had started a national campaign to have Justice David Souter's home in New Hampshire condemned and taken by eminent domain.

In her Washington hotel room, Susette panicked. In twelve hours she'd be testifying before the U.S. Senate and she didn't have her opening statement written. She had already submitted carefully prepared written testimony, but she wanted to make a separate, personal statement when she appeared before the committee.

With so much going on at once, she couldn't think straight anymore. Desperate, she telephoned Mitchell back in New London for help.

"All right, calm down," Mitchell said. "I'll dictate something to you."

"Son of a bitch!"

"What?"

"I don't even have anything to write on."

Mitchell couldn't help laughing.

"Wait, I've got a napkin," Susette said. "Okay. I'm ready. I'm ready."

Over the next thirty minutes, Mitchell helped her craft an

opening statement. Susette thanked her, promising to call her after the hearing.

Before Susette fell asleep, Von Winkle called. He had just returned from City Hall. "You missed the show of the year," he told her. "The place was packed."

"I'd rather be there than here right now," she said.

Von Winkle assured her she'd do just fine in front of the senators. "Go get 'em, Red," he said.

43

LIVING PROOF

September 20, 2005

As a little girl, on her first day of elementary school, Susette had been surprised when her class went to a cafeteria at lunchtime. She hadn't known what lunch was. In her house she had had only two meals a day, breakfast and dinner. She liked school because it offered a hot meal every day.

Entering the U.S. Capitol for the first time, she felt a little like a child all over again. She never realized that people like her—a working-class nurse without a college degree—could get an audience with senators. "Boy, there sure are a lot of people here," she said, taking a deep breath as Scott Bullock ushered her into the hearing room. She took her place at the witness table beside the mayor of Hartford, who had come to testify in favor of eminent domain.

Proud to be on the other side, Susette figured she owed it to millions of other working Americans to do her best to convince the senators that politicians like the one seated next to her didn't care about the little guys.

Susette looked over her shoulder and smiled nervously at Bullock. He gave her a look of confidence. The Susette Kelo in front of him wasn't the same Susette he had met the first time he visited her home, in 2000. During five intense years of ups and downs, victories and setbacks, she had evolved into the leader of a national movement. She wasn't polished and programmed.

346

But that was what made her so effective. You couldn't stage genuineness.

Susette didn't need notes to tell the senators how she found her house and fixed it up on her own, met Tim LeBlanc and fell in love, and thought she was on her way to living happily ever after until she discovered a condemnation notice taped to her door on the day before Thanksgiving 2000. "We did not have a very pleasant holiday," she said, "and each Thanksgiving since has been bittersweet for all of us. We're happy that we are still in our homes but afraid we could be thrown out any day."

Though often distracted at hearings, the senators couldn't help focusing on Susette. Unlike the suits that so often parade before committees—corporate executives, lawyers, lobbyists, and special-interest representatives—she *was* the people, a plain-talking woman with a story that was too infuriating to be made up.

"My neighborhood was not blighted," she said. "None of us asked for any of this. We were simply living our lives, working, taking care of our families, and paying our taxes. The city may have narrowly won the battle on eminent domain, but the war remains, not just in Fort Trumbull but also across the nation. Special interests who benefit from this use of government power are working to convince the public and legislatures that there isn't a problem. But I am living proof that there is. This battle against eminent domain abuse may have started as a way for me to save my little pink cottage, but it has rightfully grown into something much larger—the fight to restore the American Dream and the sacredness and security of each one of our homes."

Bullock wanted to clap.

Senators and their staff surrounded Susette as soon as the hearing concluded. Some praised her courage and determination. Others expressed dismay at the Court's ruling. A staffer from Senator Edward Kennedy's office handed Susette the senator's card. "If you need anything, call his office," she said. "He'll do anything to help you."

Once outside, Bullock patted her on the shoulder. "You did great in there today," he said.

"Well . . . I tried," she said.

44

▲

LEAVE NO FOOTPRINTS

Mathew Greene liked and respected Dave Goebel. He always had. Without him, Greene believed, the NLDC would have crashed and burned a couple of years earlier. As soon as Goebel came on board as chief operating officer under Claire, he had almost single-handedly made the agency run effectively. The guy was immensely organized, paid strict attention to detail, and knew how to run a complicated organization with many moving parts.

Goebel's best asset was his military background, but it was also his biggest liability, Greene had come to observe. The military couldn't survive without a rigid, top-down approach of giving orders and getting results. But democracy only worked when power flowed from the bottom up—from the people to elected leaders. Goebel never seemed to appreciate the public-relations implications of trying to run the politically empowered NLDC like a military unit. There might have been legal grounds to issue eviction notices, for example, but it was a lot like spanking a child in public: the law might permit it, but it always looks brutal when a big person strikes a little one.

Under Goebel's leadership, the NLDC had gone too far this time. The city council was looking for a reason to can him, and the eviction notices fit the bill. Greene knew the city would not back down—Goebel had to go. And so did Joplin.

To save the agency, Greene felt obligated to speak his mind. "I have a lot of respect for you," Greene told Goebel. "You've taken a lot of hits. But I think you should resign."

Goebel disagreed.

Greene tried again. "You can stay on as a consultant," he said. "But you can't be the lead guy. We gotta move forward."

Steve Percy jumped to Goebel's defense, lecturing Greene and declaring adamantly that Goebel would not step aside. Ignoring Percy, Greene told Goebel that he had met face-to-face with members of the city council and learned that the council was considering a lawsuit against the agency.

"Mat, you don't know everything," Goebel said.

Greene didn't like the sound of that. "Well, I'm your legal counsel. I should know everything."

The implication was that the NLDC was also contemplating legal action against the city council.

Greene reminded the board that the NLDC had been created to do a specific job. "We weren't created to become a political body," he said. "Let's do it and get it done." The board was not persuaded. It decided to back Goebel and Joplin. Steve Percy publicly dismissed the city council's demand to remove Goebel and Joplin. "The loss of their leadership would significantly undermine the ability of the NLDC or anyone to carry out the goals of the MDP [municipal-development plan]," he told the press.

Greene resigned and washed his hands of the agency he had represented for nearly eight years. Three days later, the city council formally voted 6–0 to cut ties with the NLDC within two weeks.

The state knew it had a serious problem on its hands. If New London dissolved the NLDC, state law required the city to appoint a successor, a new agency to implement the municipal-development plan. Additionally, the NLDC had its name on scores of contracts with vendors, developers, and lending agencies. Every contract would have to be revised to reflect the change in agencies. All of this was going to take lots of time, money, and lawyers to sort out. Clearly the city council hadn't considered any of this. Rather than looking ahead at the long-term implications, the city council had reflexively decided to teach Goebel and Joplin a lesson.

Despite the state's dissatisfaction with the NLDC, the prospect of seeing the development plan fall into the hands of an inept city council was pretty scary. The state had $70 million on the line. It didn't want to see a dysfunctional political body of ever-changing personnel and unpredictable personalities end up in charge.

Governor Rell turned to her deputy commissioner of economic development, forty-one-year-old Ron Angelo, a fast-rising star in the administration who had the kind of skill set a governor needed in times of political crisis. Angelo had an instinct for seeing the finish line and knowing what kind of tough decisions had to be made to get there. Best of all, he left no footprints.

Remarkably, Angelo had almost no political experience. Before joining the governor's administration a couple of years earlier, he had owned two highly successful companies and had spent some time in the banking industry. His approach to business and problem solving had been influenced by the lessons he had learned from his father. One simple lesson had come from their many hours of playing chess together. Angelo's father had helped him see that to succeed in chess you have to execute each move in anticipation of the next two or three moves.

Politics is a lot like chess. And when Angelo sized up the situation in New London, he saw a city council that had focused on only one move: wiping out the NLDC. Angelo called the city's new mayor, Beth Sabilia, and said the state had real concerns about the city's plans for the NLDC. Angelo suggested a more cautious approach.

Sabilia said the city council was tired of taking a beating for the NLDC's methods. Dave Goebel, she said, looked like a hatchet man.

Angelo got all that. The state wasn't too pleased with Goebel either. Calling Susette a liar and serving eviction notices was pouring salt into open wounds. From the state's perspective Goebel was the wrong man in the wrong place, doing the wrong thing at the wrong time. But blowing up the NLDC wasn't the right move, at least not before executing some other moves.

Angelo's message got through. Behind the scenes, the city council modified its approach. Reading between the lines, city officials suspected that the state was sufficiently irritated with Goebel that it wouldn't protect him. On the other hand, it seemed equally clear that the state wanted Joplin to stay on board to ensure some stability and hands-on experience atop the agency. Desperate to do something to restore its political credibility with the public, the city council decided to focus exclusively on Goebel: either he would go, or the city would follow through on its unanimous vote to disband the agency.

This time Goebel and the NLDC's board acknowledged they were in check. Ending the feud with the city, Goebel resigned. As soon as he did, the city council reversed its 6–0 vote and agreed to keep the NLDC intact. Joplin stayed on as the president.

45

JUST PRAY

Susette believed in luck. And the four-month period since the Supreme Court decision had come down proved to be the hottest good-luck streak of her life. It seemed like every time her phone rang something else good had happened. The city council was imploding. Dave Goebel got toppled. Eminent-domain-reform legislation was making its way through statehouses across the country. Grassroots movements were active in many of the country's major cities. Best of all, Susette and her neighbors were still in their homes.

It was late in October when Susette got a call from Von Winkle. "Have you talked to Rich?" he asked her.

She usually didn't talk with Beyer unless something was up with the city or the NLDC. She figured something must have happened. "No, I haven't talked to him. Why do you ask?"

"Oh, I was just wondering if you had talked to Rich," Von Winkle said before making small talk and hanging up.

A short while later, the phone rang again. It was Beyer calling from Yale–New Haven Hospital.

"Susette?"

She could tell Beyer was crying. She had a feeling the group's luck had just gone bad. "What's the matter, Rich?" she asked.

"My little girl," he said, his voice trailing off.

"Rich, what's the matter?"

Beyer started sobbing.

"Rich, you gotta tell me what's the matter. What's the matter?"

"My little girl is dying."

Attempting to calm him down, Susette asked for more information.

Beyer's eight-year-old daughter had suffered a deadly asthma attack and had been rushed to the hospital in New London before being transferred to Yale–New Haven on life support. Her brain was no longer functioning due to lack of oxygen.

"What can I do? What can I do?" Beyer pleaded.

Susette knew where this was headed. She had administered to children with acute asthma. First came respiratory arrest, followed by cardiac arrest. Without life support, the child's heart would simply stop and she would die.

"Rich," she whispered, choking back tears, "I think the only thing you can do is pray. Just pray, Rich."

She hung up and buried her face in her hands. Then she called Von Winkle and exploded at him for not warning her before she talked to Beyer. "Why didn't you tell me?" she shouted.

"Well, I thought he would have called you."

"You should have told me," she cried. "You should have told me!"

There was a long pause.

"What do you think is going to happen?" Von Winkle said softly.

"She's going to die, Billy," she said. "She's going to die."

Von Winkle didn't know what to say next.

Susette gathered her composure. "I want to go down to New Haven and see Rich. Will you take me?"

"No. I'm not going."

"Why?"

"Susette, let me tell you right now. If anything like that ever happens to me, just leave me alone."

The next day, Beyer's daughter passed away.

A consultant specializing in conflict resolution, Dr. Robert Albright II got a clear mandate from the governor to find a way to settle the standoff in Fort Trumbull that totally averted forced evictions. And to do it quickly.

Albright had mediated bitter disputes involving steelworkers and miners and their respective management in America's rust belt. In such cases, he always began by getting the heads of the labor unions and management to simply start a dialogue. Albright decided on the same approach in New London, reaching out to Londregan and Bullock.

Bullock welcomed Albright's arrival and wasted no time submitting a comprehensive proposal to resolve the standoff. Rich Beyer, the Cristofaro family, and Byron Athenian and his mother were willing to have their houses on Parcel 3 relocated to Parcel 4-A. This approach would completely free up Parcel 3 for development. It would also confine all the holdouts' properties to a small cluster on Parcel 4-A, where the city had no development plans. Bullock pointed out that this would save the state a significant amount of money because none of the property owners would have to be paid compensation and the city could commence construction immediately. "It could be a classic 'win-win' solution for all concerned," Bullock told Albright.

But Londregan shot down the idea. At this stage, why deviate from the ruling? The city had waited seven years to carry out its development scheme. The last four and a half years had been stalled by tough, expensive litigation. Along the way, the city had taken a tremendous beating. For starters, all the negative publicity around the lawsuit had prompted Pfizer to back away from its previous commitment to help pay for the hotel. Without Pfizer's occupancy guarantee, the developer no longer wanted to proceed with the hotel construction.

On a much broader scale, lenders and investors had fled the overall redevelopment project due to the stigma slapped on it by the eminent-domain dispute. No institution wanted to back a project built on land that had been acquired under one of the most despised Supreme Court decisions in decades.

Rather than compromise, Londregan dug in. He told Albright that law, ethics, and precedent made it impractical and improper for the city to go along with Bullock's suggestion to relocate the homes. Instead, Londregan gave Albright a simple response: Albright should tell the state to refuse to consider Bullock's proposal.

From Bullock's standpoint, it was Londregan—not the homeowners—who had most hurt the city. More than anyone, Londregan had led the city's relentless quest to defeat the seven property owners. This obsessive approach had put the entire ninety-acre development plan at risk. Now his equally stubborn position had everyone on a fast track to a confrontation in the streets of Fort Trumbull.

"Londregan is unbelievable!" Bullock told Susette. "He truly doesn't care about New London. The new city council needs to fire him, fast. Rell is pretty smart, though. I think she will choose 90 percent of the public over Tom Londregan!"

46

OPEN THE CHECKBOOK

Frustrated, Bullock reached out directly to Governor Rell's chief council, Kevin Rasch, pointing out that Londregan's arguments were silly and dead wrong.

The dialogue didn't sound encouraging to the governor. She asked Albright for a progress report.

Albright had underestimated the depth of the distrust and disdain between the two sides. He had even tried talking directly to city council members and the holdouts. But that proved difficult too. Individual council members had personal scores to settle and had competing ideas on who was at fault. None of them had a solution to the standoff. About the only aspect they were in sync on was the position that the city would not back down to the holdouts. And when it came to the homeowners, most of them wouldn't even return Albright's calls.

All his years dealing with unions and management had not prepared Albright for the situation in New London. "I gotta tell you, this one is as polarized as anything I have ever encountered," he told the governor's advisors.

That wasn't what the governor's advisors wanted to hear. They wanted a quick fix.

Albright tried explaining that the animosity and distrust in New London had built up over eight years. It wasn't realistic to expect it to dissipate in a few months.

But the state wanted results. Albright had been on the job for five months with a mandate to settle the dispute and so far no one had agreed to settle. It was now time to resort to the most reliable tool for fixing any legal dispute: money.

The governor had set aside $1.4 million to compensate the holdouts. Her staff implored Albright to find out if generous financial incentives might entice any of the holdouts to go peacefully.

Albright went back to work.

March 13, 2006

Word quietly spread through Fort Trumbull that Matt Dery's eighty-eight-year-old mother, Wilhelmina, had finally succumbed, dying in the same house she had been born in. That was all she had ever wanted when the battle to save her home had started, eight years earlier—the opportunity to exit life in the same place where she had entered it.

Her age and the relentless stress of the litigation had prevented Wilhelmina from attending all the court proceedings, legislative hearings, press conferences, and protests. The fear of losing the only home she had ever known had been hard enough to cope with even so. Friends and family were convinced it had shaved a few years off her life.

But her quest to hold on to her home had kept Matt going when he often had felt like giving up. He had owed it to his mother to press on. In one respect, her death marked a milestone and a victory for Matt and his family: they had hung on until Wilhelmina let go.

With the governor's checkbook at his disposal, Albright met with the city first. Any attempt to pay Fort Trumbull property owners more than the fair market value of their properties would require the city to sign off on it. The city council and Londregan said they would go along with the offers since the state was footing the bill. But they insisted on a deadline. The city council thus passed a resolution saying that anyone who didn't accept the state's offer of cash settlement by May 31st would be out of luck. After that, the city would withdraw its consent and would commence evictions.

With the city on board, Albright reached out directly to the holdouts he thought were most likely to listen. As soon as Bullock found out about it, he lost respect for Albright. Mediators, he reasoned, are supposed to be neutral. By flashing money around, Albright looked more like someone doing the city's bidding on the state's dime. The whole approach was an insult to what this case was all about. He called Albright and expressed his displeasure. "This case was never about money," Bullock told Albright.

May 28, 2006

With the deadline just days away, Susette and some of her neighbors were discussing their options over beers at Matt Dery's house. Susette didn't know what to think. The governor had been the holdouts' best ally since the Supreme Court decision. But nearly a year had passed and the city hadn't backed down. It now appeared that the governor was losing her patience with the whole situation and just wanted to see it go away, one way or another.

Suddenly the phone rang. Matt's wife, Sue, took it in another room. When she returned moments later, her face looked like she had seen a ghost.

"I have very bad news," she said.

Everyone stopped talking.

"Derek Von Winkle was shot and killed tonight," she continued.

Susette put her hand over her mouth. "Oh my God," she whispered.

Twenty-five-year-old Derek Von Winkle was Billy's son. Earlier that afternoon, police had found him and his stepbrother, who was confined to a wheelchair, dead in their duplex in a neighboring town. Both had been shot to death. Investigators arrested an eighteen-year-old acquaintance of the men and charged him with two counts of felony murder, robbery, possession of a sawed-off shotgun, possession of marijuana with intent to sell, and possession of hallucinogens with intent to sell.

The news rocked the holdouts. In a seven-month span following the Supreme Court decision, three family members from the fort had died: Beyer's daughter, Dery's mother, and now Von Winkle's son.

Susette wanted to go find Billy right away. But she remembered what he had said when Byron's daughter died: "If something like that ever happens to me, leave me alone."

Instead, she went home and cried.

May 31, 2006

Bob Albright was concerned. Deadline day had arrived and no one had said yes to the state's money. Convinced that getting one holdout to break ranks would loosen the logjam and create momentum for others to follow, Albright had offered $980,000 to Matt Dery for the family's various Fort Trumbull properties, plus an assurance that the city would waive all back taxes, occupancy fees, and sewer and water bills from the previous four-plus years. In fact, the NLDC had owned the properties since 2000 and was therefore solely responsible for the taxes. And a pretrial agreement approved by the court protected the plaintiffs against occupancy fees. Nonetheless, Albright was applying heat and offering way more money than the NLDC had ever offered.

Before sunup, Albright headed to New London intent on sealing the deal. He made Dery a persuasive pitch. The city was at the point where it felt it had waited long enough to carry out its development plan. At midnight the city would walk away from the table and commence eviction actions. With no legal means to stop the city, the state would withdraw its money from the mix and the holdouts would finally lose their homes. In addition, by the time the city slapped on all the back taxes, occupancy fees, and outstanding water and sewer bills that had accumulated during the legal battle, the holdouts would end up homeless—and penniless.

Dery couldn't ignore the grim reality. At this stage, refusing to settle looked like financial suicide. Dery had another reason to put down the sword. His mother had been a driving force in his willingness to fight on for so long, and with her recent passing that was no longer the case. At least he could rest knowing he had achieved his mother's wish, even if he accepted the offer.

Convinced he really had no choice, Dery succumbed and settled.

As soon as Dery settled, his friend and neighbor Byron Athenian and Byron's mother figured they didn't have any choice either. The state offered to pay them $189,652 for their home and moving expenses. That was almost triple what the NLDC had offered to pay them in the beginning.

By 9 a.m. Londregan knew that Dery and Athenian were going. Pleased, he turned up the heat on the others. In an e-mail to Bullock he said the city would grant Von Winkle an extra two weeks to make up his mind on account of his son's murder. "As for Kelo, Beyer, and Cristofaro," he told Bullock, "the city needs their answer today."

Bullock knew beforehand that Dery was going to settle. But Athenian had surprised him. Nonetheless, the others were holding firm, and Bullock had no intention of letting Londregan bully them into changing their minds. He phoned Susette and shared Londregan's e-mail.

She didn't like what she heard. It sounded like Londregan and Albright were in cahoots and the holdouts now had no choice.

"What do you think?" she asked.

"I think it's a bluff," Bullock said.

She wanted some assurance. Bullock said he couldn't be certain, but he suspected that the governor would do anything to avoid the prospect of forcing people from their homes. He said he'd call Albright and talk with him.

Under immense pressure from the state, Albright now made his best pitch to Bullock. The city was done playing. And when they quit playing, the incentive for the state to keep its money on the table would also disappear. Albright had been dealing directly with the governor's chief of staff and the clear message she had sent was that today was do or die. "We need an answer today, Scott, or I think it's done," Albright told him. "I think the governor will walk away."

Bullock told Albright he'd get back to him by the end of the day. He checked in with each of the remaining holdouts except Von Winkle and explained the situation. The dispute had come down to a high-stakes game of chicken. By breaking the deadline, the holdouts risked losing their homes and being saddled with enormous back taxes and occupancy fees. But the state, Bullock argued, was taking an even bigger chance. If it walked away from the table at the midnight deadline, the state risked the spectacle of the city dispatching law-enforcement officials to drag Susette and others from their homes on national television.

"I'm staying," Susette said.

The others agreed.

Bullock got hold of Albright. "We're not settling today and you can walk away if you want."

Albright contacted the governor's office with good news and bad news. Two had settled; four had not.

The governor wanted a read on the remaining four.

Albright had made little headway with them. Von Winkle was, for now, out of the picture, due to his son's death. As a nonresident of New London, Beyer remained a possible candidate for settlement if the state came up with enough money. But the Cristofaros and Susette were adamantly opposed to settling under any terms.

What now?

One thing was clear: money and a drop-dead deadline weren't going to do the trick. And no doubt Londregan and the city were ready to pull the trigger on eviction proceedings. The governor needed a new plan, and she needed it fast.

With three hours to go until midnight, a satellite broadcast truck from the Fox News Network's *Hannity & Colmes* show was stationed on the street in front of Susette's house. A massive spotlight illuminated her house as the program came on the air.

"The nationwide battle over eminent domain began with this home one year ago with the Supreme Court's landmark decision in *Kelo v. the City of New London, Connecticut.* Tonight marks the deadline given by the city for the homeowners to sell off their properties. The city council can begin eviction procedures with a vote on Monday. Joining us now from her home is Susette Kelo. And joining us from Washington is her attorney Scott Bullock. Susette, welcome," said Alan Colmes. "I guess right in back of you is the home that started this whole case. And you're not going to sell, correct?"

"Correct," she said. "I think we need to understand that none of us are selling. Our properties were taken by eminent domain."

Colmes turned to Bullock. "What happens now? She doesn't sell. The city says the deadline is right here? So what happens after this?"

"We hope that cooler heads prevail," Bullock said. "This is land that isn't needed for development."

"Hey, Susette, it's Sean Hannity here. Did you ever dream that one day you'd have a landmark Supreme Court decision with your name on it?"

"It's more like a living nightmare than a dream."

Hannity told Susette he'd probably side with the city if they wanted her home to make way for a school or a highway. But he knew that wasn't the case. "If they're going to knock your house down so they can build a bigger house with bigger tax revenue," Hannity said, "that seems like legalized stealing."

"What they're doing is wrong," Susette said. "It was wrong when it started nine years ago. And it's still wrong today. I don't even know what to say anymore."

Hannity looked to Bullock. "Susette's not going to leave. Are they going to arrest her? Are they going to take her out in hand-cuffs? Are they going to throw her out of her house? Are they going to evict her? Maybe David Souter ought to come down there and take a look at her being evicted from her house."

"Well, I certainly hope that doesn't happen because it is completely unnecessary," Bullock said. "That's the amazing thing about this whole situation. This doesn't have to happen."

"Unbelievable," Hannity said.

"Susette," Colmes said, "we thank you for fighting the good fight. We'll continue to follow this story. We thank you very much for being with us tonight."

Suddenly the spotlight went dark and Susette's earpiece went dead. The cameraman approached and removed the microphone from her sweater and shook her hand. "Good luck with what you're doing," he told her. "We support you."

The crew packed their equipment into the truck and drove off, leaving Susette standing alone in the middle of her empty, dark street. None of the other holdouts were on hand. No supporters were standing by. For the first time in eight years, Susette felt completely and totally alone in the struggle against the city. And for the first time, she got a sense of what it would feel like if she prevailed and got to stay in the fort—awfully lonely.

Now she wanted to leave. The thought of staying behind in an abandoned neighborhood without her friends felt terribly depressing.

Yet she couldn't pack it in now. She had an obligation to the nation. Letting go was not an option.

She looked up at her house. "There's no way I can let these people knock my home down," she said out loud.

She went inside and went to bed, wondering what the city would do in the morning.

Governor Rell didn't need reminding that the national media had its eye on whether the city would close in on the remaining holdouts. She pressed her staff and they pressed Albright.

He lobbied for a little more time and a lot more money to work on Beyer and Von Winkle. Neither of them lived in the fort neighborhood, and both of them were businessmen with a considerable amount of money tied up in their buildings. If the state came up with more resources, these two would probably make the smart business decision and finally bow out.

Rell committed another $1.2 million to be made available for settlement funds and she agreed to extend the deadline to June 15. But the state needed a fallback position for Susette and the Cristofaro family. They lived in their homes and had made it abundantly clear no amount of money would get them to go. The governor didn't want to see them forced out, but the state couldn't force the city to return their property deeds. The governor and her staff formulated a contingency plan to deal with Susette and the Cristofaro family. Then Rell faxed a letter to Mayor Sabilia explaining the governor's position. It read: "The State of Connecticut recommends that the City offer to relocate their primary residences (but not investment properties) to an appropriate location on Parcel 4-A, accompanied with a deed to the parcel upon which their homes will be relocated. Such deeds should include restrictive covenants to protect the development and cause title to the properties and all improvements to revert to the City upon transfer or death of the title holder."

The ball was now in the city's court.

47

THE ENDGAME

June 1, 2006

"Did I wake you?" Bullock asked Susette.

"Are you kidding me? I've already had fourteen calls this morning."

It was 7 a.m., and Susette's appearance on the Fox News channel ten hours earlier had triggered a new round of offers from people around the country who wanted to help protect her home from the city. Some of the callers had scared Susette. A militia group that opposed the government's actions wanted to send men with guns to fend off the city.

"This shit is getting out of control," Susette said.

"No matter what you do, stay away from those people," Bullock said.

"For God's sake, I am," she said, shaken by the fact that violent fanatics might soon be on her doorstep. "But if the city doesn't back down they're going to have blood in the streets."

Bullock had a more immediate problem to address: Governor Rell's letter to the city. He was not surprised that the governor had extended the deadline a couple more weeks and was prepared to pump more money into settlements. But he was furious at her fallback position—allowing the holdouts to maintain lifetime use of their properties—but with the titles reverting back to the city at death. "That's completely unacceptable," Bullock said. "That's not true ownership."

"It sounds like Governor Rell is abandoning us," Susette said. "Why doesn't she stand up to the city?"

"I don't know," he said. "But we're going after the governor."

By the time she hung up with Bullock, Susette was late for work. Racing out of her neighborhood she spotted Von Winkle working behind the window in his shop. It was the first time she'd seen him since his son's murder.

Eager to talk to him, she telephoned him as soon as she reached her office. She figured she'd begin by asking him about the governor's mediator.

"Albright call you?" she asked.

"No. Did he call you?"

"Nope."

She told him that Matt Dery and Byron Athenian had settled.

Von Winkle didn't say much. The swagger in his manner had disappeared, the humor in his voice snuffed out by a bullet.

"I probably can't do anything for you," Susette told him. "But I feel really bad, Billy. If you're going to stay, I'll stay."

"You're not going to drive me crazy today, are you, Red?"

She sensed a faint tone of sarcasm. Boy, she missed the old Billy.

Bullock and Kramer worked up a press release that portrayed the governor as a flip-flopping politician who was abandoning the homeowners at the eleventh hour. Bullock then called the capitol building in Hartford and got Representative Bob Ward, one of the ranking Republican legislators. Ward had come out hard against the Supreme Court decision and had previously called the NLDC stupid. More importantly, he had a direct line to the governor.

Bullock read the merciless press release nailing the governor for abandoning the homeowners and mocking her proposal to give the homeowners lifetime use of their properties. "That's the legal equivalent of being a serf," Bullock said.

A practical politician who didn't want to see a Republican

governor take a hit in the national media, Ward clearly got the picture. "Give me two hours," he told Bullock.

Later that afternoon, Governor Rell revised her position. "I believe strongly that the residents of Fort Trumbull have a right to hold property, to hold the title to that property and to pass that title on to their children," she wrote in a follow-up letter to Mayor Sabilia.

Bullock agreed to quash the press release. The way had been paved for Susette and the Cristofaros to keep their homes. The governor had made clear her intentions. If the last two holdouts didn't want to accept the state's money, their titles should be returned and the city should move forward with its development plans.

Beth Sabilia had been mayor for less than six months. It had been six of the worst months of her life. The pressure stemming from the standoff had engulfed her administration and her personal life. No matter what she did, constituents were screaming at her. The acrimony had gotten so out of hand that Sabilia couldn't even shop for groceries without being confronted by someone who was furious over the inability to resolve the dispute in Fort Trumbull.

The heat went up a few more degrees when Sabilia read Governor Rell's second letter in as many days. By going on record with a statement in favor of unconditionally returning the deeds to Susette and the Cristofaros, the governor had sent a clear message to the city: if it didn't compromise with these final two holdouts, it would be all alone to deal with the public scorn that would rain down on the city when marshals tried to pull these last few folks from their homes.

Sabilia got the point, but she didn't appreciate it. She was willing to entertain the possibility of lifetime use of the properties, but not complete ownership. A lawyer by profession, Sabilia had adopted Londregan's view: the city had battled through the courts and had won. She had to stay the course for the city. "Otherwise," she said, "everything was for naught. All the litigation and arguments made to the Supreme Court and all of our policy arguments would be eviscerated."

She quickly drafted a testy response to the governor. "The City Council's position has been consistent," Sabilia wrote. "The deeds of anything more than life-time possession will not return to the former property owner. The proposal outlined in your letter of today is not consistent with the Municipal Development Plan, with the City of New London's Zoning Regulations, nor with the directives set forth in the State of Connecticut's financial endorsement of the revitalization of the Fort Trumbull area."

After Londregan reviewed the letter, Sabilia faxed it to Rell.

Sabilia's letter came at the state like a brushback pitch, thrown right at the governor's chin. The state got the hint: if push came to shove, the city would drag Susette and the others out of their homes, no matter what it looked like on the evening news.

To drive the point home, the city turned a deaf ear to overwhelming sentiment from city residents and voted at its next city-council meeting to commence evictions.

All along Governor Rell had thought New London had been wrong in its decision to use eminent domain and had been unreasonable in its unwillingness to reconsider. The city's latest actions confirmed those views. Emboldened, Rell vowed not to let the tensions escalate into a street brawl. She needed someone to get to Susette. Robert Albright wasn't the answer. He had performed valiantly, but the governor needed a closer.

She turned to her deputy Ron Angelo. "You are going to resolve this thing," she said.

Rich Beyer had consistently brushed off Bob Albright. Each time Albright offered more money Beyer told him money wasn't the issue. But when Albright called him after the deadline had passed, there was a sense of finality in his voice. And the offer was far greater than any number previously tossed out: $500,000. "I'm told to tell you this is the amount we have to give you," he said.

Beyer said he'd get back to him. In Beyer's mind, half a million was still not close to what he would have earned off the properties had he simply been permitted to complete the renovations and sell them. But at this point he was simply trying to break even on his investment. And this time he was convinced the game was over.

He called Bullock. "Scott, this is looking pretty serious," he told him. "We're going to have to take the money, or we're going to walk away with a loss on this. There's no fighting this anymore."

Bullock encouraged him to do what was best for his family and his business.

Loyal to the cause, Beyer didn't do anything until talking it all over with Susette. She agreed he should probably take the money. At this point, even the governor didn't back the idea of returning the deeds for investment properties.

Beyer called Albright back and agreed to settle for $500,000, plus $15,000 in relocation costs.

Right after Beyer settled, the state made a final run at Von Winkle. It agreed to give him $1.8 million for his buildings. The price floored the NLDC, which felt that Von Winkle was getting far more than he deserved. But the state was looking forward, not backward. Von Winkle decided to take the same approach. Besides, what good would it do to hold on to a couple of buildings in an abandoned, demolished neighborhood?

Von Winkle settled.

Only Susette and the Cristofaro family remained.

"What should I do?"

The question was driving Susette mad. Other than a catnap here and there and an occasional snack, she hadn't slept or eaten in days. Other than Michael Cristofaro, all the people she had fought beside for nearly a decade were now bowing out and moving on. She didn't have that luxury. Although she had never asked to be the lead plaintiff and have her name on an infamous Supreme Court decision, that was where she found herself. Whether she liked it or not, no one could take her place as the leader of the movement. There was only one Kelo in *Kelo*.

She couldn't help resenting her situation.

Then a friend reminded her that Rosa Parks hadn't set out
to become the mother of the modern civil rights movement
when she refused a Montgomery bus driver's order to vacate
her seat for a white passenger. Her civil disobedience sparked
the Montgomery bus boycott, which elevated Martin Luther
King Jr. to national prominence and ushered in a movement
that forever changed America. Every so often, an ordinary person has the chance to do an extraordinary thing that alters
history. That chance had come to Susette Kelo.

As a former businessman, Ron Angelo understood why Rich
Beyer and Billy Von Winkle had settled. But as a homeowner,
he also understood why Susette and the Cristofaro family still
hadn't. He agreed with the governor—the city had treated these
people unjustly for almost a decade.

Angelo called Bullock to establish a dialogue and set some
ground rules. "Let's not bullshit each other," Angelo began.
"Otherwise, we're wasting our time."

Bullock couldn't have agreed more.

Personally, Angelo didn't agree with the city's use of eminent
domain in Fort Trumbull and he believed that Bullock's clients
had been unnecessarily beaten down. Repeated assaults on the
fundamental urge to own a home had caused deep wounds and
left nasty scars. Angelo knew it would take a lot more than a couple of blank checks to make these people feel whole. It was going
to take a fresh approach. He had no intention of trying to force
them to do something they didn't want to do. But he wanted to
take one last look at whether there was anything besides money
that would satisfy Susette and the Cristofaro family.

Bullock liked Angelo's approach. He agreed to discuss the
idea with his clients.

Susette and Michael Cristofaro traveled to Washington in mid-
June to attend a dinner recognizing the achievements of the Castle Coalition. Heavy hitters, from bank CEOs to national media
figures, were on hand, and Susette had agreed to be the keynote
speaker. All these important people wanted their picture taken

with Susette. When it was over, Susette told Bullock she wanted to talk with him alone in the hotel lobby.

She had been doing a lot of thinking. She knew the city wasn't going to let her stay in the neighborhood. And with everyone else leaving, she no longer wanted to stay. To her, loneliness was worse than illness.

"You know . . ." she said, her voice trailing off as she looked up at the ceiling.

Bullock put his hand on her knee. "It's okay," he whispered.

"This is hard."

"Tell me what you are thinking."

She lowered her eyes. "I'm not quitting," she said. "I have an idea."

She wanted to leave Fort Trumbull and take her home with her. The city could have her land. But she wasn't giving up her house, not to them at least. She figured the structure could be moved to a location outside the Fort Trumbull area.

Bullock was intrigued. By saving Susette's house and relocating it elsewhere, it could become a historic landmark and a fitting tribute to the historic battle they had waged. It could even become a museum serving an educational purpose. Best of all, it would deny some NLDC and city officials the victory they lusted after most, the demolition of Susette's emblematic pink house.

Susette confided she had another reason for choosing this course. The calls from angry fanatics were increasing, along with their rhetoric of violent opposition. If she stayed put and the city tried to force her out, Susette feared what might happen.

The institute had the same concerns. They had garnered a lot of goodwill through litigation and lawful civil disobedience. A violent standoff would mar the entire effort.

If the state would compensate her enough to find another home and also pay for the relocation of her pink house, she'd agree to leave the neighborhood. She had only one condition: she would not settle until the city and the state took care of the Cristofaro family.

The Cristofaro family had come up with its own conditions for leaving. First, they wanted to take some of the shrubs from the property; Pasquale Cristofaro had transplanted the shrubs decades earlier when the city had taken his first house through eminent domain. Second, they wanted a plaque erected in the fort neighborhood in honor of Margherita Cristofaro, the family matriarch who had died during the battle with the city. And third, if the city ended up building new upscale housing where their homes had once stood, the family wanted an exclusive right to purchase one at a fixed price so it could return to the neighborhood.

Bullock brought these terms and conditions to Ron Angelo.

He had heard all the rumors: Susette was impossible to deal with. She was greedy. She was holding out for more money.

Ron Angelo was on his way to her house to find out for himself. Before closing any deal, he wanted to sit down with her face-to-face, something no one in the Rell administration had ever bothered to do.

When he arrived, Susette met him at the door. "This is my son Willis," she said, introducing her twenty-eight-year-old son, a student working on his master's degree in biology. "He'll be the one you're going to talk to."

"My mother's done talking," Willis said.

Angelo said he understood. Susette looked like a woman carrying the weight of the world.

The three of them sat down. Willis got right to the bottom line. "This is what my mother wants," he said. "She has a little house on a little hill overlooking the water. And that's what she's going to end up with."

It was simple. She wanted the deed back to her pink house and enough money to move it outside the fort and establish it as a historic site. And she wanted enough money to purchase a home that resembled what she'd be leaving behind.

"You gotta understand," Willis told Angelo. "This is no longer about my mother. The whole country is watching to see whether she stays and gets dragged out. If you knew my mother, you'd understand that she says what she means, and she means what she says. My mother isn't afraid of you or anybody else."

Angelo said he understood, and he apologized. But he wanted Susette to understand something too. The Rell administration had inherited this mess from the Rowland administration. Angelo hadn't chosen the job of picking up the pieces. Rather it had been dumped in his lap.

"Is your mother proud of you for the job you're doing?" Susette asked.

Angelo didn't take offense. Instead, he revealed something. His daughter in middle school was doing a project on the case and she sided with the homeowners. She wasn't pleased with her father.

His honesty impressed Susette.

Susette's grit impressed Angelo. Nobody knew what it felt like to walk in her shoes, he knew. By the time he left her house, he decided he wanted to go to bat for her.

Initially, Tom Londregan and the city council had the same response when Angelo first told them what Susette and Michael Cristofaro wanted: "No way." They were not interested in seeing Susette's house saved, and they sure as hell didn't want the Cristofaro family to move back into the neighborhood when or if high-end housing went up. And the city didn't want to see them get as much money as the state seemed willing to pay them.

Bullock said that Susette and Michael Cristofaro had a simple response if their demands were not met: Bring on the marshals.

Then the council reflected. The NLDC had had enough and wanted out at any cost. Mayor Sabilia feared Susette wouldn't go. And Londregan knew that Angelo held a trump card: Although the state couldn't force the city to settle, it could make life very difficult when the city tried to proceed with the development. Virtually every aspect of the plan required state sign-offs from the Department of Economic and Community Development and the Department of Environmental Protection. If the city wanted to go forward, it was time to play ball.

Finally, the city said okay.

June 30, 2006

Susette signed a settlement contract entitling her to $442,000 for her building lot. She could use her own money to pay for her house to be disassembled, relocated, and rebuilt on a private lot elsewhere in the city. Avner Gregory, who had done original restoration work on the house decades earlier, donated a lot for the reconstruction and offered to act as the home's caretaker.

Michael Cristofaro received $475,000, and the city also met the other three terms he had set.

Shortly after signing the papers, Angelo and Susette and Bullock ran into each other on the street in New London. The state had forked out $4.1 million to settle with six holdouts. "It was expensive," Angelo admitted. "It wasn't pretty. But it worked."

There was no way Susette would consider living in New London again. In the hunt for a place to live, she drove across the Thames River into Groton and started driving up and down waterfront streets in search of "For Sale" signs. Coming down a small side street, she saw a sign that read, "FOR SALE BY OWNER" in front of a small bungalow. The property abutted historic Fort Griswold, which, like Fort Trumbull, had been attacked by Benedict Arnold for the British in the Revolutionary War. It was almost directly across the river from Fort Trumbull.

Susette parked the car and approached the house. From the doorstep, she could see her old neighborhood across the water. She rang the doorbell.

An Asian man answered.

"Is your house still for sale?" she asked.

"Yes," said the man, eager to describe his modest three-bedroom house. It needed renovation, and his asking price was $224,000.

Even without inspecting she could see the place needed a lot of work. But she knew it was what she wanted: a little house on a little hill overlooking the water. She knew right away she was going to buy this house.

Suddenly a smile swept across the man's face. "Hey, I know

who you are," he said. "You're the lady from right over there." He pointed across the river to the Fort Trumbull area.

Susette grinned and nodded.

"I read about you all the time in the newspaper," he said. "Come in. Come in."

EPILOGUE

In the summer of 2007, Susette's pink house was successfully disassembled—board by board—and moved elsewhere in the city, on Avner Gregory's land. A year later the Institute for Justice held a ceremony, officially dedicating the house as a historic landmark. A plaque in the front yard denotes the importance of the little pink house that changed the country. It remains an emblem of the fight waged in Fort Trumbull and other places throughout the country.

Susette bought and renovated the small house next to Fort Griswold. She lives there with Tim LeBlanc, who has completed a miraculous recovery from his accident. Susette still works two jobs as a nurse, one for the hospital and one for the City of New London. She set aside the remainder of her settlement money for her five sons.

Every plaintiff from the eminent-domain lawsuit has left New London, vowing not to return.

Governor John Rowland pled guilty to felony conspiracy and was sentenced to one year and a day in federal prison.

Peter Ellef was sentenced to thirty months in prison for his part in the corruption scandal.

Claire Gaudiani resides in New York City and teaches at New York University's Heyman Center for Philanthropy and Fundraising.

In 2002 George Milne retired from Pfizer after thirty-two

years. He is now an active venture capitalist and an adjunct lecturer at Harvard and MIT.

Jay Levin continues to practice law.

Scott Sawyer and John and Sarah Steffian are still battling the city and the NLDC in court. Their two environmental lawsuits are currently on appeal.

The U.S. Supreme Court's *Kelo* decision has become a catalyst for change. Scott Bullock and Dana Berliner continue to litigate eminent-domain and other constitutional cases at the Institute for Justice. In July 2006, they won the first major post-*Kelo* case decided by a state Supreme Court, when the Supreme Court of Ohio unanimously rejected the *Kelo* decision under the state Constitution and struck down the taking of homes to give to a private developer to build a shopping mall. Also, as of 2008, seven states have passed constitutional amendments to ban taking private property for economic development and forty-two of the fifty states have passed legislation to protect property owners from abusive eminent-domain practices.

Notably, Connecticut, the Constitution state, is one of the few states that haven't changed their eminent-domain law in any way.

As of the fall of 2008—more than three years after the Supreme Court approved the City of New London's plan to take private homes and replace them with buildings capable of generating higher tax revenues—the NLDC still has not broken ground. In the summer of 2008, the NLDC announced that its developer, Corcoran Jennison, had failed to secure adequate financing for the building project. Nonetheless, every home in the ninety-acre redevelopment area has been demolished. The former Fort Trumbull neighborhood is a barren wasteland of weeds, litter, and rubble.

ACKNOWLEDGMENTS

W hat took you so long?"
That's how Susette Kelo greeted me the first time I knocked on her door. It was November 28, 2005, and I had come to introduce myself and seek her cooperation on a book I was contemplating about the Supreme Court case bearing her name.

She invited me in, saying she had been hoping I would look into the dispute that had played out in her neighborhood. That afternoon I questioned her for three hours, sizing up her ability to recall facts and probing her motives for waging a battle that had lasted eight years. Before I left, Susette confirmed she would fully cooperate—no strings attached and seeking nothing in return—if I decided to go forward.

Her willingness to submit to relentless questioning and constant prying over a two-year period was a vital key to writing this book. Some of my questions probed very sensitive personal matters well outside the scope of her case. I am grateful for her trust and the privilege of chronicling her story.

Another key to telling this story was cooperation from the Institute for Justice. The attorneys and staff bent over backward to accommodate my never-ending requests for information. John Kramer was machinelike in his ability to crank out documents, photographs, and video footage in response to my queries. And Scott Bullock, in particular, was extremely patient and forthcoming.

Similarly, Bullock's counterpart, Tom Londregan, New London's city attorney, also went out of his way to assist me in my reporting. He too was candid and open. In addition to granting repeated interviews and requests for follow-up information and clarifications, Londregan did it all with a wonderful sense of humor. While adversaries throughout this case, both Bullock and Londregan were nothing but gentlemen and true professionals in their conduct toward me.

I am also very grateful to Claire Gaudiani and George Milne for their willingness to be interviewed, along with Claire's former secretary Claudia Shapiro, who is undoubtedly one of the sweetest human beings I've ever met.

Likewise, I'm very appreciative to some key players who opposed—to one degree or another—some of the initiatives led by Gaudiani and Milne. They include: Tony Basilica, John Markowicz, Fred Paxton, Steve and Amy Hallquist, and Kathleen Mitchell.

Others whose positions didn't necessarily line up in this saga were also generous with their time and forthcoming with their words: Reid MacCluggage, the former publisher of the *Day*; Wesley Horton, the attorney who defended the city's use of eminent domain before the U.S. Supreme Court; former New London Mayor Lloyd Beachy; and Pfizer's point man on real-estate development, Jim Serbia. Of course, a book like this would not be possible without the cooperation of many. Ultimately, almost everyone I approached for interviews ended up talking. There are too many to list here. I simply say thanks to all those who trusted me enough to open up and let me in.

I'm also indebted to a man whom I regretfully left out of this story, Neild Oldham. Frankly, without him, this story would have turned out a lot different. He carried the banner of the Fort Trumbull residents with unmatched courage and passion. Oldham's actions deserve to be chronicled. But shortly after I met Mr. Oldham, he died, foreclosing any opportunity to interview him on the record. Many rightfully see him as an unsung hero.

I'd be remiss if I didn't mention that during the course of writing this book I joined the faculty of Southern Virginia University, where I teach advanced writing and current affairs. President Rodney Smith promised me a great environment for writing, and he delivered on that promise.

I conclude with those whom I treasure most—my professional colleagues and my family.

My publisher, Jamie Raab, and associate publisher, Les Pockell, have been great to me and my family. And they have been bullish about this story since the first draft pages hit their desks. I'm deeply grateful for the privilege of writing under Grand Central Publishing's imprint.

Many people at Grand Central Publishing—from Sales to Advertising to Marketing—got behind this book in a big way. I'm indebted to all of them. And a few require special mention. No detail was too small for production editor Dorothea Halliday, who was relentless in her pursuit of excellence as we refined the narrative and polished the presentation. Chris Nolan's insight, experience, and mastery of words brought clarity to the story and tightened key passages. And Tracy Martin and Evan Boorstyn logged long hours on the little things that go a long way to a book's success. This A-team was led by my editor, Rick Wolff, who saw the power of this story long before it was written and whose enthusiasm never wavered.

Rick is much more than an editor to me. He offered me my first commercial-publishing contract back when I was a first-year law student with no writing pedigree to speak of. What can I say? The guy changed my life by giving me a chance to write. And he's just a wonderfully decent, honest human being with incredibly high professional standards. I'm blessed to be his close colleague.

My agent, Basil Kane, is simply one of my dearest friends. We sometimes talk two or three times a day. Rarely does a week go by that we don't speak. He's been my confidant, and he's been at my side through thick and thin for all twelve years of my writing career. I'm not sure I deserve such good company.

My personal assistant in Connecticut, Donna Cochrane, has been with me long enough that she is like family. Her loyalty and goodness are priceless human qualities.

My children are my pride and joy. I love writing, but I love them a lot more. Tennyson Ford, Clancy Nolan, Maggie May, and Clara Belle are what makes me rich and keeps me humble.

My wife, Lydia, is a daring woman. She jumped off a cliff with me when I decided to write this book without a contract. For two years I researched and wrote with no guarantee that this story would ever get published. Her faith inspired me to press on and on and on. She's the one I owe the most. She's my true north. She's simply the one, the beautiful one.

SOURCE NOTES

The primary sources for this book include interviews conducted by the author, correspondence with the author, public and private papers, and photography (both still and motion pictures).

THE INTERVIEWS

Close to three hundred on-the-record interviews and countless off-the-record interviews and background conversations were conducted. Many of these were tape-recorded and most sources were interviewed more than once. Some principal characters were interviewed more than a half dozen times, and a couple of principals were interviewed in excess of twenty-five times.

The book's dialogue and direct quotes are largely a result of two techniques: multiple interviewing and tape recording. Participants in the reported conversations—and in some cases, the witnesses to these conversations—were asked to provide their best recollection of what was said. In all, interviews were conducted with officials from the State of Connecticut, Pfizer Inc., the City of New London, New London Development Corporation, Connecticut College, the Institute for Justice, the Coalition to Save Fort Trumbull Neighborhood, the Fort Trumbull Conservancy, and the residents of the Fort Trumbull neighborhood.

Despite my requests, the following principal characters declined to be interviewed: Governor John Rowland, Peter Ellef, Jay Levin, David Goebel, Stephen Percy, Sarah Steffian, and Edward

O'Connell. Quotes attributed to them come from transcripts, public records, published reports, and interviews with individuals who were parties to conversations depicted in this book.

John Steffian also declined to be interviewed. But he did provide a written statement—through his attorney, Scott Sawyer—in response to a question from the author.

THE CORRESPONDENCE WITH THE AUTHOR

In response to queries for very specific details, I received more than a hundred written answers from individuals. Most of these responses came via e-mail. A few came in the form of letters and memos.

PUBLIC AND PRIVATE PAPERS

Under the Freedom of Information Act, I received access to more than one thousand pages of documents from Connecticut's Department of Economic Development and the Department of Environmental Protection. These included confidential memos, correspondence and contracts between Peter Ellef and Jay Levin, as well as records of invoices and payments between the State of Connecticut and Jay Levin. Additionally, state records turned over to the author included scores of e-mails and memos between Claire Gaudiani, state officials, and Pfizer.

I was also granted access to public records through the City of New London, the Town of Preston, the Norwich Superior Court, and the New London Superior Court.

I obtained minutes from New London Development Corporation meetings, as well as motions the agency passed.

The Institute for Justice provided thousands of pages of documents in the form of briefs, memorandums, deposition transcripts, and court transcripts. The institute also permitted me to conduct research at its Arlington, Virginia, law office, providing access to files, records, and photography.

The following individuals granted me access to private papers that included handwritten notes, diaries and journals, personal correspondence, and minutes: Susette Kelo, attorney Thomas Londregan, attorney Scott Bullock, John Markowicz, Steve and

Amy Hallquist, Professor Fred Paxton, publisher Reid MacClug-gage, and Kathleen Mitchell.

In the case of Susette Kelo, she turned over numerous boxes of documents, diaries, photo albums, personal papers, correspondence, financial records, and various other documents, including vital records. She also permitted me to dig through files and belongings in her home.

Thomas Londregan provided me with personal correspondence and letters, as well as notes containing his thoughts and remarks at various key junctures reported in this book. Mr. Londregan's brother Frank Londregan provided written responses to questions about the Londregan family history in New London.

Scott Bullock provided copies of his personal notes reflecting his thoughts, strategies, and remarks at various points in this history.

John Markowicz, Steve and Amy Hallquist, and Fred Paxton are meticulous keepers of copious notes and records. All four generously shared their notes, minutes, and records with me. And all four submitted to tape-recorded interviews that expanded on their notes.

Reid MacCluggage provided personal letters and correspondence. He also submitted to a lengthy tape-recorded interview and various follow-up interviews to elaborate on the nature and context of his private papers turned over to me.

Kathleen Mitchell maintained perhaps the most comprehensive archive of e-mails spanning the years covered in this book. These e-mails are to and from members of the New London City Council, members of the New London Development Corporation, members of the media, lawyers, state officials, members of the Coalition to Save Fort Trumbull Neighborhood, and residents of the neighborhood. Upon request, she shared many of these e-mails with me.

Finally, a source provided hundreds of documents consisting of personal e-mails, internal correspondence, and confidential memos. Many of these documents are originals (not photocopies) and some are handwritten.

PHOTOGRAPHY

I solicited scores of photographs of the people, places, and scenes depicted in this book. Many of these were taken by amateurs and contained in individuals' private collections. Others came from more traditional or professional sources, such as newspapers and magazines, historical societies, and law firms. Audio and video recordings of meetings, rallies, and speeches were also obtained.

The still photography was used primarily to describe background scenery, such as clothing colors, weather, and other details. The video and audio recordings were used primarily to corroborate dialogue and quotes.

The secondary sources for the book include books, articles, government reports, court records, laws, legal opinions and court decisions, press releases, and various other reference materials.

Many news organizations covered the *Kelo v. City of New London* case and I relied on countless reports from all forms of news media. But the *Day* newspaper warrants special mention here. No news organization covered the *Kelo* case more consistently and comprehensively than New London's hometown paper. When using a quote that appeared originally in the *Day*, I attempted to independently confirm the quote's accuracy. In some instances this was not possible, and I relied on the paper's accuracy.

The following organizations provided me with records, reports, and other documents that were used in background research: Harrall-Michalowski Associates, Inc.; Landmarks; the Coalition to Save Fort Trumbull Neighborhood; and Connecticut College.

INDEX

ABOUT THE AUTHOR

Jeff Benedict is an award-winning writer and is considered one of America's top investigative journalists. He has published seven critically acclaimed books, including *Pros and Cons, Out of Bounds, Without Reservation, No Bone Unturned,* and *The Mormon Way of Doing Business.* His articles have appeared in *Sports Illustrated,* the *New York Times,* the *Los Angeles Times,* and ESPN's online magazine, and his reporting has been the basis of a documentary on the Discovery Channel, as well as segments on *60 Minutes, Dateline, 20/20,* and HBO's *Real Sports.* He is a frequent guest on network news and cable stations, and in 2007 he produced his first documentary film for public television. You can visit his Web site at www.jeffbenedict.com.